The Male Body

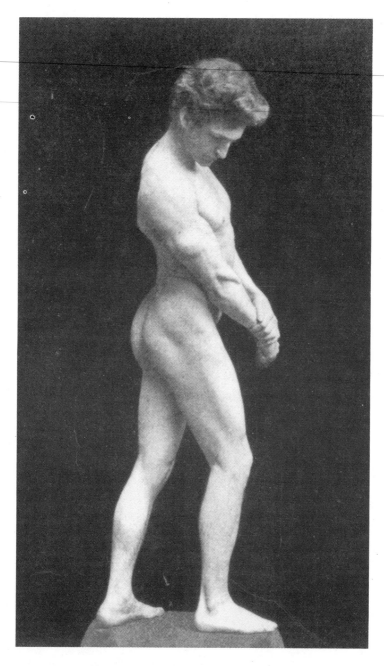

Frontispiece for Bernarr Macfadden's best-selling book, *The Virile Powers of Superb Manhood: How Developed, How Lost, How Regained* (New York: Physical Culture Publishing Co., 1900).

The Male Body

Features, Destinies, Exposures

Laurence Goldstein, Editor

Ann Arbor

THE UNIVERSITY OF MICHIGAN PRESS

1997   1996   1995   1994   4   3   2   1

Library of Congress Cataloging-in-Publication Data

The male body : features, destinies, exposures / Laurence Goldstein,
    editor.
         p.   cm.
    Includes bibliographical references.
    ISBN 0-472-09597-8 (alk. paper). — ISBN 0-472-06597-1 (pbk. :
alk. paper)
    1. Body, Human—Social aspects. 2. Body, Human in literature.
3. Men in literature. 4. Masculinity (Psychology) I. Goldstein,
Laurence, 1943– .
GT495.M36   1994
391'.6—dc20   94-24555
                                                              CIP

A CIP catalogue record for this book is available from the British Library.

CONTENTS

LAURENCE GOLDSTEIN

INTRODUCTION

This anthology of writings, adapted from a special issue of *Michigan
Quarterly Review*, is the inevitable companion volume to *The
Female Body*, published by the University of Michigan Press in
1991. In my introduction to that collection I noted that some
authors and colleagues had inquired, sometimes with good humor
and sometimes not, why I had chosen *this* gender as a site for extensive commentary. "Why does it always have to be the *female* body
that's presented as exotic, other, fascinating to scrutinize and imagine?" one woman asked me. "Why is it never the *male* body?" It was
a legitimate question for a feminist to direct to the male editor of
such a volume, and I took it to heart. Even as I pondered the possibility of producing a mate for *The Female Body*, however, a legion
of scholars had begun to engage the same question. The subject of
masculinity, always implied in feminist discourse, has now emerged
from the shadows and become what Margaret Atwood called the
female body in 1990: "a hot topic."

Indeed, it is self-evident that feminist scholarship and feminist
polemics have resulted in the flood of publications relating to manhood and its history. It is not so much that men want to answer back
to the critics of patriarchy, though some best-selling books clearly
have that intention, as that they have been prompted to rethink
their own nature now that its consequences have been examined by
the opposite sex with such thoroughness in the last three decades. Or
rather, the notion that men have an essential "nature" endowed
upon them by the iron laws of biology now seems as dubious as the
feminine mystique itself. If recent writings, including those in this
collection, are any indication, the task of men's studies is to recover
from history, and from empirically-observed behaviors in the
present day, that sense of choice and variety in self-definition that so
many women have embraced as a means of personal and social

liberation. Though women have reason to be suspicious about the boom in masculinity discourse, as if it's all just a strategy to reassert patriarchal control over the literature of gender, they also have reason to welcome it as a reciprocal testament that their voices have been heard, and that the male body, like the female, will never look quite the same again.

Is all this attention to the body a good thing? Or is it, as some critics have charged, a self-indulgent chronicle of anxiety, resentment, and self-pity fabricated by intellectuals for one another while the rest of the world's problems languish in neglect? It may be useful to remind ourselves why the literature of the body has become so popular, and not just in the academy. By way of explanation I can do no better than refer the reader to Ivan Ilich's essay, "A Plea for Body History," in the Spring 1987 issue of *Michigan Quarterly Review*. Ilich states that his research for the recently-published *Medical Nemesis* had persuaded him that twentieth-century people have allowed a medical establishment and its subsidiary profit-making agents to colonize the human body in unhealthy ways. In some happier time the body was appreciated as the free realm of enjoyment and purposeful action, as well as suffering. The late Middle Ages and early Renaissance had conceived, in their brightest moments, that "the Western Self is experienced as flesh and blood" and that this "birth of selfhood endowed Europe with a body of experience unlike any other." Each epoch since has offered the world an enhanced definition of the body's self, amplifying the opportunities for new identities. Following the Enlightenment and the Romantic era, the body as an agent of desire seemed to have been fully liberated, a "body electric," as Walt Whitman hopefully prophesied, its nature as various as nature itself.

Even a puritanism notoriously suspicious of bodily functions, and ever-inventive of ways to curb nature's impulses, could not retard the steady growth of "physical culture" as a social ideal. Michael S. Kimmel helps us to see how remarkable Whitman's vision was in a nineteenth century obsessed with masculine vigor of a specific kind, and terrified by effeminacy. "Our cities are populated by weaklings," wrote an alarmed Bernarr MacFadden, who published guides to good health in order to counteract the degeneration he witnessed around him. Kimmel's survey of the popular literature of the era devoted to body-building and character-building demonstrates how persistently and desperately male Americans have turned to the exercise appliance, the gymnasium, the sports field, and the wide open spaces to construct their masculinity lest they lose their gender distinction. A society suspicious of sexuality and geared toward "training the boy" to pursue a monolithic ideal of masculinity endowed our own century with a complex of values that challenges us in the 1990s.

The task of defining and improving upon those values is not one of spoiled self-pity but the opposite. In Ilich's terms, masculinity studies are one means of resisting, on behalf of women as well as men, the tendency in our culture to institutionalize "the topology of depression, lassitude, irritation, [and] pain." Like so much recent historiography that has focused on the private sphere, body history seeks to redirect attention away from leaders, policies, and organizations, and toward the daily physical life of ordinary people. The body needs to be rescued from its captivity by an unwholesome form of culture, though paradoxically the means of release must be another round of therapeutic examinations. As the contents of this book make clear, a rigorous diagnosis of the contemporary body/politic is likely to reveal ideological and commercial forces more harmful in their combined effects than any single nemesis, medical or otherwise. What seems not only useful but urgent in our *fin-de-siècle* moment is the close observation and evaluation of what Ilich calls "the unique enfleshment of an age's ethos."

Certainly there are masculine forms that seem unique in our time, such as the steroid-engorging bodybuilder and the hyperkinetic rock star. Speaking of the former, Sam Fussell asserts that pumping up is "perfectly postmodern, where surface is substance and larger-than-life is life." If the body is all we have, having lost the soul hypothesized by old-time religion, then making a spectacle of abundant material possessions is our era's special form of devotional piety and bourgeois vanity alike. Similarly, Fred Pfeil demonstrates in his case studies of Bruce Springsteen and Axl Rose how each represents in his music and body language a style of "authenticity" consoling to a generation uncertain about how to behave—literally, how to comport one's body—at a time when rock 'n roll has become the dominant art for a self-selected community of followers. Only in the Dionysian rite of the rock concert, as in the gymnasium or sports arena, do large portions of the general public feel real and ecstatically "enfleshed."

Are these positive images of the male body? They are certainly aggressive, reckless, and excessive in ways that are worrisome. "Men's bodies are the most dangerous things on earth," Margaret Atwood remarks. The male of the species seems to have a hormonal drive toward extravagance, risk-taking, and intimidation that has always been a fundamental part of his definition. John Updike calls it a "pain-smothering adrenalin rush" to "test the limits." The sense of brute power is part of the carnal enjoyment that constitutes masculinity, acted out not only at rock concerts and bodybuilding competitions and in popular movies, but in ways both socially bonding and antisocially dismembering in everyday life. As Updike notes, this sense of power gives the impression of being exempt from time, transcendent — part of the unique rapture of the male in his first few decades.

But time takes its toll on the young warrior, the graceful athlete, the indefatigable lover. The pathos of decline has always been a part of the literature of masculinity, and this pathos threatens to be doubly intense in our own era when surface and spectacle and "muscle" so radically outweigh their former rivals for respect and cultural authority. Margaret Morganroth Gullette shows how an exploitive market economy has begun to prey upon male anxieties about growing older and losing that self-defining macho glamour. Because the midlife male body "experiences itself mainly through the mesh of culture" and because at the end of this century "we find ourselves entering a new cultural situation," men and women alike must join together to resist the depredations of a meaning-making establishment as sinister as Ilich's demonic model of the medical profession. It is in the best interests of cosmetic surgeons, pharmaceutical companies, fashion designers, and product-makers of all kinds to raise the anxiety level of men, as they have done so successfully for women. Now it is time, Gullette asserts, for both sexes to fight back for the dignity and unique pleasures of the midlife body.

The sign of the male body is of course the penis, or the "phallus" if one wishes to speak symbolically. It designates the male, and its sexual power enables both the enjoyment and sorrow that fill the literature of all nations. Edward Field speaks for all men when he addresses his penis lyrically as a boon companion essential for his psychic wellbeing. "Stand up, friend, with me," he urges hopefully. John Updike points out that an erection is a gravity-defying act with metaphorical affinities to the compulsive male movement in space, earthly and heavenly. The penis is "the disposable rocket," a mechanical wonder that is also a cultural force of potentially unlimited meanings. In everyday idiom, however, we recognize that it is not meaningful enough: being called a "prick" is not a compliment but a hostile act. Charles Johnson reminds us how the black body has been stereotyped as a phallus to suit the needs of a racist society. When a body is "epidermalized," he remarks, "the thickness of the world's texture is thinned," the interaction of persons is degraded and the "interiority" of people of color annihilated. The black "tool" is a taboo instrument that discloses the most deeply-hidden racial and sexual anxieties in our civilization.

But whatever color it is, the penis remains a mysterious, even occult object in our culture. As Susan Bordo notes, it "has grown more, not less culturally cloaked over time." The gingerly ways it was indicated during the Clarence Thomas/Anita Hill hearings provided amusement for the nation. ("Having a body is not altogether serious," Margaret Atwood remarks.) But precisely because it is the symbol of a vulnerable body, a source of shame as well as authority, "patriarchal power generally wants it out of sight." As Bordo points out, the feminist and gay movements have complicated the meanings of the phallus, and of genital sexuality, probably for all time. Hardness and softness as metaphors for the male and female respectively have contributed to an ethos of male violence offensive to our postmodern sensibility. "It is necessary to re-think and re-vision the qualities of penetrability and impenetrability," she writes, ". . .in terms of their broadest meanings: emotional, intellectual, and social as well as sexual."

When an author depicts the male body he or she constructs a meaning for it that elaborates or subverts the reader's own views of the matter. David Lehman remarks in his poem, "If the poets of sex / Are right, the exchange of bodily fluids is a function // Of natural thirst, and love is the speechless joy / That lasts until it dies." But the poets of sex speak in many tongues and their messages are polysemous. Evelyn Lau's poem on a sadomasochistic relationship crosses Victorian romance with the practices revealed by psychoanalysis and the candor of journalism. In Joyce Carol Oates's short story the curious girl who looks at a dirty picture is terrified by an abuse of masculine power that proves to be unforgettable. And in Cathy Song's poem "Vasectomy," the husband's "broken sex" and its mirror image, the "rotting eggs" of the wife, redefine sexuality as something far different than the natural thirst summoned by the idealistic poets of sex. How different sexuality looks, too, when it is displaced in the testimony of other writers to diverse parts of the body: the male nipple coveted by Brenda Hillman, the weary blue eyes envied by Mitch Berman's protagonist, the groin injury suffered by Nicholas Samaras, the stomach praised by Robert Bly for "father[ing] the children of heat."

Personal testimony in the form of autoerotic self-regard is the basic act of body-imaging, perhaps of all narrative. There can be no credible account of general history without the individual profiles authored by those who gaze at themselves while holding up the mirror for their readers. The memoirs of Leo Braudy and Phillip Lopate are exemplary of what the more discursive essays describe: a masculine consciousness dominated by sexuality but not confined by it, not reducible to it. In a fine ironic touch, Braudy is recalled to memories of teenage sexual obsession during an episode of midlife urination at a scholarly retreat in Italy. His account reminds us how often teenage boys depend on obscene language and crude *frottage* to explore the terrain of adolescent sexuality and satisfy what Susan Bordo calls "the human need for transgression, excess, and extremity." Lopate examines various parts of his anatomy to emphasize that the male body is much more meaningful than is commonly acknowledged. The nose, the back, the legs—what a pleasure it is to bring these body parts into the light of consciousness for sustained attention, if only to emphasize that the "male member" must share its pride of place in the whole congregation. Significantly, he concludes by noticing the fingers that enable his body to be typed out, inscribed and circulated to readers of *The Male Body*.

The prose work by German author Mario Wirz is a much different document of self-criticism. In one sense it is a memoir, for we know from his other writings that the author has AIDS and that the details about childhood and adolescence in this work match his own biography. But Wirz's modernist monologue effectively distances his subject, so that his own view of himself veers often into the view of others, unsympathetic others, whose hostility toward his gay identity he has internalized as an infection metaphorically equivalent to his fatal disease. Wirz remains in an "inbetween zone" of solitude and self-pity. He travels inward and backward, discovering in his adolescent personality and the disdain of his classmates toward "soft as pudding . . . little Miss Sensitive" the origins of his present condition. The male body emerges as an immensely complicated object in his metafiction, vulnerable to psychic rupture when biology and psychology drive it beyond the cultural norm.

Nobody who keeps an eye out for changes in modern taste can miss the fact that the male body, like the female, is increasingly being imagined at a point of extremity that the nineteenth century considered indecorous, when it considered the subject at all. The milder form of this phenomenon is the modernist impulse to submit heroic models to parodic diminishment, as Christianne Balk observes in her poem on one commercial use of Michelangelo's heroic David. As Andrew Campbell and Nathan Griffith point out in an essay on the portfolio of artworks they have curated for this book, contemporary artists have extended this practice in ingenious ways, as in the manner one artist adapts the "Dying Slave" of Michelangelo to explore the erotics of pain, and another substitutes a male nude for Canova's "Venus." The plenitude of role changes and gender confusions of contemporary art represent strategies, by gay and heterosexual artists alike, for enhancing the opportunities of more intense sensation, of excess and transgression.

Throughout the cycles of individual life, and of history, this question of what it means to be enfleshed remains inescapable. Ruth Behar considers it in a brief meditation on her preschool son. Alan Soldofsky's poem focuses on insecurities beginning with adolescence. Brad Sewell's short story gives us a case history to illustrate how relentlessly these insecurities press on males in our historical moment. Two members of a high school wrestling team share a peer environment that bonds them, not only as athletes but as factory workers after graduation. But the more muscled and "masculine" of the two goes on to a future less hopeful than his smarter double, whose more capacious idea of the body, thanks to a self-consciousness that kept him from the wholehearted admiration of his fellow athletes, makes a better fit with social requirements for advancement and elevation into the professional world. Like my poem on the sports complex, Sewell's story considers how "the incessant untrophied training till death" marks our unheroic era, where bodies are so easily imaginable as industrial products.

How does the male body imagine itself, and how do others see it? These are the most basic questions, not just for literary discourse but in the daily personal experience of every male. The body is the essential carrier of life, the sign of the future. As Stephen Dobyns puts it in his volume, *Body Traffic*:

Whatever lifts the body up — muscles,
sinews, joints, whatever wrestles against
gravity itself — the raised step, the lifted arm —
these form the body's hope. But also hunger,

selfishness, desire, all that leads us
to put one foot in front of the other,
these too form the body's hope, whatever
combats that urge to lie down — greed,

anger, lust — these feelings keep us going.

The central narrative of all body histories is precisely this forward-ness, this persistence in pleasing the body so that it will keep going day after day toward its variety of goals. What others see when they observe a male body in action is this self-interested quest, sometimes vain and exploitative, sometimes admirable to the point of heroism.

When I told a friend that I was assembling material on this subject, she said, "It won't be easy. The male body simply isn't as interesting as the female body." I could not help but feel personally aggrieved by the remark, though I understood the semiotic sense in which she was speaking. My editorial effort has been to gather materials to disprove her thesis, to demonstrate that the male body is no less fascinating and complex than the female body, in part because so much of what we find interesting about the female body can also be located in the male entity, now more than ever. In shaping a companion volume for *The Female Body* I have enjoyed having my opinion confirmed, and I hope that readers will likewise find that the topic rewards the closest attention we can pay to it as men and women who have a compelling stake in discovering who we are.

MARGARET ATWOOD

ALIEN TERRITORY

1.

He conceives himself in alien territory. Not his turf — alien! Listen!
The rushing of the red rivers, the rustling of the fresh leaves in the
dusk, always in the dusk, under the dark stars, and the wish-wash,
wish-wash of the heavy soothing sea, which becomes — yes! — the
drums of the natives, beating, beating, louder, faster, lower, slower.
Are they hostile? Who knows, because they're invisible.

He sleeps and wakes, wakes and sleeps, and suddenly all is movement and suffering and terror and he is shot out gasping for breath
into blinding light and a place that's even more dangerous, where
food is scarce and two enormous giants stand guard over his wooden
prison. Shout as he might, rattle the bars, nobody comes to let him
out. One of the giants is boisterous and hair-covered, with a big
stick; the other walks more softly but has two enormous bulgy comforts which she selfishly refuses to detach and give away, to him.
Neither of them looks anything like him, and their language is
incomprehensible.

Aliens! What can he do? And to make it worse, they surround him
with animals — bears, rabbits, cats, giraffes — each one of them
stuffed and, evidently, castrated, because although he looks and
looks, all they have at best is a tail. Is this the fate the aliens have in
store for him, as well?

Where did I come from? he asks, for what will not be the first
time. *Out of me,* the bulgy one says fondly, as if he should be
pleased. Out of *where?* Out of *what?* He covers his ears, shutting out

the untruth, the shame, the pulpy horror. It is not to be thought, it is not to be borne!

No wonder that at the first opportunity he climbs out the window and joins a gang of other explorers, each one of them an exile, an immigrant, like himself. Together they set out on their solitary journeys.

What are they searching for? Their homeland. Their true country. The place they came from, which can't possibly be here.

2.

All men are created equal, as someone said who was either very hopeful or very mischievous. What a lot of anxiety could have been avoided if he'd only kept his mouth shut.

Sigmund was wrong about the primal scene: Mom and Dad, keyhole version. That might be upsetting, true, but there's another one:

Five guys standing outside, pissing into a snowbank, a river, the underbrush, pretending not to look down. Or maybe *not* looking down: gazing upward, at the stars, which gives us the origin of astronomy. Anything to avoid comparisons, which aren't so much odious as intimidating.

And not only astronomy: quantum physics, engineering, laser technology, all numeration between zero and infinity. Something safely abstract, detached from you; a transfer of the obsession with size to anything at all. Lord, Lord, they measure everything: the height of the Great Pyramids, the rate of fingernail growth, the multiplication of viruses, the sands of the sea, the number of angels that can dance on the head of a pin. And then it's only a short step to proving that God is a mathematical equation. Not a person. Not a body, Heaven forbid. Not one like yours. Not an earthbound one, not one with size and therefore pain.

When you're feeling blue, just keep on whistling. Just keep on measuring. Just don't look down.

3.

The history of war is a history of killed bodies. That's what war is: bodies killing other bodies, bodies being killed.

Some of the killed bodies are those of women and children, as a side effect you might say. Fallout, shrapnel, napalm, rape and skewering, anti-personnel devices. But most of the killed bodies are men. So are most of those doing the killing.

Why do men want to kill the bodies of other men? Women don't want to kill the bodies of other women. By and large. As far as we know.

Here are some traditional reasons: Loot. Territory. Lust for power. Hormones. Adrenaline high. Rage. God. Flag. Honor. Righteous anger. Revenge. Oppression. Slavery. Starvation. Defense of one's life. Love; or, a desire to protect the women and children. From what? From the bodies of other men.

What men are most afraid of is not lions, not snakes, not the dark, not women. Not any more. What men are most afraid of is the body of another man.

Men's bodies are the most dangerous things on earth.

4.

On the other hand, it could be argued that men don't have any bodies at all. Look at the magazines! Magazines for women have women's bodies on the covers, magazines for men have women's bodies on the covers. When men appear on the covers of magazines, it's magazines about money, or about world news. Invasions, rocket launches, political coups, interest rates, elections, medical breakthroughs. *Reality.* Not *entertainment.* Such magazines show only the heads, the unsmiling heads, the talking heads, the decision-making heads, and maybe a little glimpse, a coy flash of suit. How do we know there's a body, under all that discreet pinstriped tailoring? We don't, and maybe there isn't.

What does this lead us to suppose? That women are bodies with heads attached, and men are heads with bodies attached? Or not, depending.

You can have a body, though, if you're a rock star, an athlete, or a gay model. As I said, *entertainment*. Having a body is not altogether serious.

5.

Or else too serious for words.

The thing is: men's bodies aren't dependable. Now it does, now it doesn't, and so much for the triumph of the will. A man is the puppet of his body, or vice versa. He and it make tomfools of each other: it lets him down. Or up, at the wrong moment. Just stare hard out the schoolroom window and recite the multiplication tables and pretend this isn't happening! Your face at least can be immobile. Easier to have a trained dog, which will do what you want it to, nine times out of ten.

The other thing is: men's bodies are detachable. Consider the history of statuary: the definitive bits get knocked off so easily, through revolution or prudery or simple transportation, with leaves stuck on for substitutes, fig or grape; or in more northern climates, maple. A man and his body are soon parted.

In the old old days, you became a man through blood. Through incisions, tattoos, splinters of wood; through an intimate wound, and the refusal to flinch. Through being beaten by older boys, in the dormitory, with a wooden paddle you were forced to carve yourself. The torments varied, but they were all torments. *It's a boy*, they cry with joy. *Let's cut some off!*

Every morning I get down on my knees and thank God for not creating me a man. A man so chained to unpredictability. A man so much at the mercy of himself. A man so prone to sadness. A man who has to take it like a man. A man, who can't fake it.

In the gap between desire and enactment, noun and verb, intention and infliction, *want* and *have*, compassion begins.

6.

Bluebeard ran off with the third sister, intelligent though beautiful, and shut her up in his palace. *Everything here is yours, my dear,* he said to her. *Just don't open the small door. I will give you the key; however I expect you not to use it.*

Believe it or not, this sister was in love with him, even though she knew he was a serial killer. She roamed over the whole palace, ignoring the jewels and the silk dresses and the piles of gold. Instead she went through the medicine cabinet and the kitchen drawers, looking for clues to his uniqueness. Because she loved him, she wanted to understand him. She also wanted to cure him. She thought she had the healing touch.

But she didn't find out a lot. In his closet there were suits and ties and matching shoes and casual wear, some golf outfits and a tennis racquet, and some jeans for when he wanted to rake up the leaves. Nothing unusual, nothing kinky, nothing sinister. She had to admit to being a little disappointed.

She found his previous women quite easily. They were in the linen closet, neatly cut up and ironed flat and folded, stored in mothballs and lavender. Bachelors acquire such domestic skills. The women didn't make much of an impression on her, except the one who looked like his mother. That one she took out with rubber gloves on and slipped into the incinerator in the garden. *Maybe it was his mother*, she thought. *If so, good riddance.*

She read through his large collection of cookbooks, and prepared the dishes on the most-thumbed pages. At dinner he was politeness itself, pulling out her chair and offering more wine and leading the conversation around to topics of the day. She said gently that she wished he would talk more about his feelings. He said that if she had his feelings, she wouldn't want to talk about them either. This intrigued her. She was now more in love with him and more curious than ever.

Well, she thought, *I've tried everything else; it's the small door or nothing. Anyway, he gave me the key.* She waited until he had gone to the office or wherever it was he went, and made straight for the small door. When she opened it, what should be inside but a dead child. A small dead child with its eyes wide open.

It's mine, he said, coming up behind her. *I gave birth to it. I warned you. Weren't you happy with me?*

It looks like you, she said, not turning around, not knowing what to say. She realized now that he was not sane in any known sense of the word, but she still hoped to talk her way out of it. She could feel the love seeping out of her. Her heart was dry ice.

It is me, he said sadly. *Don't be afraid.*

Where are we going? she said, because it was getting dark, and there was suddenly no floor.

Deeper, he said.

7.

Those ones. Why do women like them? They have nothing to offer, none of the usual things. They have short attention spans, falling-apart clothes, old beat-up cars, if any. The cars break down, and they try to fix them, and don't succeed, and give up. They go on long walks, from which they forget to return. They prefer weeds to flowers. They tell trivial fibs. They perform clumsy tricks with oranges and pieces of string, hoping desperately that someone will laugh. They don't put food on the table. They don't make money. Don't, can't, won't.

They offer nothing. They offer the great clean sweep of nothing, the unseen sky during a blizzard, the dark pause between moon and moon. They offer their poverty, an empty wooden bowl; the bowl of a beggar, whose gift is to ask. Look into it, look down deep, where potential coils like smoke, and you might hear anything. Nothing has yet been said.

They have bodies, however. Their bodies are unlike the bodies of other men. Their bodies are verbalized. *Mouth, eye, hand, foot,* they say. Their bodies have weight, and move over the ground, step by step, like yours. Like you they roll in the hot mud of the sunlight, like you they are amazed by morning, like you they can taste the wind, like you they sing. *Love,* they say, and at the time they always mean it, as you do also. They can say *lust* as well, and *disgust*; you wouldn't trust them otherwise. They say the worst things you have ever dreamed. They open locked doors. All this is given to them for nothing.

They have their angers. They have their despair, which washes over them like gray ink, blanking them out, leaving them immobile, in metal kitchen chairs, beside closed windows, looking out at the brick walls of deserted factories, for years and years. Yet nothing is with them; it keeps faith with them, and from it they bring back messages:

Hurt, they say and suddenly their bodies hurt again, like real bodies. *Death,* they say, making the word sound like the backwash of a wave. Their bodies die, and waver, and turn to mist. And yet they can exist in two worlds at once: lost in earth or eaten by flames, and here. In this room, when you re-say them, in their own words.

But why do women like them? Not *like,* I mean to say: *adore.* (Remember, that despite everything, despite all I have told you, the rusted cars, the greasy wardrobes, the lack of breakfasts, the hopelessness, remain the same.)

Because if they can say their own bodies, they could say yours also. Because they could say *skin* as if it meant something, not only to them but to you. Because one night, when the snow is falling and the moon is blotted out, they could put their empty hands, their hands filled with poverty, their beggar's hands, on your body, and bless it, and tell you it is made of light.

JOHN UPDIKE

THE DISPOSABLE ROCKET

Inhabiting a male body is much like having a bank account; as long as it's healthy, you don't think much about it. Compared to the female body, it is a low-maintenance proposition: a shower now and then, trim the fingernails every ten days, a haircut once a month. Oh yes, shaving—scraping or buzzing away at your face every morning. Byron, in *Don Juan*, thought the repeated nuisance of shaving balanced out the periodic agony, for females, of childbirth. Women are, his lines tell us,

> Condemn'd to child-bed, as men for their sins
> Have shaving too entail'd upon their chins, —

> A daily plague, which in the aggregate
> May average on the whole with parturition.

From the standpoint of reproduction, the male body is a delivery system, as the female is a mazy device for retention. Once the delivery is made, men feel a faint but distinct falling-off of interest. Yet against the enduring female heroics of birth and nurture should be set the male's superhuman frenzy to deliver his goods: he vaults walls, skips sleep, risks wallet, health, and his political future all to ram home his seed into the gut of the chosen woman. The sense of the chase lives in him as the key to life. His body is, like a delivery rocket that falls away in space, a disposable means. Men put their bodies at risk to experience the release from gravity.

When my tenancy of a male body was fairly new—of six or so years' duration—I used to jump and fall just for the joy of it. Falling—backwards, downstairs—become a specialty of mine, an attention-getting stunt I was practicing into my thirties, at suburban parties. Falling is, after all, a kind of flying, though of briefer duration than would be ideal. My impulse to hurl myself from high

8

windows and the edges of cliffs belongs to my body, not my mind, which resists the siren call of the chasm with all its might; the interior struggle knocks the wind from my lungs and tightens my scrotum and gives any trip to Europe, with its Alps, castle parapets, and gargoyled cathedral lookouts, a flavor of nightmare. Falling, strangely, no longer figures in my dreams, as it often did when I was a boy and my subconscious was more honest with me. An airplane, that necessary evil, turns the earth into a map so quickly the brain turns aloof and calm; still, I marvel that there is no end of young men willing to become jet pilots.

Any accounting of male-female differences must include the male's superior recklessness, a drive not, I think, toward death, as the darker feminist cosmogonies would have it, but to test the limits, to see what the traffic will bear — a kind of mechanic's curiosity. The number of men who do lasting damage to their young bodies is striking; war and car accidents aside, secondary-school sports, with the approval of parents and the encouragement of brutish coaches, take a fearful toll of skulls and knees. We were made for combat, back in the post-simian, East-African days, and the bumping, the whacking, the breathlessness, the pain-smothering adrenalin rush form a cumbersome and unfashionable bliss, but bliss nevertheless. Take your body to the edge, and see if it flies.

The male sense of space must differ from that of female, who has such interesting, active, and significant inner space. The space that interests men is outer. The fly ball high against the sky, the long pass spiraling overhead, the jet fighter like a scarcely visible pinpoint nozzle laying down its vapor trail at forty thousand feet, the gazelle haunch flickering just beyond arrow-reach, the uncountable stars sprinkled on their great black wheel, the horizon, the mountaintop, the quasar — these bring portents with them, and awaken a sense of relation with the invisible, with the empty. The ideal male body is taut with lines of potential force, a diagram extending outward; the ideal female body curves around centers of repose. Of course, no one is ideal, and the sexes are somewhat androgynous subdivisions of a species: Diana the huntress is a more trendy body-type nowadays than languid, overweight Venus, and polymorphous Dionysus poses for more underwear ads than Mars. Relatively, though, men's bodies, however elegant, are designed for covering territory, for moving on.

An erection, too, defies gravity, flirts with it precariously. It extends the diagram of outward direction into downright detachability — objective in the case of the sperm, subjective in the case of the testicles and penis. Men's bodies, at this juncture, feel only partly theirs; a demon of sorts has been attached to their lower torsos, whose performance is erratic and whose errands seem, at times, ridiculous. It is like having a (much) smaller brother toward whom you feel both fond and impatient; if he is you, it is you in curiously simplified and ignoble form. This sense, of the male body being two of them, is acknowledged in verbal love play and erotic writing, where the penis is playfully given its own name, an individuation not even the rarest rapture grants a vagina. Here, where maleness gathers to a quintessence of itself, there can be no insincerity, there can be no hiding; for sheer nakedness, there is nothing like a hopeful phallus; its aggressive shape is indivisible from its tender-skinned vulnerability. The act of intercourse, from the point of view of a consenting female, has an element of mothering, of enwrapment, of merciful concealment, even. The male body, for this interval, is tucked out of harm's way.

To inhabit a male body, then, is to feel somewhat detached from it. It is not an enemy, but not entirely a friend. Our essence seems to lie not in cells and muscles but in the traces our thoughts and actions inscribe on the air. The male body skims the surface of nature's deep, wherein the blood and pain and mysterious cravings of women perpetuate the species. Participating less in nature's processes than the female body, the male body gives the impression — false — of being exempt from time. Its powers of strength and reach descend in early adolescence, along with acne and sweaty feet, and depart, in imperceptible increments, after thirty or so. It surprises me to discover, when I remove my shoes and socks, the same paper-white hairless ankles that struck me as pathetic when I observed them on my father. I felt betrayed when, in some tumble of touch football twenty years ago, I heard my tibia snap; and when, between two reading engagements in Cleveland, my appendix tried to burst; and when, the other day, not for the first time, there arose to my nostrils out my own body the musty attic smell my grandfather's body had.

A man's body does not betray its tenant as rapidly as a woman's. Never as fine and lovely, it has less distance to fall; what rugged beauty it has is wrinkle-proof. It keeps its capability of procreation indecently long. Unless intense athletic demands are made on it, the thing serves well enough to sixty, which is my age now. From here on, it's chancy. There are no breasts or ovaries to admit cancer to the male body, but the prostate, that awkwardly located little source of seminal fluid, shows the strain of sexual function with fits of hysterical cell replication, and all that beer and potato chips add up in the coronary arteries. A writer, whose physical equipment can be minimal, as long as it gets him to the desk, the lectern, and New York City once in a while, cannot but be grateful to his body, especially to his eyes, those tender and intricate sites where the brain extrudes from the skull, and to his hands, which hold the pen or tap the keyboard. His body has been, not himself exactly, but a close pal, pot-bellied and balding like most of his other pals now. A man and his body are like a boy and the buddy who has a driver's license and the use of his father's car for the evening; he goes along, gratefully, for the ride.

MICHAEL S. KIMMEL

CONSUMING MANHOOD: THE FEMINIZATION OF AMERICAN CULTURE AND THE RECREATION OF THE MALE BODY, 1832–1920

*"You can't have a firm will with-
out firm muscles."*

G. Stanley Hall

It's a psychoanalytic commonplace that what we lose in reality we recreate in fantasy. Those objects, relationships, and experiences that give life meaning, that make us feel full, satisfied, secure, are snatched from us, leaving us insecure, frightened, and desperate. Part of our normal, garden-variety neurosis is the creation of a stockpile of symbols that remind us of those lost qualities, a secret symbolic treasure chest we can occasionally raid to recreate earlier moments of fulfillment.

American men have been searching for their lost manhood since the middle of the nineteenth century. Plagued by chronic anxiety that our masculinity is constantly being tested, American men have raided that cultural treasure chest for symbolic objects that might restore this lost manhood. At times such raids exhibit neurotic tendencies of psychic retreat to earlier mythic times of gender identity security; at other times, though, men have been subject to more serious breaks with reality and the effort to live in that symbolic fantasy world.

This essay will examine some of those efforts to rescue and retrieve masculinity during a pivotal moment of historical transition during which masculinity was widely perceived as in crisis and in radical need of such restoration. First, I will describe the ways that a secure

12

sense of masculinity was gradually destabilized in the first few decades of the nineteenth century, and describe some of the mechanisms that men employed to reground their eroding sense of manhood. These included increasing restrictions on the male body through proscriptions of sexuality; the exclusion of all "others" — such as women, non-native-born whites, men of color, and, later in the century, homosexuals — from the increasingly problematic public area; and fantasies of escape. I'll also explore the rediscovery of the male body at the turn of the century as a gendered testing ground, a site of demonstration of masculinity, especially in consumerist fantasies of physical prowess.

1. The Terrors of the Self-Made Man

At the turn of the nineteenth century, the term manhood was synonymous with the term adulthood, the opposite of childhood. Virility was counterposed to puerility, not femininity. To be manly was to accept adult responsibilities as a provider, producer, and protector of a family. Manhood was grounded in property ownership — whether of landed estates or of the workingman's physical body which was his to deploy as he saw fit. Two models of manhood prevailed. The term "Genteel Patriarch" describes the manhood of the landed gentry: refined, elegant, and given to casual sensuousness, he was a devoted father who spent his time on his estate with his family. Urban craftsmen and shopkeepers subscribed to a model of "Heroic Artisan," who embodied the physical strength and republican virtue of the Jeffersonian yeoman farmer and independent artisan. Also a devoted father, the Heroic Artisan taught his sons his craft, supporting them through ritual apprenticeship to master status, as his father had earlier initiated him. An economic liberal who cherished his workplace autonomy, he was also a democrat, delighting in the participatory democracy of the town meeting.

By the 1830s, a new version of masculinity emerged in the eastern cities. "Marketplace Manhood" describes this "new man" who derived his identity entirely from success in the capitalist marketplace, from his accumulated wealth, power, and capital. The manhood of the urban entrepreneur, the businessman, was restless, agitated, devoted to his work in the homosocial public arena. He was thus an absentee landlord at home and an absent father to his children. When Henry Clay called America "a nation of self-made men," it was of Marketplace Man that he was speaking.

The frenzy for self-making spelled the historic doom of both Heroic Artisans and Genteel Patriarchs. Even today, once-heroic artisans fight against being transformed into faceless proletarians, which means the loss of workplace autonomy, small-town communal political power and domestic patriarchy, while the gentility of the old gentry is now ridiculed as the effeminacy of the urban dandy and fop. The triumph of marketplace masculinity pushed these two remnants of the old regime into the realms of the non-men.

For Marketplace Man himself, the psychological consequences of self-making were striking, and immediately evident to the sensitive eye. As manhood became dislodged from traditional moorings, it was thrown into constant question in the unstable world of economic competition. Masculinity became a homosocial enactment, to be proved in the marketplace, a "site of humiliation" according to Henry David Thoreau. No wonder that perceptive French aristocrat Alexis de Tocqueville noticed this irony at the core of the American temperament:

> An American will build a house in which to pass his old age and sell it before the roof is on; he will plant a garden and rent it just as the trees are coming into bearing; he will clear a field and leave others to reap the harvest; he will take up a profession and leave it, settle in one place and soon go off elsewhere with his changing desires. . . . At first sight there is something astonishing in this spectacle of so many lucky men restless in the midst of abundance.[1]

What a lucky man, indeed — chronically restless, temperamentally anxious, a man in constant motion to prove what ultimately cannot be proved: that he is a real man and that his identity is unthreatened by the actions of other men.

How could American middle-class men, these new self-made men, ever find relief from their relentless efforts to prove their manhood? Participants in the marketplace, which promises orderly rational accounting, ultimately became preoccupied with a world increasingly out of control. To a young man seeking his fortune in such a free and mobile society, identity was no longer fixed, and there were no firm familial foundations to ground a secure sense of himself as a man. Achieving manhood became a concern for men; for the first time in American history, young men experienced "identity crises." "Sons had to compete for elusive manhood in the market rather than grow into secure manhood by replicating fathers. Where many could never attain the self-made manhood of success, middle class masculinity pushed egotism to extremes of aggression, calculation, self-control and unremitting effort."[2]

These young men solved this first "crisis of masculinity" in American history in a variety of ways: they went to work, making sure to keep women out of the workplace and ensure it as a homosocial preserve. They went to war, pitting the manhood of the industrial workers and heroic artisans of the north against the chivalric yeoman farmers of the south. They also went to war against their selves, pitting their manly will and resolve against the raging desires and animal lusts that their bodies experienced. And they went west, to start over, to make their fortunes, to escape the civilizing constraints of domestic life represented by the Victorian woman.

To succeed in the market, the American middle-class man had to first gain control over his self. And by this he increasingly meant his body—its desires, its sensations. In the 1830s and 1840s, a spate of advice manuals counseled these young men on how to do just that.[3] The concern was so widespread, the advice books so popular, and the link between economic and sexual behavior so explicit, in fact, that one modern writer coined the phrase "spermatic economy" to describe the fusion of sexual and marketplace activities. Simply put, the self-control required of marketplace success required the sexual control of a disciplined body, a body controlled by the will. Conservation of sperm signified conservation of energy for its deployment in the market. "Sturdy manhood," one writer claimed, "loses its energy and bends under too frequent expenditure of this important secretion."[4]

Conforming to the spermatic economy meant, first of all, gaining control over the body, often imagined in these advice books as a well of carnal desires and diffuse energy. Like premature Freudians, advice manual writers sought to control these desires and harness the energy toward productive activity. Young men were counseled to avoid certain behaviors and activities likely to elicit carnal appetites over their more productive competition. Above all, these manuals were frantically concerned about masturbation, which would sap men's vital energies and enervate them for the tasks ahead.

The American edition of S. A. Tissot's classic French work *A Treatise on the Diseases Produced by Onanism* in 1832 captured the public imagination and allowed fears to congeal on the secret vice. Self-control, so necessary for success in the world of men, meant sexual control—control over what the body did—and control over appetite for vice. By the 1850s, several advice books—among them William Alcott's *The Young Man's Guide* (1846), George Burnap's *Lectures to Young Men* (1848), George Peck's *The Formation of a Manly Character* (1853), and Timothy Arthur's *Advice to Young Men* (1855)—addressed men's need for self-control over passion and temptation directly, and masturbation indirectly, occasionally in a coded language that readers no doubt understood.

Among the most successful of these advice books were Sylvester Graham's *A Lecture to Young Men* (1834), and his later *Lectures on Science and Human Life* (1839) and John Todd's *The Student's Manual* (1835). Todd, a New England minister, who became one of the nation's foremost campaigners against women's rights, and Graham, a health reformer and the inventor of the cracker that bears his name, were the preeminent experts who addressed themselves to the problems of becoming and remaining a successful man in the mid-nineteenth century. In his autobiographical work, *John Todd, The Story of his Life, Told Mainly By Himself* (1876), Todd claimed to have been "an orphan, shelterless, penniless" as a boy; he was, therefore, a prime example of the self-made man. (With one small exception—it was all a lie. Todd had been raised by his mother and two aunts after his father died.) *The Student's Manual* struck a nerve among American youth; by 1854 it had gone through 24 editions.

Graham laid out an elaborate plan for dietary and behavioral reforms that would allow men to live secure, happy, and successful lives. Concerned that the inner "vital economy" of the body was becoming enervated and insecure because of sexual excess, vice, and masturbation, Graham offered a set of bodily do's and don't's, a prescription of dietary and sexual temperance. All desire, Graham wrote, "disturbs and disorders all the functions of the system." To combat desire, Graham advocated a diet of farinaceous foods, properly prepared, like "good bread, made of coarsely ground, unbolted wheat, or rye-meal, and hominy, made of cracked wheat, or rye, or Indian corn." Young men should avoid full and large suppers, and should eat no animal meat whatever, since he was convinced that one is more susceptible to sins of the flesh if one eats another's flesh, advice for which Graham was twice attacked by Boston butchers. He advocated strenuous exercise, the avoidance of "every kind of stimulating and heating substances" and sleeping on a hard wood bed, since feather beds would wrap the sleeper in indolent luxury and thereby enervate him. Graham warned that socializing boys to bad habits of "luxury, indolence, voluptuousness and sensuality" (many of the qualities once praised among Genteel Patriarchs), would lead them to surrender their "nobleness, dignity, honor, and manhood" and become

> the wretched transgressor [who] sinks into a miserable fatuity, and finally becomes a confirmed and degraded idiot, whose deeply sunken and vacant, glossy eye, and livid shrivelled countenance, and ulcerous, toothless gums, and fetid breath, and feeble, broken voice, and emaciated and dwarfish and crooked body, and almost hairless head — covered perhaps with suppurating blisters and running sores — denote a premature old age! a blighted body — and a ruined soul!5

Such dire warnings indicate that, for Graham, the real demon that haunted young men was the specter of male sexual desire. Male sexuality was, by definition, predatory, lustful, and amoral, the chief obstacle to public order. Sexuality in all its forms must be suppressed and controlled. Sexual relations between husbands and wives needed to be regulated and their frequency curtailed — Graham suggested no more than once a month — lest a variety of illnesses befall the husband.6 Even sexual fantasies — "those lascivious day-dreams and amorous reveries" which are so common among "the idle, and the voluptuous, and the sedentary, and the nervous" — must be suppressed, Graham argued, lest the daydreamer succumb to "debility, effeminacy, disordered functions, and permanent disease, and even premature death, without the actual exercise of the genital organs!" Seemingly harmless sexual fantasies lead to desire and motivation, a blood-boiling lust, that must find an outlet, either with a woman or by oneself.

There were many other members of this antebellum vice squad eager to assist self-made men in their efforts at self-control. Dr. Augustus Kingsley Gardner advised parents that even if their children attempt to hide their practice of the solitary vice, sooner or later the "hysterias, epilepsies, spinal irritations, and a train of symptoms" would give them away to a watchful eye. Another writer counseled parents to employ several innovative treatments for sexual intemperance and especially masturbation, including a straight-jacket, to help boys keep their hands to themselves, and tying the feet so that the thighs would remain separate. If these didn't work, he contrived "cork cushions" which could be placed inside the thighs to pry them apart, and a "genital cage," a metal truss of silver or tin in which the boy's penis and scrotum were placed and held by springs. (Several patents for these devices, including one that sounded an electrical alarm in the event of an erection, were issued at the turn of the century, as competition in the war against venery heated up.) R. J. Culverwell invented a chair that served as a kind of douche-bidet for the sexually tempted. An armchair was fitted with an open seat, beneath which a pan of cold water, or "medicated refrigerant fluid" would be placed. By means of a pump, a young man could direct this cold water to his genitals, thus "cooling" his sexual urges, and making himself more capable of self-control.[7]

This obsessive repression of all things sexual indicates more than sexual prudishness or puritanical repression. It reveals an increasing preoccupation with the body and a correspondingly decreasing interest in the soul. That body was a sexual body, a body of desires, of dangerous fluids, of blind passions. This preoccupation with carnality, fueled by fears of loss of control, led to extraordinary measures to reassert control. If the young man wanted to become a successful Marketplace Man, he would have to control his body, to turn it into a tempered instrument that he could, by his will, deploy in an uncertain sea of fortune, confident that it was able to withstand fitful storms and still remain afloat.

This sexual panic had serious consequences, not only for the young men involved, but also for women, and for non-white, or immigrant men—those screens against which white, native-born American men constructed their identities. These "repressed middle class sexual energies were then channeled into a xenophobic hostility toward the immigrant and the black, then projected into fantasies incorporating the enviable and fully expressed sexuality of these alien groups" as well as projected onto women, who were cast simultaneously as seductive temptresses, brimming with carnal desires they were unable to control, or pious, asexual angels, for whom the merest mention of the body and its desires, would cause them to faint straightaway.[8] Sexual anxieties projected onto blacks, women, and immigrants prompted men to devise social, economic, political, and ideological controls, to keep others out of the way, clearing the field for white, native-born men.

2. The Crisis of Masculinity at the Turn of the Century

By the last few decades of the century, the realm of production had been so transformed that men could no longer anchor their identity in their position in the market. Now, new symbols were created, the consumption of which reminded men of that secure past, before identity crises, before crises of masculinity. Manhood had earlier meant economic autonomy — control over one's own labor, cooperative control over the labor process, ownership of the products of one's labor. It had meant political patriarchy — the control of domestic and political life by native-born white men whose community spirit and republican virtue was respected in small-town life. And it had meant the freedom symbolized by the west — vast, uncivilized, primitive — where men could test and prove their manhood away from the civilizing influence of women. When these avenues of demonstrating manhood were suddenly closed, it touched off a widespread cultural identity crisis. As historian Elliot J. Gorn writes:

> Where would a sense of maleness come from for the worker who sat at a desk all day? How could one be manly without independence? Where was virility to be found in increasingly faceless bureaucracies? How might clerks or salesmen feel masculine doing 'women's work'? What became of rugged individualism inside intensively rationalized corporations? How could a man be a patriarch when his job kept him away from home for most of his waking hours?[9]

And so men began to search for ways to reconstitute gender identity, to recreate ways to feel secure and confident as men. Some sought to return to those earlier years, by proclaiming the Heroic Artisan as working-class hero, by excluding women, blacks, and immigrants, or by globalizing the frontier through imperial expansion. But the most striking efforts had to do with the body — both in renewed efforts to control the disorderly body, and the fantasy efforts to clothe the body in the accoutrements of a wild and rugged, primitive masculinity. "As men felt their own sense of masculinity eroding, they turned to fantasies that embodied heroic physical action, reading novels of the Wild West and cheering the exploits of baseball and football players."[10] If manhood could no longer be produced, then it could be consumed, by the appropriation of symbols and props that signified earlier forms of stability.

Historians have long noted the turn of the century as an era of transition from a "culture of production" to a "culture of consumption." Identity was based less on what one did and more upon how one lived. In his classic study *The Lonely Crowd*, sociologist David Riesman discerned the shift in identities and ethics, between the "inner directed" nineteenth-century man, a man of strong character animated by an inner sense of morality, and the twentieth-century "other directed" man, a sensitive personality animated by a need to fit in, to be liked. Inner directed men went their own way, could stand alone, tuned to the hum of an internal gyroscope; other directed men scan a mental radar screen for fluctuations in public opinion. For the other directed man, having a good personality was the way to win friends and influence people.

The new man was perfectly suited for the emerging culture of consumption. These new values were reinforced in new institutions such as the department store, vaudeville stage, baseball diamond, and the advertising industry. They also underscored the search for a new foundation upon which to ground manhood for the coming century. Such a search involved a sweeping critique of the "feminization" of American culture. As the traditional bases for manhood were eroding, Americans had lost the hardy virtues of rugged manliness and were becoming soft, effete, enervated. To some, this was a symptom of a widespread cultural degeneration, of race mixing, the dilution of native blood stock. To others, rapid industrialization and urbanization had created a class of robotic workers and a new class of "brain workers," men who sit at desks all day and never physically exert themselves. Others were preoccupied with the feminization of young boys: since the separation of spheres required that men be away from home all day, the socialization of young boys had been completely taken over by women — as mothers, teachers, and Sunday School instructors. To reconstitute American manhood meant literally to rescue boys from the feminizing clutches of adult women.

Efforts to reconstitute male identity in the realm of consumption required several psychological and cultural inversions of earlier ways to demonstrate manhood. Early nineteenth-century capitalism required adventurous producers, men willing to take risks in the marketplace. Late nineteenth-century industrial capitalism, by contrast, requires adventurous consumers and cautious, timid, and obedient workers. As historian Stephanie Coontz poses the problem:

> As an impersonal work and political order ignored men's individual values, skills, and reputation, masculinity lost its organic connection with work and politics, its material base. The loss of opportunities for middle-class men to succeed to self-employment and the growing subordination of skilled workers to management contradicted traditional definitions of manliness. The qualities men now needed to work in industrial America were almost feminine ones: tact, teamwork, the ability to accept direction. New definitions of masculinity had to be constructed that did not derive directly from the workplace.[11]

New definitions, for example, that indicated a historic shift in language — from *manhood*, the inner directed autonomous American producer, to *masculinity*, the set of qualities that denoted the acquisition of gender identity. While "manhood" had historically been contrasted with "childhood," to suggest that manhood meant being fully adult, responsible, and autonomous, the new opposite of "masculinity" was "femininity," traits and attitudes associated with women, not children. Manhood was an expression of inner character; masculinity was constantly in need of validation, of demonstration, of proof.

It was in patterns of consumption, leisure, and recreation that American men found the danger, adventure, and risk-taking that used to be their experience in their working lives. Now they found the excitement at the baseball park, at the gymnasium, or sitting down to read *Tarzan* or a good western novel. Suddenly, books appeared about the urban "jungle" or "wilderness" so that men could experience manly risk and excitement without ever leaving the city — books like Upton Sinclair's classic muckraking exposé of the Chicago meat-packing industry, *The Jungle* (1902), or Robert Woods's work on settlement houses, *The City Wilderness* (1898). Or they could flip through the pages of *National Geographic* to experience the primitive "other."

One could replace the inner experience of manhood — a sense of security that radiated outward from the virtuous self into a sturdy and muscular frame that had taken shape from years of hard physical labor — and transform it into a set of physical characteristics obtained by hard work in the gymnasium. The ideal of the self-made man gradually assumed increasingly physical connotations, so that by the 1870s, the idea of "inner strength" was replaced by a doctrine of physicality and the body. By the turn of the century, a massive, nationwide health and athletics craze was in full swing, as men compulsively attempted to develop manly physiques as a way of demonstrating that they possessed the virtues of manhood. The self-made man of the 1840s "shaped himself by acting upon the material world and [testing] himself in the crucible of competition"; by century's end, he was making over his physique to appear powerful physically, perhaps to replace the lost real power he once felt. If the body revealed the virtues of the man, then working on the body could demonstrate the possession of virtues that one was no longer certain one possessed.[12]

3. The Feminization of American Culture

In his popular novel *The Bostonians* (1885), Henry James confronted the feminization of American culture. After pursuing the young feminist visionary Verena Tarrant for what seems like an eternity, Basil Ransome explodes in a rhetorical torrent:

> The whole generation is womanized; the masculine tone is passing out of the world; it's a feminine, nervous, hysterical, chattering, canting age, an age of hollow phrases and false delicacy and exaggerated solicitudes and coddled sensibilities, which, if we don't soon look out, will usher in the reign of mediocrity, of the feeblest and flattest and most pretentious that has ever been. The masculine character, the ability to dare and endure, to know and yet not fear reality, to look the world in the face and take it for what it is . . . that is what I want to preserve, or rather . . . recover; and I must tell you that I don't in the least care what becomes of you ladies while I make the attempt![13]

Here was the critique of the feminization of American culture in condensed form. Something had happened to American society that had led to a loss of cultural vitality, of national virility.

Some writers believed that cultural feminization was the natural consequence of the invasion of cultural outsiders, the "others," whose manhood was suspect to begin with. Fears of cultural degeneration were fueled by the entry of supposedly weaker and less virile races and ethnicities into the growing northern industrial city. To others, it was the city itself that bred feminization, with its conformist masses scurrying to work in large bureaucratic offices, sapping innate masculine vitality in the service of the corporation. "Our cities are populated by weaklings," wrote health reformer Bernarr MacFadden in a letter to President Theodore Roosevelt in 1907. A few years earlier, Frank Lloyd Wright had hurled a series of expletives at the city as evidence of his disdain for its enervating qualities:

> . . . a place fit for banking and prostitution and not much else . . . a crime of crimes . . . a vast prison . . . triumph of the herd instinct . . . outgrown and overgrown . . . the greatest mouth in the world . . . humanity preying upon humanity . . . carcass . . . parasite . . . fibrous tumor . . . pig pile . . . incongruous mantrap of monstrous dimensions . . . Enormity *devouring manhood*, confusing personality by frustration of individuality. Is this not Anti-Christ? The Moloch that knows no God but more?[14]

Many believed that feminization of American culture was synonymous with the feminization of American boyhood, the result of the predominance of women in the lives of young boys — as mothers left alone at home with their young sons, and as teachers in both elementary and Sunday schools. The turn of the century witnessed a gradual feminization of public school teaching. In 1870, about two-thirds of all teachers in public and private school were women; by 1900, nearly three-fourths were women, and almost 80% by 1910. The "preponderance of women's influence in our public schools," warned Rabbi Solomon Schindler in 1892, was feminizing our boys; a "vast horde of female teachers" were teaching boys how to become men, added psychologist J. McKeen Cattell. A 1904 report of a British group sent to the United States to observe American education and head off a similar problem in Britain concluded that the preponderance of women teachers meant that "the boy in America is not being brought up to punch another boy's head; or to stand having his own punched in an healthy and proper manner" (although the report did not specify the proper manner for having one's head punched).[15]

Observers were alarmed about the effect of pedagogical feminization on young boys. One writer posed two unpleasant outcomes: the "effeminate babyish boy" and "the bad boy," and suggested that masculine influence "is necessary for the proper development" of young boys. Another writer in *The Educational Review* in 1914 complained that women teachers had created "a feminized manhood, emotional, illogical, non-combative against public evils." This psychic violence to "masculine nature," he argued, was beginning to "warp the psyches of our boys and young men into femininity."[16]

To others, the problem wasn't women but the demands of the culture itself that made men "weak, effeminate, decaying and almost ready to expire from sheer exhaustion and decrepitude" as an editorial in the *North Carolina Presbyterian* put it in 1867. The demands of the workplace, the rapid pace of urban life, the clanging, roaring, churning energy of a society driven by marketplace masculinity — relentlessly on-the-go, anxious and eager to succeed — had simply worn men out by the end of the century. Over-civilization had made men "over-sophisticated and effete;" their energies had been spent, not saved — their manhood dissipated into countless economic and social directions. Suddenly new words such as "pussyfoot" and "stuffed shirt" were in common parlance, as men sought to demarcate themselves from those who had fallen victim to moral and gendered lassitude. Women "pity weakly men," O. S. Fowler warned, but they love and admire those "who are red faced, not white livered; right hearty feeders, not dainty; sprightly, not tottering; more muscular than exquisite, and powerful than effeminate, in mind and body."[17]

Most terrifying to men, and most indicative of this fear of cultural feminization, was the specter of the sissy. The term sissy was also coined in the last decade of the century, and came to encapsulate all the qualities that men were not. Above all, the sissy was outwardly feminine in demeanor, comportment, and affect. If manhood is defined by justice, courage, generosity, modesty, dignity, wrote Rafford Pyke in his 1902 diatribe against sissies in *Cosmopolitan* magazine, then the sissy was "flabby, feeble, mawkish," "chicken-hearted, cold and fearful." He was "a slender youthful figure, smooth faced, a little vacuous in the expression of the countenance, with light hair and rather pale eyes a little wide apart; a voice not necessarily weak, but lacking timbre, resonance, carrying power." Dr. Alfred Stillé, president of the American Medical Association, weighed in with a claim that "a man with feminine traits of character, or with the frame and carriage of a female, is despised by both the sex he ostensibly belongs to, and that of which he is at once a caricature and a libel."[18]

The emergence of a visible gay male subculture in many large American cities at the turn of the century gave an even greater moral urgency to men's hysterical flight from the perception of being a sissy. Here were real-live gender inverts, men acting like women — and therefore any manner of behavior or action that was reminiscent of these inverts might be a man's undoing. To be seen as a sissy was the worst thing imaginable — it meant being everything that a man wasn't. And everything that a woman (and therefore gay man) was. Thus did masculinity become a set of attitudes, traits, and characteristics that were defined by their opposition to femininity, to the realm of women. Men were fanatical in their resolute avoidance of all emotions or behaviors seen as even remotely feminine. This concern with the sissification of American manhood was so pronounced by the turn of the century that men sought to demarcate themselves from women by any means at their disposal. Beards and moustaches experienced a cultural revival, as men sought to sharpen the distinctions in manner, appearance, and style between the sexes as a way of muting the increasing similarities of everyday life, and thus mask men's increasing gender anxiety. To those concerned with feminization, American manhood was seen as listless, lifeless, lethargic. It needed a quick pick-me-up, a jolt of energy, a vitality booster. American manhood needed to pump up.

4. Men's Bodies, Men's Selves

And pump up men did — in droves. The turn of the century witnessed a nationwide health craze, as thousands of American men sought to acquire manly physiques, shore up flagging energy, or develop masculine hardiness as ways of countering the perceived feminization of culture. The health craze was vital to the perpetuation of a virile nation; claimed one contemporary observer:

> Gymnasiums, athletic clubs, outdoor sports, and methods of exercise and other artificial means of contributing to and continuing the physical vigor and virility of the race take the place of the hard physical labor of the earlier periods, or the love of luxury and ease, when physical development is no longer a necessity, overcomes the promptings of intelligence and experience, and the moral illness of the civilization has begun its work of devastation and destruction.[19]

This preoccupation with the physical body facilitated the transition from inner directed men, who expressed their inner selves in the workplace and at home — that is, in their "real" lives — to other directed men, concerned with acquiring the culturally defined trappings that denoted manhood. The increasing importance of the body, of physicality, meant that men's bodies carried a different sort of weight than expressing the man within. The body did not contain the man; it was the man.

Turn of the century men flocked to healers who prescribed tonics and elixirs guaranteed to put hair on their chests and life in their step. Men like Russell Trall, founder of the New York Hydropathic and Physiological School, who proclaimed the virtues of hydropathy — the famed "water cure" which involved steam-induced sweats or plunges in ice water. Or Robert Edis, who saw impurities hiding everywhere in the feminized household and railed against wallpaper, draperies, carpets and Europeanized furniture. Or Horace Fletcher, whose proposal that we masticate each bit of food 1,000 times before swallowing was proclaimed as a way to recover health and challenge the "gobble, gulp, and go" table manners of marketplace masculinity. Or Bernarr MacFadden, the celebrated founder of Physical Culture, who promoted a new muscular manhood to be built from purified blood, deep breathing exercises, vigorous workouts with barbells, and large doses of his breakfast cereal, Strengthro. (MacFadden was also the proud inventor of a "peniscope," a cylindrical glass tube with a rubber hose at one end attached to a vacuum pump, designed to enlarge the male organ.)

And men consumed vast quantities of these manly concoctions. Like Sylvester Graham's crackers earlier in the century, or C. W. Post's new Grape Nuts (1901) promoted as brain food for the burgeoning white collar class because "brain workers must have different food than day laborers." Or J. H. Kellogg's rolled flakes of whole corn, which were but a part of his total health regimen. In 1900 one firm published a list of 63 imported and 42 domestic bottled waters for sale, complete with the geographic source of each water, and a brief note alerting potential purchasers to their specific medicinal properties. And men bought enormous numbers of the advice manuals and guide books to find out how to become and remain manly in the face of constant threats — books such as William Haikie's *How to Get Strong and How to Stay So* (1879), and MacFadden's own

Superb Manhood were turned into best-sellers, the first self-help books of the new century.[20]

As earlier in the century, when the world is experienced as out of control, one remedy is to gain control over the body. Many turn of the century health reformers continued their predecessors' morbid fascination with controlling male sexuality, especially the body's fluids, as a way to gain control of the forces that were sapping men's energies. A recurring economic metaphor marks many post-bellum advice books, as men were encouraged to save, conserve, and invest their seed, the fruits of their productive bodies, and to avoid unnecessary expenditure or profligate waste.[21]

Crusaders against masturbation were divided about the immediate effects of the solitary vice. To some, it resulted in the immediate onset of sexual depravity — consorting with prostitutes, unbridled lusts that the young man could no longer contain, and ultimately, insanity and early death. Masturbation was a crime that "blanches the cheek, that shakes the nervous system into ruin, that clouds the intellect, that breaks down the integrity of the will, that launches emasculated ruin into asylums of hopeless insanity, collapsing in premature death," wrote G. Douglas in 1900. To others, masturbation would so drain its practitioner that he would have no ardor left over for sexual activity. Winfield Hall's advice book, *From Youth to Manhood*, published by the YMCA in 1900, claimed that since masturbation is unnatural, it is "more depleting than is normal sexual intercourse." Thus, as if in compensation, nature would exact its revenge, "removing, step by step, his manhood."[22]

One could counteract these tendencies through physical and dietary regimens. Eating Corn Flakes for breakfast, for example, designed by J. H. Kellogg as a massive anaphrodisiac, to temper and eventually reduce sexual ardor in American men. Kellogg was perhaps the most creative and hysterical turn of the century health reformer. Kellogg's books, like *Man the Masterpiece* (1886) and *Plain Facts for Young and Old* (1888), were best sellers of popular self-improvement, providing a guide for young men and their parents about clean and healthful living.

Kellogg was fanatical in his pursuit of masculine purity. His general health regime included:

1. Kneading and pounding on the abdomen each day to promote evacuation before sleep and thus avoiding 'irritating' congestions.

2. Drinking hot water, six to eight glasses a day (same end in view).

3. Urinating several times each night (same end in view).

4. Avoiding alcohol, tobacco, and tea because they stimulated lecherous thoughts.

5. Taking cold enemas and hot sitz baths each day.

6. Wearing a wet girdle to bed each night.[23]

But his chief concern was masturbation. In *Plain Facts for Old and Young* (1888), Kellogg provided anxious parents with a frighteningly systematic list of thirty-nine signs of masturbation, including physical and behavioral changes. Such a list could provoke anxiety in virtually every parent. What could they do about this plague? In a chapter called "Treatment for Self-Abuse and Its Effects," Kellogg listed a set of chilling home remedies. In addition to bandaging the genitals, and covering the organs with cages, and tying the hands, Kellogg also recommends circumcision, "without administering an anaesthetic, as the brief pain attending the operation will have a salutary effect upon the mind, especially if it be connected with the idea of punishment." Parents of older boys may be forced to have silver sutures placed over the foreskin of their sons' penises to prevent erection. "The prepuce, or foreskin, is drawn forward over the glans, and the needle to which the wire is attached is passed through from one side to the other. After drawing the wire through, the ends are twisted together, and cut off close. It is now impossible for an erection to occur, and the slight irritation thus produced acts as a most powerful means of overcoming the disposition to resort to the practice." (Although the extent to which Kellogg's sadistic suggestions were followed by terrified parents is impossible to know, one can only cringe at the possibility that any did.)

By the 1910s, much of this sexual panic began to subside, in part because of the popularization of Freudian psychoanalysis. If nothing else, Freud was a fierce opponent of sexual puritanism, and the ideology of the spermatic economy. To Freud the sexual instinct was just that, an instinct, inherited and normal. In "Sexual Morality and Modern Nervousness" (1908), Freud argued that the notion of physical depletion had it backward — it was *continence* not expenditure of semen, that was injurious to men. The only harm from masturbation was the guilt that traditionally attended it. "Masturbation as a rule does not much harm beyond that which we believe it to be wrong," was how one physician put it — as close as one can come to an iatrogenic, or, more accurately, a cultural etiology of disease.

Yet no sooner was the fear of depletion through masturbation ushered out as a problem for men than problems with male sexuality found another new, or, rather, a very old, cause. Dr. William Robinson's *Sexual Impotence* (1912) was an enormously popular treatment of male sexual problems, going through thirteen editions. Robinson argued that "older doctors" had exaggerated the ills associated with masturbation; it certainly was not the cause of impotence. In fact, men were not to be blamed for impotence; women were, since it was women's lack of responsiveness to male sexual ardor which exacerbated and sometimes even caused impotence. The problem was, as he coined the term, "frigidity" in women, which "will not call out his virility." Once again, male sexuality was women's concern.[24]

By the end of the century, psychiatrists and psychologists were blaming modern society for many of men's psychological problems. Some reformers suggested that it was the pace of society that caused men's problems — the rush of the modern, the clanking barrage of stimuli, the productive frenzy. Men simply wore themselves out mentally as well as physically. Dr. Edward Jarvis, speaking before the American Institutions for the Insane in 1851, pointed his finger at mobility and industrialization:

> No son is necessarily confined to the work . . . of his father . . . all fields are open . . . all are invited to join the strife. . . . They are struggling . . . at that which they cannot reach . . . their mental powers are strained to their utmost tension. . . . Their minds stagger . . . they are perplexed with the variety of insurmountable obstacles; and they are exhausted with the ineffectual labor.

And Dr. Peter Bryce, head of the Alabama Insane Hospital, found in 1872 that mental illness was most common among men "at the most active time of life," ages 35 to 40. "Habitual intemperance, sexual excesses, overstrain in business, in fact, all those habits which tend to keep up too rapid cerebral action, are supposed to induce this form of disease. It is especially a disease of *fast life*, and fast business in large cities."[25]

No one understood the psychological and somatic effects of modern civilization better than George Beard and Dr. S. Weir Mitchell. Beard's *American Nervousness* (1881) and *Sexual Neurasthenia* (1884; revised 1902) introduced a new psychological malady into American life: neurasthenia, or, as it quickly became known in the popular press, "brain sprain." Neurasthenia, Beard claimed, was the result of "overcivilization" — changes such as steam power, the periodical press, the telegraph, the sciences. The outcome was a host of symptoms, including insomnia, dyspepsia, hysteria, hypochondria, asthma, headache, skin rashes, hay fever, baldness, inebriety, hot flashes, cold flashes, nervous exhaustion, brain collapse. "Modern nervousness is the cry of the system struggling with its environment."[26]

Mitchell agreed. In his best selling *Wear and Tear: Hints for the Overworked* (1891), Mitchell observed that the "growth of nerve maladies has been inordinate" because the "nervous system of certain classes of Americans is being sorely overtaxed." The cause was modern life itself:

> the cruel competition for the dollar, the new and exacting habits of business, the racing speed which the telegraph and railway have introduced into commercial life, the new value which great fortunes have come to possess as means towards social advancement, and the overeducation and overstraining of our young people.

As a result of this "wear and tear," the "incessant cares of overwork, of business anxiety," Americans were suffering from "dyspepsia, consumption, and maladies of the heart."[27]

Never before had a cultural diagnosis resulted in a more gendered prescription and cure. Neurasthenia tended to invert gendered health, masculinizing women and feminizing men. So neurasthenic women were therefore to be confined to their beds, to remain completely idle and unstimulated; they had to reinvent their femininity. For example, Charlotte Perkins Gilman was diagnosed as having neurasthenia in 1885, when she was 25, by none other than Dr. Mitchell. "Live as domestic a life as possible," he advised her. "Have your child with you all the time. Lie down an hour after each meal. Have but two hours intellectual life a day. And never touch a pen, brush, or pencil as long as you live." Gilman was obedient; she "went home, followed those directions rigidly for months, and came perilously close to losing my mind," she wrote in her diary. (Her short story "The Yellow Wallpaper" offers a chilling description of her experience, and what might have happened had she not had the strength to get out of bed.) Men, by contrast, were pushed out to western dude ranches to take in the masculinizing freshness of the out-of-doors. Men, after all, had to reinvent their masculinity. Riding the range, breathing the fresh country air, and exerting the body and resting the mind were curative for men, and in the last two decades of the century large numbers of weak and puny eastern city men—like Theodore Roosevelt, Owen Wister, Frederic Remington and Thomas Eakins—all went west to find a cure for their insufficient manhood. That each returned a dedicated convert, trumpeting the curative value of the strenuous life, is part of the story of how we were won over to the west.

5. Recreating Manhood in the Out-of-Doors

The effort to recreate American manhood went outside the home or the bedroom, outside the factory or the corporation, into leisure and recreation, to include the rediscovery of the tonic freshness of the wilderness. Teenagers, college students, and young male clerks filled diaries with an endless list of their outdoor activities—everything from boxing to hiking, from ice skating to football and baseball. One physician proposed that a certain cure for hay fever was a "season of farm work," not because contact with the allergen would cure the malady, but because outdoor work would cure virtually anything. "Get your children into the country," one real estate advertisement for Wilmington, Delaware, urged potential buyers in 1905. "The cities murder children. The hot pavements, the dust, the noise, are fatal in many cases and harmful always. The history of successful men is nearly always the history of country boys." And if not to purchase, at least to rent or visit. "Thousands of tired, nerve-shaken, over-civilized people are beginning to find out that going to the mountains is going home; that wilderness is a necessity," wrote John Muir. And George Evans advised:

> Whenever the light of civilization falls upon you with a blighting power, and work and pleasure become stale and flat, go to the wilderness. The wilderness will take hold on you. It will give you good red blood; it will turn you from a weakling into a man.

Perhaps, but for many wilderness explorers or visitors to newly-minted "dude ranches" — which were often nothing more than failed cattle ranches reopened as consumer health spas — the west had been transformed into a gigantic theme park, safely unthreatening, whose natural beauty was protected as in an art museum. The three men who so graphically memorialized the premodern west — novelist Owen Wister, painter Frederic Remington, and naturalist President Theodore Roosevelt — were all effete eastern intellectuals who spent time on these civilized western ranches and rediscovered their manhood — and spent the rest of their adult lives sharing news of their conversion.[28]

Hunting experienced a renaissance at the turn of the century. Just as modern methods of slaughtering beef had been developed, and the hunt was no longer a material necessity for survival, it returned as recreation and fantasy in the proving of manhood. Theodore Roosevelt organized the Boone and Crockett Club to encourage big-game hunting. "Hunting big game in the wilderness," he and co-founder George Bird Grinnell wrote in 1893, "is a sport for a vigorous and masterful people." William Kent, a California congressman concerned about the degeneration of the race since the disappearance of the cave man, rejoiced in the savagery of the hunt. After a kill, Hunt declared, "you are a barbarian, and you're glad of it. It's good to be a barbarian . . . and you know that if you are a barbarian, you are at any rate a man."[29] Some commentators didn't care how the meat was obtained, as long as it was consumed. Many health reformers, including Graham, had shunned meat eating, believing that it excited the system and stimulated animal passions. To the masculinist health reformers, meat eating was a potent answer to feminized manhood; some claimed that a diet devoid of red meat would prevent the building of full manly power. George Beard described his encounter with a vegetarian in gendered terms; the hiker's "pale and feminine features, tinged with an unnatural flush" repelled Beard. Following a popular medical belief, Woods Hutchinson claimed that one needs blood to make blood, muscle to make muscle, and that the way to health was through consumption of large quantities of barely cooked beef. Hutchinson taunted vegetarians for being repelled by "Meat! R-r-red meat, dr-r-ripping with b-l-lood, r-r-reeking of the shambles." By eating red meat, men were literally consuming manhood.[30]

6. Sports Crazy

In the late nineteenth century, America went "sports crazy," as the nation witnessed a bicycle craze, a dramatic increase in tennis, golf, bicycling, weightlifting, and boxing, new excitement over football and racing, keen interest in basketball, and the spectacular rise of baseball. Sports were heralded as character-building; health reformers promised that athletic activity would make young men healthier and instill moral virtues. Sports were a central element in the fight against feminization; sports made boys into men. Sports were necessary, according to D. A. Sargent, to "counteract the enervating tendency of the times and to improve the health, strength, and vigor of our youth" since they provided the best kind of "general exercise for the body, and develop courage, manliness, and self-control." Sports aided youth in "the struggle for manliness," wrote G. Walter Fiske in *Boy Life and Self-Government*. Manhood required proof; sports were its central testing ground, where men proved they were men, and not women or homosexuals. One English newspaper championed athletics for substituting the "feats of man for the 'freak of the fop,' hardiness for effeminacy, and dexterity for luxurious indolence."[31]

More than physical manhood, sports were celebrated for instilling moral virtue as well. Here, especially, the masculinist response to the crisis of masculinity resonated with the anti-urban sentiments of those who feared modern industrial society. Sports developed "courage, steadiness of nerve," "resourcefulness, self-knowledge, self-reliance," "the ability to work with others" and "readiness to subordinate selfish impulses, personal desires, and individual credit to a common end," claimed Frances Walker, president of M.I.T., in an address to the Phi Beta Kappa at Harvard in 1893. The Wesleyan University *Bulletin* observed in 1895 that the end of the century "is an era of rampant athleticism. But these contests play their part in making sturdy citizens, and training men in the invaluable qualities of loyalty, self-sacrifice, obedience, and temperance." Sports could rescue American boys from the "haunts of dissipation" that seduced them in the cities — the taverns, gambling parlors, and brothels, according to the *Brooklyn Eagle*. Youth needs recreation, the *New York Herald* claimed, and "if they can't get it healthily and morally, they will seek it unhealthily and immorally at night, in drink saloons or at the gambling tables, and from these dissipations to those of a lower depth, the gradation is easy."[32]

So America went off to the sporting green. The first tennis court was built in Boston in 1876, the first basketball court in 1891. The American Bowling Congress was founded in 1895, and the Amateur Athletic Union in 1890. Sports offered a counter to the "prosy mediocrity of the latter-day industrial scheme of life," as Thorstein Veblen put it in *The Theory of the Leisure Class*, revitalizing American manhood while it replaced the frontier as "the outlet through which the pressure of urban populations was eased." Nowhere was this better expressed than in boxing and in the rapid rise of baseball, both as participatory and spectator sports. These were among the central mechanisms by which masculinity was reconstituted at the turn of the century, as well as vehicles by which the various classes, races, and ethnicities that were thrown together into the urban melting pot accommodated themselves to class society and developed the temperaments that facilitated the transition to a consumer culture.[33]

Here's what one boxing fan wrote in 1888: "This vaunted age needs a saving touch of honest, old fashioned barbarism, so that when we come to die, we shall die leaving men behind us, and not a race of eminently respectable female saints."[34] He certainly got his wish; boxing was increasingly popular at the turn of the century. As with other sports, boxing was defended as a counter to the "mere womanishness" of modern, overcivilized society. But boxing was more than mere manhood; it heralded the triumphant return of the Heroic Artisan as mythic hero. No sooner had the Heroic Artisan virtually disappeared into enormous, impersonal factories lined with rows and rows of unskilled workers, than he staged his triumphant return in the boxing ring. If the workaday world undermined working class manhood — requiring obedience to rules and docility toward managers — then boxing celebrated his traditional virtues — toughness, prowess, ferocity. If men could not make things with the skill of their hands, they could, at least, destroy things, or others, with them.

In his fascinating study of bare-knuckle prize fighting in America, *The Manly Art*, Elliot Gorn describes the way that working-class bachelor subcultures in the late nineteenth-century city resurrected the language of skilled artisans in their descriptions of boxing matches. Just as industrialization had destroyed traditional skills and crushed artisanal autonomy, boxing revived it in a frenzied fantasy of violence. Boxing was a "profession," and boxers were "trained" in various "schools" of fighting. Newspapers reported that the combatants "went to work," or one "made good work" of his opponent. Admirers spoke of the way that particular fighters "plied their trades" or understood the "arts and mysteries" of the pugilistic métier. Words like "art," "science" and "craft" were tossed about as often as in universities. Boxers resisted proletarianization; they controlled their own labor and were free of work discipline and authority relations. Here was a "manly art," which instilled and expressed violent masculine power, and required craftsmanlike skill and artistic deftness. Boxers symbolized autonomous artisanal manhood at the very moment of its disappearance.[35]

No one symbolized this cult of "elemental virility" better than John L. Sullivan, a walking embodiment of the remasculinization of America, perhaps the "greatest American hero of the late 19th century." With his manly swagger and well-waxed moustache, this Irish fighter recalled a lost era of artisanal heroism, "the growing desire to smash through the fluff of bourgeois gentility and the tangle of corporate ensnarements to the throbbing heart of life." And no one could symbolize the demise of this triumphant return of artisanal manhood than the emergence of Jack Johnson, the first black heavyweight boxing champion. Flamboyant and powerful, Johnson was the black specter that haunted white workingmen's sense of manhood since antebellum days — the specter that unskilled free blacks would triumph over skilled white workers in the workplace, the bedroom, and now, in the sporting world they held dearest in their artisanal hearts: the boxing ring.[36]

Baseball, too, encapsulates how sports were used to recreate a threatened manhood at the turn of the century. Theodore Roosevelt listed baseball in his list of "the true sports for a manly race." Just as horse racing had resulted in better horse breeding, Edward Marshall claimed in 1910, so baseball "resulted in improvement in man breeding." "No boy can grow to a perfectly normal manhood today without the benefits of at least a small amount of baseball experience and practice," wrote William McKeever in his popular advice manual, *Training the Boy* (1913). Perhaps novelist Zane Grey said it best. "All boys love baseball," he wrote. "If they don't they're not real boys."[37]

And they're not real Americans, for baseball was heralded as promoting civic, as well as gendered, virtue. A.J. Spalding enumerated, alliteratively, in his *America's National Game* (1911):

> American Courage. Confidence. Combativeness; American Dash. Discipline, Determination; American Energy. Eagerness, Enthusiasm; American Pluck, Persistence, Performance: American Spirit, Sagacity. Success; American Vim, Vigor, Virility.

Such American values were Christian values, replacing the desiccated immorality of a dissolute life with the healthy vitality of American manhood, a "remedy for the many evils resulting from the immoral associations boys and young men of our cities are apt to become connected with" and therefore deserving "the endorsement of every clergyman in the country." Baseball was good for men's bodies and souls, imperative for the health and moral fiber of the body social. From pulpits and advice manuals, the virtues of baseball were sounded.[38]

Those virtues stressed, on the surface, autonomy and aggressive independence — but they simultaneously reinforced obedience, self-sacrifice, discipline, and a rigid hierarchy. While sport "gives a product of exotic ferocity and cunning," a "rehabilitation of the early barbarian temperament," as Thorstein Veblen put it, its training regimen also "conduces to economic serviceability." Sports reproduced those character traits required by industrial capitalism, and participation by working-class youths was hailed as a mechanism of insuring obedience to authority and acceptance of hierarchy. Baseball's version of masculinity thus cut with a contradictory edge: if the masculinity expressed on the baseball field was exuberant, fiercely competitive, wildly aggressive, it was so only in a controlled and orderly arena, closely supervised by powerful adults. As such, the masculinity reconstituted on the baseball field also facilitated a docility and obedience to authority that would serve the maintenance of the emerging industrial capitalist order.[39]

Baseball was fantasy, and it was diversion, a safety valve, allowing the release of potential aggression in a healthy, socially acceptable way. "One thing in common absorbs us," wrote the Rev. Roland D. Sawyer in 1908, "we rub shoulders, high and low; we speak without waiting for an introduction; we forget everything clannish, all the petty conventionalities being laid aside." Novelist and former minor league ballplayer Zane Grey echoed these sentiments:

> Here is one place where caste is lost. Ragamuffins and velvet-breeched, white collared boys stand in that equality which augurs well for the future of the stars and stripes. Dainty clothes are no bar to the game if their owner is not afraid to soil them.[40]

It was not just "masculinity" that was reconstituted through sports, but a particular kind of masculinity — white and middle class. Baseball perpetuated hierarchy even as it seemed to challenge it. By the end of the second decade of the century, some of the innocence of this illusory solution was lost. In 1919, this world was shaken during the World Series scandal that involved the infamous Chicago "Black Sox," who had apparently "fixed" the series. The scandal captivated American men. Commercialism had "come to dominate the sporting quality of sports"; heroes were venal and the pristine pastoral was exposed as corrupt, part of the emergent corporate order, and not the alternative to it that people had imagined.[41] But by then it was too late: the corporate order would face less and less organized opposition from a mobilized and unified working class. The reconstituted masculinity that was encouraged by baseball had replaced traditional definitions of masculinity, and was fully accommodated to the new capitalist order. The geographic frontier was replaced by the outfield fence, workplace autonomy by watching a solitary pitcher and batter square off against one another.

From the bedroom to the baseball diamond, from health bars to barbells, from the cleansing sanitarium to the neighborhood gymnasium, American men went searching for a sense of manhood that had somehow been lost. The turn of the century found men looking, as we have always looked, for increasing control over our bodies, an indication that we had mastered an unruly self, and were able to turn ourselves into productive machines. How ironic that our efforts to resist being turned into machines in the arena of production had us turn ourselves into machines of consumption; the secular body was less a temple than a template of the healthy, self-controlled and therefore self-possessed man. Alongside these increasingly desperate efforts to control the body and its desires and appetites, American men retreated to masculinist fantasy camps, the untamed outdoor baseball diamond or dude ranch, to experience vicariously the rugged manhood that we imagined of our mythic ancestors.

Today, of course, the body remains no less a site of masculine proof, the ultimate testing ground for identity in a world in which collective solutions to the problem of identity seem all but discredited. If manhood-as-character does not emanate from inside to be expressed through the body, perhaps masculinity-as-personality can be applied to the body, as evidence of that inner experience, even in its absence. If we do not experience that manhood in the workplace, we metaphorically recreate the workplace in the realm of consumption, as we "work out," or as we experience "performance anxiety" that our "tools" will not perform adequately to "get the job done" — this in an activity that was once considered pleasure. Or we head off to the corporate "jungle" replete with signifiers of earlier rugged manhood — driving Jeep Cherokees, wearing power ties, Timberland shoes, Stetson or Chaps cologne, before we head off to bond with other men for the weekend at a Robert Bly retreat. Now, as then, what we lose in reality we recreate in fantasy.

NOTES

[1]Alexis de Tocqueville, *Democracy in America*, translated by George Lawrence, ed. J.P. Mayer (New York: Anchor, 1969), 536.

[2]Charles Sellers, *The Market Revolution: Jacksonian America, 1815–1846* (New York: Oxford University Press, 1992), 246.

[3]Such books were enormously popular. William Alcott's *The Young Man's Guide* (1833) ran through 21 editions by 1858. The first edition of Daniel Eddy's *The Young Man's Friend* sold 10,000 copies. In 1857, Albert Barnes noted "the unusual number of books that are addressed particularly to young men" and the way in which "our public speakers everywhere advert to their character, temptations, dangers and prospects with deep solicitude." Cited in Joseph Kett, *Rites of Passage* (New York: Basic Books, 1977), 95.

[4]Cited in G. J. Barker-Benfield, *The Horrors of the Half-Known Life: Male Attitudes Toward Women and Sexuality in Nineteenth Century America* (New York: Harper and Row, 1976), 179. "Men were preoccupied with the fear of a loss of sperm, connected as it was to the whole question of manhood and to a man's hopes for some kind of immortality," the author remarks. "Men believed their expenditure of sperm had to be governed according to an economic principle" (180–1; see also chapters 15–16).

[5]Sylvester Graham, *A Lecture to Young Men* (Providence: Weeden and Cory, 1834), 25, 39, 73, 33–4, 58.

[6]These included:

Languor, lassitude, muscular relaxation, general debility and heaviness, depression of spirits, loss of appetite, indigestion, faintness and sinking at the pit of the stomach, increased susceptibilities of the skin and lungs to all the atmospheric changes, feebleness of circulation, chilliness, head-ache, melancholy, hypochondria, hysterics, feebleness of all the senses, impaired vision, loss of sight, weakness of the lungs, nervous cough, pulmonary consumption, disorders of the liver and kidneys, urinary difficulties, disorders of the genital organs, weakness of the brain, loss of memory, epilepsy, insanity, apoplexy — and extreme feebleness and early death of offspring. . . .

In part, the cautions against sexual expression were based on a volcanic theory of the orgasmic eruption. The nervous system, Graham warned, is almost unbearably fragile, and is unable to bear "the convulsive paroxysms attending venereal indulgence":

> The brain, stomach, heart, lungs, liver, skin — and the other organs — feel it sweeping over them, with the tremendous violence of a tornado. The powerfully excited and convulsed heart drives the blood, in fearful congestion, to the principal viscera, — producing oppression, irritation, debility, rupture, inflammation, and sometimes disorganization; — and this violent paroxysm is generally succeeded by great exhaustion, relaxation, lassitude, and even prostration (1834: 20).

[7]Gardner, cited in Barker-Benfield, *The Horrors*, 272–3. See also John Haller and Robin Haller, *The Physician and Sexuality in Victorian America* (New York: Norton, 1977), 208. R. J. Culverwell, *Professional Records: The Institutes of Marriage, Its Intent, Obligations, and Physical and Constitutional Disqualifications* (New York, 1846), 5.

[8]Charles Rosenberg and Carroll Smith-Rosenberg, "The Female Animal: Medical and Biological Views of Woman and Her Role in Nineteenth Century America" in *Journal of American History*, 2, 1973, 353.

[9]Elliot J. Gorn, *The Manly Art: Bare-Knuckle Prize Fighting in America* (Ithaca: Cornell University Press, 1986), 192.

[10]E. Anthony Rotundo, "Body and Soul: Changing Ideals of American Middle-Class Manhood, 1770–1920" in *Journal of Social History*, 16;4 (1983), 32. See also his *American Manhood* (New York: Basic, 1993), which appeared too late to be incorporated into this essay.

[11]Stephanie Coontz, *The Social Origins of Private Life* (New York: Verso, 1988), 339.

[12]Roberta J. Park, "Physiologists, Physicians, and Physical Education: Nineteenth Century Biology and Exercise, Hygienic and Educative" in *Sport and Exercise Science*, ed. J. W. Berryman and R. J. Park (Urbana: University of Illinois Press, 1992), 141.

[13]Henry James, *The Bostonians* (New York: Modern Library, 1984), 293.

[14]Bernarr MacFadden, "An Open Letter to President Roosevelt," in *Physical Culture* 18, 1907, 75. Frank Lloyd Wright is cited in Herbert Muschamp, *Man About Town: Frank Lloyd Wright in New York City* (Cambridge: The MIT Press, 1983), 13. Anti-urbanism as a theme in the critique of feminization is discussed by T. J. Jackson Lears, *No Place of Grace: Anti-Modernism and the Transformation of American Culture, 1880–1920* (New York: Pantheon, 1981).

[15]Rabbi Solomon Schindler, "A Flaw in our Public School System" in *Arena* 6 (June 1892), 60; J. McKeen Cattell cited in William O'Neill, *Divorce in the Progressive Era* (New Haven: Yale University Press, 1967), 221. The British report is mentioned in Luther Gulick, "The Alleged Feminization of Our American Boys" in *American Physical Education Review* 10 (September 1905), 214.

[16]Alfred Cleveland, "The Predominance of Female Teachers" in *Pedagogical Seminary* 12 (September 1905), 301, 303. A. Chadwick, "The Woman Peril" in *Educational Review* 47 (February 1914), 115–16, 118.

[17]See John Higham, *Strangers in the Land: Patterns of American Nativism, 1860–1925* (New York: Atheneum, 1970), 78–9. O. S. Fowler, *Private Lectures on*

Perfect Men, Women and Children in Happy Families. . . . (Sharon Station, NY: privately printed by Mrs. O. S. Fowler, 1883), 5. William James argued that there is "no more contemptible type of human character than that of the nervous sentimentalist and dreamer, who spends his life in a weltering sea of sensibility and emotion, but who never does a concrete manly deed." Cited in Robert N. Bellah, et al., *Habits of the Heart* (New York: Harper and Row, 1985), 120. See also Henry Childs Merwin, "On Being Civilized Too Much" in *Atlantic Monthly* 79 (June 1897).

[18]Rafford Pyke, "What Men Like in Men" in *Cosmopolitan*, August 1902, 405–6. Stille cited in Morris Fishbein, *A History of the American Medical Association* (Philadelphia: W. B. Saunders, 1947), 82–3.

[19]George Ruskin Phoebus, "Civilization—Physical Culture" in *Physical Culture* 3, 1900, 21–2.

[20]See Harvey Green, *Fit for America: Health, Fitness, Sport and American Society* (New York: Pantheon, 1986). See also G. Carson, *Cornflake Crusade.* (New York: Rinehart and Co., 1957).

[21]One medical text in 1883 anthropomorphized and assigned political tendencies to male and female reproductive cells, claiming that "the male element is the originating factor, and the female the perpetuating factor; the ovum is conservative, the male cell, progressive." William Keith Brooks, *The Law of Heredity* (Baltimore: J. Murphy, 1883), 94; see also Cynthia Eagle Russett, *Sexual Science: The Victorian Construction of Womanhood* (Cambridge: Harvard University Press, 1989), 94, and H. W. Foster, "Physical Education and Degeneracy" in *The Independent* 52, August 2, 1900.

[22]G. Douglas, "Social Purity" in *Official Report of the 12th International Christian Endeavor Convention* (New York, 1900), 254; Winfield Hall, *From Youth to Manhood* (New York: Association Press, 1900), 54. Hall was elaborate in his advice on the methods to avoid the evils of masturbation. He counseled boys and young men to sleep on hard beds, "throw your whole energy into your work," and perform a regimen of ritual ablution and purification: "Arise three quarters of an hour before breakfast every morning, take a cold sponge or shower bath; drink two glasses of cold water; dress and go out and walk around the block before breakfast" (58).

[23]J. H. Kellogg, *Man the Masterpiece, or Plain Truths Plainly Told About Boyhood, Youth and Manhood* (Burlington, Iowa: I. F. Segner, 1886), 445–453; see also J. H. Kellogg, *Plain Facts for Old and Young, Embracing the Natural History and Hygiene of Organic Life* (Burlington, Iowa: I. F. Segner, 1888); Joseph Kett, *Rites of Passage, [previously cited work]* 165; John Money, *The Destroying Angel* (Buffalo: Prometheus Books, 1985), and T. J. Jackson Lears, *No Place of Grace,* 14.

[24]Cited in Kevin Mumford, "Lost Manhood Found: Sexual Impotence and the Contradictions of Victorian Culture," in *American Sexual Politics,* J. C. Fout and M. S. Tantillo, eds. (Chicago: University of Chicago Press, 1993), 96.

[25]Jarvis cited in Barker-Benfield, *The Horrors of the Half-Known Life,* 29; Bryce cited in John Starrett Hughes, "The Madness of Separate Spheres: Insanity and Masculinity in Victorian Alabama" in *Meanings for Manhood: Constructions of Masculinity in Victorian America,* M. Carnes and C. Griffen, eds., (Chicago: University of Chicago Press, 1991), 60.

[26]George Beard, *American Nervousness* (1881), 138; see also Tom Lutz, *American Nervousness, 1903: An Anecdotal History* (Ithaca: Cornell University Press, 1991), and Edward Wakefield, "Nervousness: The National Disease of America" in *McClure's Magazine* 2, February 1894.

[27]S. Weir Mitchell, *Wear and Tear: Hints for the Overworked* (Philadelphia: J. Lippincott, 1891), 28, 9, 67.

28See E. Anthony Rotundo, "Body and Soul," 28; Leon Fink *Workingmen's Democracy: The Knights of Labor and American Politics* (Urbana: University of Illinois Press, 1983), 9; Delaware ad cited in Kenneth Jackson, *Crabgrass Frontier* (New York: Oxford University Press, 1985), 138; John Muir cited in David Shi, *The Simple Life: Plain Thinking and High Thinking in American Culture* (New York: Oxford University Press, 1985), 197; George Evans, "The Wilderness," in *Overland Monthly* 43 (January 1904), 33.

29Roosevelt and Grinnell, 1893, 14–15; Kent is cited in Roderick Nash, *Wilderness and the American Mind* (New Haven: Yale University Press, 1967), 153.

30Woods Hutchinson, *Instinct and Health* (New York: Dodd and Mead, 1909). See also Martin Holbrook, *Eating for Strength; or, Food and Diet and their Relationship to Health and Work* (New York: Holbrook, 1888).

31Sargent, cited in Joe Dubbert, *A Man's Place: Masculinity in Transition* (Englewood Cliffs: Prentice-Hall, 1979), 169. Fiske is cited in Donald Mrozek, *Sports and American Mentality* (Knoxville: University of Tennessee Press, 1983), 207. British paper cited in Melvin Adelman, *A Sporting Time: New York City and the Rise of Modern Athletics, 1820–1870* (Urbana: University of Illinois Press, 1986), 284.

32Walker and Wesleyan Bulletin cited in Louise Knight, "The 'Quails': The History of Wesleyan University's First Period of Coeducation, 1872–1912," BA honors thesis, Wesleyan University, 1972. I am grateful to Ms. Knight for sharing her work with me. New York newspapers cited in Melvin Adelman, *A Sporting Time*, 277. See also George Frank Lydston, *Diseases of Society and Degeneracy* (The Vice and Crime Problem) (Philadelphia: J. Lippincott, 1904), 582.

33Thorstein Veblen, *The Theory of the Leisure Class* (New York: Modern Library, 1964), 208.

34Cited in Michael C. Adams, *The Great Adventure*, 41.

35Elliot Gorn, *The Manly Art*, 138.

36Elliot Gorn, *The Manly Art*, 247.

37Marshall, cited in Albert Spalding, *America's National Game* (New York: American Sports Publishing Co., 1911), 534. William McKeever, *Training the Boy* (New York: Macmillan, 1913), 91. Zane Grey, "Inside Baseball," in *Baseball Magazine*, 3; 4, 1909. Much of the material in this section is condensed from my "Baseball and the Reconstitution of American Masculinity, 1880–1920" in *Baseball History* 3, 1990.

38A. J. Spalding, *America's National Game*, 4. Cited in Melvin Adelman, *A Sporting Time*, 173.

39Thorstein Veblen, *The Theory of the Leisure Class*, 204. Veblen was one of many who were less sanguine about sports' curative potential. His blistering critique of the nascent consumer culture suggests that organized sports are an illusory panacea. For the individual man, athletics are no sign of virtue, since "the temperament which inclines men to [sports] is essentially a boyish temperament. The addiction to sports therefore in a peculiar degree marks an arrested development of the man's moral nature." And culturally, sports may be an evolutionary throwback, as they "afford an excerise for dexterity and for the emulative ferocity and astuteness characteristic of predatory life." Veblen, *The Theory of the Leisure Class*, 200, 203. Boy Scout leader Ernest Thompson Seton thought that watching would lead to "spectatoritis," and turn manly men into "mollycoddles of the bleachers." "The Dangers of Athletic Training," *American Medicine* 13, 1907, 500.

40Rev. Roland D. Sawyer, "The Larger Side of Baseball" in *Baseball Magazine*, 1; 6, 1908, 31–2; Zane Grey, "Inside Baseball," 12.

41Peter Filene, *Him/Her Self: Sex Roles in America* (Baltimore: The Johns Hopkins University Press, 1986), 139.

Arnold Schwarzenegger, in the film *Pumping Iron* (1977).

SAM FUSSELL

BODYBUILDER AMERICANUS

> *Fashion is that by which the fantastic becomes for a moment universal.*
>
> Oscar Wilde

1. Setting the Stage

Our fin de siècle is looking distinctly fin de siècle. Floppy berets, velveteen jackets and lilies are out, but in their place are triceps, traps and delts. Muscles are the latest props of the dandy. The modern male would no more leave his condo without his costume than the eighteenth-century rake would willingly part with his peruke, beauty spot and whiteface.

Open a magazine. Turn on the television. You can't blame Grandpa for wiping his glasses. It does look as if everyone has swallowed an air hose. From the gargantuan contestants on crash television shows like *American Gladiators* to Presidents Reagan, Bush, and Clinton prodded in photo-ops to "pump a little iron," it's everywhere. Current estimates put the figure at twenty million Americans who do it, and lest you doubt, grab a side table at cocktail hour and witness the nightly stampede from the office to the gym.[1] Take your ticket to the turnstile and watch the world's highest-paid movie stars, Stallone and Schwarzenegger, flex and fight, chop and charm. Catch the Calvin Klein models in clothing magazines, every one of whom puts Charles Atlas to shame. Note the bank line, and the customer before you, another self-styled wide guy, whose shaved and shaped chest looks like the burnished Roman breastplate of a city centurion. Muscles. Not fifteen years ago the symbol of deviance, this form is now the norm.

Of course, there's nothing new about caricatural distortion. Think

43

of the Chinese and bound feet or Victorian matrons squeezing their charges into the corset. Or, in our own day, the Ubange sporting lip and ear spools the size of hubcaps, the Burmese Padaung wearing hoops from chin to clavicle to create their giraffe necks, tribal scarification, or the wasp-waists of the New Guinean Ibitoe. But what is unprecedented is this specific exterior template, this superstructure of muscles. And it's as uniquely twentieth century as blinking neon.

How sports purists loath bodybuilders. Rick Telander of *Sports Illustrated* speaks for the majority when he confesses: "If you ask me, the whole bodybuilding subculture is like a freak show at a circus."[2] While Discobulus has his discus, and David his slingshot, the accoutrements of the bodybuilder are nothing but his Day-Glo posing trunks, his bottle of tan-in-a-minute, his cassette tape of posing music, his gestures, his attitudes. That and his muscles, which seem so . . . gratuitous. Disgusted, the sportswriter drops the bodybuilder in the same bin as the professional wrestler. And why not? If sports are a ritualized performance of mock-combat, bodybuilding and pro wrestling take it one step further. They are an abstract of an abstract. With their music hall grandiloquence, they parody a parody.

It's deeper than sport. It's spectacle. And its roots really are the Big Top. It was Ziegfeld who promoted the world's first bodybuilder, Eugene Sandow, in the 1890s.[3] Under the maestro's direction, Sandow toured the U. S. in a gigantic glass bell jar, wearing nothing but a fig leaf and a smile. Modern day bodybuilders simply continue the tradition. As pro bodybuilder Aaron Baker puts it, "That's what I like: shock value. I think it's up to us as performers to entertain the crowd. This is show business."[4] Schwarzenegger says the same: "Posing is pure theater. I understand that and I love it." "My body has always been dramatic."[5] It's the Greatest Show on Earth. The bodybuilder comes complete with everything but a velvet restraining rope and castors. To this day, "freaky" is the highest compliment one bodybuilder can pay another. But the bodybuilder is less in the tradition of the circus strong man than the bearded lady. It's unnerving because it's so deeply androgynous. It's somehow simultaneously bully and sissy, butch and femme.

2. Come Back to the Bench Ag'in, Arnold Honey!

Steroids or not, a natural bodybuilder is an oxymoron. Bodybuilding is to flesh what origami is to paper. It is literally "warped."

That's the trick. The look is as carefully cultivated, as painstakingly pared as a bonsai tree. And there's nothing natural about it.

While the swimmer and the bicyclist shave to cut down on drag, on air or water resistance, the bodybuilder shaves to make sure his body is seen without obstruction. His performance lies in being looked at, ogled, appraised. For these modern-day coxcombs, using the theatricality of the street as their backdrop, the stare is the ultimate reward. It's a reversal of sex roles, with the builder taking a traditionally female role: body as object. To be "buff" or "buffed" means literally polished — not like people but furniture. Not for nothing is the bodybuilder's tan-in-a-bottle known as "bronzer." Every movement of the bodybuilder is self-conscious presentation and display. Take the distinctive and dramatic walk of the body-builder, that weightlifter's waddle of muscles on parade. With the elbows held wide from the body, thighs spread far apart, the walk is as stylized, as preening, as a model's flounce down the runway.

Quintessentially urban, bodybuilding is inextricably intertwined with homosexual camp. Susan Sontag remarks: "The whole point of camp is to dethrone the serious."[6] By making a labor of leisure, a vocation of recreation, bodybuilders lampoon wage slaves and nine-to-fivers. His is a perversion of puritanism, and utilitarianism. He doesn't use his muscles to build bridges, but to raise eyebrows. They are at once functionless, yet highly functional.

"Camp introduces a new standard: artifice as an ideal, theatricality," says Sontag. Every bodybuilder's goal is to achieve "the Apollonian Ideal," in which he embodies perfect symmetry. This is accomplished by using pulleys and barbells to increase certain bodyparts and decrease others until, at long last, the neck measures the same in circumference as the arms and the calves, while the chest measures twice one thigh.

"The essence of camp is its love of the unnatural: of artifice and exaggeration." Those who actually work with their bodies don't look remotely like bodybuilders, whether it be the village smithy or farmers under their John Deere caps. In fact, the world's strongest men (such as Russia's Vasili Alexeev) look like Jackie Gleason. But through dumbbells and cable exercises that temporarily balloon the muscle, and stringent dieting that shrinks the joints, the bodybuilder banks on artifice to give him the appearance of spectacular muscularity. Camp is "The curved line, the extravagant gesture." It's the revenge of the hip on the square or the straight. I mean this literally: the curved contours of a bodybuilder's body, every muscle a ball, are in direct contrast to the right angles and level edges that form "the straight." His is the body politic, his muscles are a raging scream of dissent. Like the transvestite, today's muscle fop wraps himself up in colossal drapery. His muscles are what Mishima calls "the fortifications of style."[7]

Bodybuilders blur the distinction between He-men and Girlygirls. He shares her obsession with the scales ("Oh my God! I'm retaining water!" is their mutual lament). Both invest food with moral properties; for him, high in protein is "good," high in fat is "bad," for her all food is bad. His testosterone tizzies or 'roid rages are her hormonal mood swings of PMS. His joy in cleavage, accentuated by the tank-top, which as a restraint to his bouncing breasts looks like nothing so much as a male halter, is her joy in cleavage, accentuated by the push-up bustier. Both bodies are testaments to physical passion, made more so, in each case, by shaving the legs and the underarms. The bodybuilder combines David with Goliath, beauty with the beast. At this point, leather is lace. It's genderbending as amusing and confusing as Carol Channing (a woman playing a man playing a woman).

Whether it be beefcake or cheesecake, it's still cake. It's no wonder that in this world He-man Mickey Hargitay met and married Girlygirl Jayne Mansfield or that, in another case of bulges meeting bulges, Mae West of *Myra Breckenridge* frolics amongst a giggling gaggle of bodybuilders in their posing trunks. The only wonder is that Arnold Schwarzenegger didn't marry Dolly Parton.

"These women are not meant to look real," says director Candida Royale, speaking of porn actresses. With their beestung lips and Lady Godiva golden tresses, heaving silicone hooters and six-inch long passion pink acrylic fingernails, "They are not representations. They are fantasy or distortion made concrete, made material."[8]

So too, the bodybuilder, with his balls of energy. He symbolizes force existing through sheer will. He symbolizes the dynamo. Reduced to his purest form, he symbolizes the penis. He glorifies his own glands, just as Jean Genet's muscular Armand, from *The Thief's Journal*, defends his "immodest attitudes:" "Women walk with their tits bulging, don't they? They parade them, don't they? Well, I've got a right to let my balls stick out so people can see them, and even to offer them on a platter."[9]

The muscleman is, quite literally, the cock of the walk. He hones his hard body (to be soft is anathema) for the boardwalks and the bedroom. The modern boulevardier is turgid himself, coursing with veins, constantly at attention, ready to explode. Bodybuilder and author Yukio Mishima took priapic delight in his workouts. He could barely contain his excitement at what he calls "The swelling of muscles encased in a sunlit skin."[10] This auto-eroticism is a fetishism of form. Don't doubt Schwarzenegger when he says: "Seeing new changes in my body, feeling them, turned me on."[11]

The sensation is masturbatory, but the roots are homosex past and present. The grandparents of Joe Weider's *Muscle & Fitness* are his *Demi-Gods* and *Young Physique*, the gay porn of its day, featuring basted bodybuilders hanging out in G-strings, caught fresh in the flush of physicality. Today's muscle magazines come wrapped in plastic, with fold-out centerfolds of your favorite flexing body-builder. The homosexual undercurrent comes to the surface in the classifieds that end each issue: "Chest Men of America" Unite, reads the fine print of *Musclemag*. Finally, a club "for muscular men into pec worship."[12]

In fact, the parallel world to "Iron Pumpers" is "Vacuum Pump-ers," men who shave their scrotum and the base of the penis to highlight the organ and extend its length through daily stretching through a custom-ordered modified vacuum tube. Many of them members of a club called BIG (which worships masculine size in all its variant forms: big biceps, big boots, big cigars, big motorcycles, etc.), their club magazine is called *Dimension*. Such size queens attend weekly "pumping parties," where they mix and mingle, all the while admiring the extended wares of the pumpees.

"Masculinity? Male homosexuality is pure masculinity,"[13] David Kopay has written, and one can see what he means in the biker films of Kenneth Anger or the pornographic pumped-up cartoons of Tom of Finland. Nazi insignia, Levis and leather are the uniform, but the clothes are only a second-skin to the pumped-up flesh. Likewise, a butch bar in Washington D. C. advertises, "If you're man enough. . . ." Charles Ludum recognized the send-up possibilities in extreme masculinity and regularly incorporated bodybuilders into the act at his Ridiculous Theater Company in the Village.

The companion piece to *Pumping Iron* isn't the war epic *Tobruk* or the sports idyll *The Endless Summer*. It's *Paris is Burning*, in which camping and kvetching den mothers primp and prepare their vogueing, stylized charges for the glittering prizes of competition. The starry-eyed aspirant yearns for "titles" (the Mr. Olympia crown or Miss Spanish Harlem tiara), and, by implication, nobility.

Bodybuilders exhibit their properties.
Photo by Ralph DeHaan (© 1988)

3. Takin' it to the Limits

To give their activity dignity, pro bodybuilders come and go talking of Michelangelo, but they themselves are something Michelangelo could cook up only on mescaline, left loose in a room with a garden trowel, an ice-cream scoop, and an egg-timer. Were Michelangelo's Moses to don posing briefs and take to today's stage, he would be hooted mercilessly and hooked shortly thereafter. The face is noble but the body's just not muscular enough for today's pros. Jesus Christ of *The Last Judgment* would receive a Bronx cheer for his poor shoulder (narrow) to waist (wide) ratio and his flabby midsection.

To become a self-willed grotesque is no mean feat. The diet is beyond the drab (how does a meal of ten egg whites and two skinless chicken breasts grab you?). No milk, yogurt, or cheese may pass their lips (dairy "clouds your skin"). The water they drink springs not from the tap, but from the bottle, to ensure a low sodium level. "Here **you** are the sport,"[14] says bodybuilder Rick Valente, and being you is a full-time job what with twice daily training, six meals per day (at a quotidian aggregate of 7,000 calories), mid-afternoon napping, consultation with the choreographer, and deep dips into that most well-thumbed of pharmacopoeias, the *Physician's Desk Reference.*

Bodybuilders are made, not born, and they are years in the making. Eight to ten years, in the case of the champions. That's two hours a session, two sessions a day, six days a week, three-hundred plus days per year, for eight to ten years. There are impediments along the way, not just 500 pound deadlifts and bench presses and squats, but the shoulder and knee surgery that often accompanies them, degenerative arthritis, cirrhosis of the liver, hypertension, heart disease, and the host of problems associated with long-time drug use.

To improve their performance in the gym, bodybuilders take to methyl-testosterone, rhesus monkey hormones, pure adrenalin, HGH stimulators, and an assortment of amphetamines.[15] For competition, they use oral and injectible steroids, diuretics, clenbuterol, thyroid, and human growth hormone (drawn from the pituitary gland of cadavers).

Hooting at health, they play with the dangerous edge. After months of hard training and force-feeding, they spend the final weeks starving themselves to achieve the "inside-out" look by the day of competition. That's the skin shrunk like Saran Wrap, the body ripped and stripped, sliced and diced of all fat. But dieting isn't enough. So today's bodybuilders inject diuretics until their skin, thin as Bible paper, is so translucent one can visibly see raw tissue and striated muscle swimming in a bowl of veins beneath. Today's top crop, Lee Haney and Victor Richards, make Schwarzenegger look like Gilligan, first mate of the SS Minnow.

But trying to transcend fixed forms is not without a cost. As the muscle troupe travels from city to city to compete, behind the red curtain (stained brown from the fake tan of the competitors), wheezing and wobbling, vomiting and fainting backstage doesn't merit a raised hand. In the clash of the titans, nose bleeds, hair coming out in clumps, the state of your kidneys and liver is irrelevant. You don't win trophies for the state of your insides, but for your outside shell.

But to the driven, the risks are worth the rewards: bursting barriers and winning the respect of your bodybuilding peers. It brings to mind Mailer on boxers: "Like men who climb mountains, it is an exercise of ego which becomes something like soul."[16] Bodybuilders are their own test pilots, breaking the bonds of gravity, stretching their own envelope, the human frame, piercing the ceiling and propelling onward into the etherized air above to the great beyond. The danger is the allure. How much are you willing to suffer to achieve your aims? Like rocket-fuel-powered drag racers, solo sailors and speed skiers, they run a fine line between bravery and bravado, fearlessness and folly.

And there is real danger. Drawn and dehydrated, Renel Janvier spent the hours after pre-judging at the 1988 NPC USA Championships hooked to an IV before he went on to win the evening show. On the Grand Prix circuit, in 1988, depleted Albert Beckles collapsed, convulsed, and nearly croaked on the parquet at a bodybuilding banquet before paramedics brought him back to life on the buffet table.

There is also death. For professional bodybuilder Steve Michalick, his fantasy on stage was to reach the finale without fainting, then hit his most muscular pose, and — God willing — spontaneously combust, leaving his audience showered in flaps of his own flesh and blood.[17] Alas, for Michalick, he couldn't quite reach his dream. Try as he night, he never actually blew up. But when death comes for the bodybuilder, it comes in the form of implosion, not explosion. Looking the perfect picture of health, twenty-three year-old Andrew Hornby dropped dead in his competition briefs at the 1991 British Amateur Bodybuilding Championships. In 1992, thirty-three year-old Mohammad Benaziza won the IFBB Dutch Grand Prix in Rotterdam. Seven hours later, he died of heart failure.

None of this is news to heavy-duty muscle fans. The myth of the outlaw lives. The Pioneer spirit survives. Take one muscle magazine writer celebrating bodybuilder Jim Quinn. "What with all the cultural astrictions such as eco-terrorists, femi-Nazis and uni-world isocrats dictating human expression, we are no longer allowed to take life to its limits. Jim Quinn, on the other hand, did."[18]

Hunter S. Thompson's Hell's Angels ask, "Whaddeyou mean by that word 'right'? The only thing we're concerned about is what's right for us. We got our own definition of 'right.'"[19] Likewise, builders answer to no one. And that includes the U.S. government. To be a professional bodybuilder, where steroid use is 100%, is to be, by definition, an outlaw. That is, using steroids for non-medical reasons is against the Anabolic Steroids Control Act of 1991. To the medical community (save renegade physicians), drug use constitutes abuse. But to the select fraternity of pro bodybuilders, defying the government en masse, there is use and necessity and moral obligation. These self-described "Dianabol Desperadoes" forged their flesh in raucous venues like Mr. America's Gym on Long Island, which featured on the walls not pictures of bodybuilding greats but close-ups of dripping 3cc steroid-filled syringes bearing the legend, "Up the Dosage!"[20]

Pity the bodybuilding bureaucrat, charged as he is with perpetual damage control. Ben Weider does his best, bleating "Bodybuilding is not body destruction. Quote me,"[21] but it most definitely is. Muscles grow because they are stressed. The rebuilding (the body's reaction to the stress) creates a larger muscle. It's inherent in the act. Turning flesh into fantasy is a game, and a dangerous one, but to these players, it's the only game in town.

4. Takin' it to the 'burbs

But wait. How could this be? Snatched from life's margins, the bodybuilder, that grotesquerie, finds himself beamed from the fringe to the fashionable. As he moves from the walls of the Post Office to the billboards of Times Square, is it amusement he feels? Is it delight? Or is it, somehow . . . dispossession? Before his eyes, yesterday's muscle pits turn into today's fern bars. In ten years, Gold's Gym has grown from one ratty room to 410 franchises. Both salon and saloon, today's gyms are chrome-mirrored juke joints for the sexes to meet and mingle alongside a battery of exotic exercise machines and a bar featuring protein milkshakes. Everyone's doin' the muscle shuffle, even display window mannequins, who boast buzz-cuts and biceps. Even *The New York Times*, which banks on boosting its circulation by promising "A Great Workout" to its read-ers. "For your body of knowledge," the ad reads, "Tone daily with *The New York Times*."[22] From totally geek to totally chic, and in only one decade!

Forget for a moment that the average world-class bodybuilder is so short that when he assumes the position on the potty his tootsies don't reach the floor (Momo Benaziza, R. I. P., stood a regal 5' 3"). Forget the fact he looks like murder, but he invariably talks like Minnie Mouse. Forget that Dr. Barry Brenner, professor of medicine at Harvard Medical School, estimates the average life span of a pro bodybuilder at 55.[23] Who but a bodybuilder is a self-made man?

With power back in fashion, we're intoxicated by the illusion, by the allure of righteous might. It's the draw of The He-Man Masters of the Universe Life Action doll. It's the pull of our highest-grossing movies: *Superman, Teenage Mutant Ninja Turtles, Rambo, Batman, Dick Tracy, Terminator I and II,* and *Robocop.* The reconstructed, pumped-up male body promises control, control over your every muscle fiber, control over your immediate environment. The irony of the illusion is that at his most powerful, our superhero, the bodybuilder, is virtually powerless. Flexing on stage, at the height of his seeming virility, he's pumped so full of steroids that he's literally impotent. But not only is he less of a man at his moment of majesty, he's actually more of a woman. Faced with a flood of surplus testosterone, the body reacts by temporarily shrinking the testicles (with a resultant sperm count drop) and releasing an estrogen counterbalance, resulting, frequently, in a bulbous swelling under the nipples known as gynecomastia, or "bitch tits."

But why sweat the details? And if bodybuilding is another in a long line of appropriation from gay subculture, well, what of it? Does your grandma, heavier than a Holstein, really **want** to know why she bought those black leather pants at the mall? Because just as disco fever, urban cowboys, XTC parties, the lumberjack look, leather kings, and vogueing all found their place from the gay subculture to the heterosexual mainstream, from homo radical to hetero chic is the traditional travel of the avant-garde. And bodybuilders, known for forty years in the gay ghetto as "rough trade," are no exception. Who is the Gold's Gym prototype but gay poster boy Mr. Clean with his bald pate, earring, white T-shirt and bulging biceps?

Truth to tell, every king is a bit of a queen. Schwarzenegger with his dyed hair and bulging breasts, his shaved legs and sly smile is the latest in a time-honored tradition. In the '60s, Joe Namath made a mint modeling pantyhose in a national TV ad. He was the first to sport femme white low-tops in the brutal NFL world of butch black hightops. Muhammed Ali, the Louisville Lip, stole his shtick from the campy wrestling legend Gorgeous George. Stroking his cheek, mugging to the camera, Ali asked, "Ain't I pretty?" And shuffling in the ring, with his red tassels dangling from his white boxing boots, he was.

"Soldiers and women, that's how the world is," says Jeannette Winterson. "Any other role is temporary. Any other role is a gesture."[24] But Bodybuilder Americanus is clearly a bit of both, and since the unisex '60s, nothing sells like the interplay between butch and femme. For instance, the '70s, in which it was *de rigueur* for the modern male to display a fruity gold necklace in his open silk shirt, providing the chest beneath it was sufficiently hairy. Or the '80s, in which Don Johnson and George Michael popularized pastel suits and hip-hugging Levis to go with the three-day stubble. Or now the '90s, in which today's man emulates top-dollar television athletes by sporting muscles alongside his ponytail and requisite earrings.

But before jockwear was rockwear, and it's rockers who bridge the gap between the sexual and artistic avant-garde and the youth who incorporate it into their own subversive style. Rock musicians and their Rapunzel hair are like bodybuilders and their curves. Alongside their aversion to "straights," they share the cult of androgyny and the image of debauchery (think of Bowie and Boy George, the New York Dolls and the mincing Jagger). "Subversive?" Keith Richards asks, "Of course we're subversive." "And that's what rock and roll is," he says, "an attitude."[25] And so is bodybuilding. With the chest out, the elbows held as high as the shoulders, the legs slightly bent, the posture is half the performance.

But not for long. Sure as Rolling Stones raunch becomes elevator muzak, takin' it to the 'burbs leaves the product defanged and Disneyfied, and bodybuilding's no exception. As suburbanites homogenize and tame the freaky look, adopting it for themselves for the comfort of fashion, for social cachet, bodybuilding moves from exotic to ersatz. The slide from revolutionary to reactionary is evident nowhere more than in today's drug culture. How far Timothy Leary's '60s drug mantra of "Tune in, Turn on, Drop out" is from "Discipline, Dedication, Determination," the gung-ho muscle mantra of the '80s! The so-called "three D's" of gymspeak are not the rebel yell, yet they are on the lips of the one million plus American males who've tried steroids. They couldn't agree more with their anabolic avatar, Schwarzenegger, when he says, "My relationship to power and authority is that I'm all for it."[26] A 1985 NCAA study of college athletes found steroid-users more conservative politically, more likely to remain home at night, and more likely to earn more money after college than non-users. Another poll, conducted by the Department of Health and Human Services, found that 86% of steroid-users shoot up for "personal appearance."[27]

But the costume of the modern American male is not complete without the other trappings of his he-ness. Not just the heavy leather weightlifting belt, which as weekend wear is as omnipresent a fashion accessory as the beeper, but his car choice as well. Note the four wheel drive Jeep Cherokees and the Ford Explorers (to navigate the difficult terrain from corner condo to supermarket), note the resurgence in popularity of the Harley Davidson cycle, note the statistical fact that pitbulls have eclipsed poodles as the pet of choice for the American family. It's a sign of the times, in this general swing to the right, that Brooks Brothers has finally relented and now offers, among the racks and rows of power suits, the letterman's jacket.

We're back to the Big Man on Campus, in likes and looks. Even his deodorant tells the tale, be it Brut or Power Stick. It's the American tradition of grandstanding—as American, in fact, as Paul Bunyan or Wild Pecos Bill. These oversized heroes who hail from "tall tales" and "stretchers" are the nineteenth-century precursors to the twentieth-century icon Superman. If muscles maketh man, then get to work as God and colonize the poles and plots of your own demesne. Become your own America, with purple mountains' majesty and deep abdominal planes. Know yourself, from terra incognita to terra firma. Franco Columbu calls the split between his upper and lower pecs "The Grand Canyon." Schwarzenegger likens his biceps to "mountains."[28] In this world, "density" is actually a compliment. The muscle magazines sell MASS FUEL and POWER MASS, industrial-size drums of anabolic musclebuilding formula for hard-gainers intent on creating more continents.

Not since the Victorian age, where corpulence was viewed as a sign of masculine prosperity, have men so stuffed themselves. Guzzling protein drinks and raw eggs, they are trying to "fill out the frame," to physically fill the masculine template. Not, this time around, to look like bloated barons of industry, but to look like laborers. Not exploiters, but exploited. Here, the muscular restructuring of the male body is a form of blue-collar worship. Just so, the bare-chested, muscled rock singers screech into the microphone, accenting their honesty by clutching their crotch. Whether it's rockers like Springsteen or rappers like LL Cool J. and Ricardo on MTV, or Marky Mark (né Wahlberg) sporting his Calvin Kleins, their shirtlessness is intended as sincerity, their exposed muscularity as dignity in labor. "Baring all" is presumably to come clean, but not when the body, polished and plucked and pumped, is another form of dress. Unwittingly their power as truth-tellers, as modern-day bards, as givers of "the low-down," is negated by the body.

It's actually bourgeois to the core. It's materialism incarnate, with muscles replacing money as numerical gradations, as incremental units of self-worth. To keep up with the Joneses means accumulating objects, in this case amassing bodyparts—traps, abs, quads, pecs. In this life of getting and spending, your bank account is public and visible. It's as American as conspicuous consumption, with status the goal, envy the motivation. British artist Richard Hamilton captures this in his collage, *Just What Is It That Makes Today's Homes So Different, So Appealing?* Our hubba-hubba hosts, the muscleman and luscious lady greet us in their gadget-filled home. They've got the latest — the television, the car insignia, the tape recorder, the Hoover (larger, in fact, than their maid), the canned ham, the newspaper. His muscles are as essential for this pride-in-ownership as her gravity-defying boobs. Both husband and wife display their shiny goods with male-and-female side-chest poses. In our world of advertising, it's no wonder why bodybuilding succeeded where powerlifting and Olym-

Richard Hamilton, *Just What Is It That Makes Today's Homes So Different, So Appealing?* 1956. Collage. Kunsthalle, Tübingen.

pic weightlifting didn't. In the atomic age, the appearance of strength is more important than the application of strength.

Not for nothing does the verb, to muscle, mean to intimidate. In the behavioral sink of the city, the message is to back off, buster, don't mess with me. Say you mean business with your T-shirt, your body, or both. So sidewalk sellers hawk T-shirts reading "Urban Jungle Gym," or tank-tops bearing guerrilla slogans like "Dedicated to Survival of the Fittest."[29] In this sublimation of war, arms are called guns. "BIG GUNS; Winning the Arms Race With Massive Triceps" is the title of one how-to article in the muscle magazines.[30] Lee Haney's instructional video on bicep-building is called "Guns. Armed and Dangerous."[31]

Now that Road Warrior chic plays in Peoria, aggression is downright fashionable. It's the language of Realpolitik. No accident that Reagan increased his popularity by aping Eastwood ("Go ahead. Make my Day.") or that Bush followed suit ("Read my lips . . ."). The threat's the thing. Even more important than the shot fired is the pistol waved, whether in the take-no-prisoners form of Los Angeles Raiderwear ("Real Men Wear Black"), or the current marketability of ghetto fury ("By Any Means Necessary").

It's the latest rage. Literally. "RAGE," a so-called muscle intensity pack, is the name of a product sold in the bodybuilding magazines. Though not yet selling as fast and furious as X caps, give it time. The '60s Power to the People has become Power to the Person. The '70s May the Force be with You has become I am the force. Now, in the '90s, pro athlete Chris Mullin in his convict's crewcut models the Nike FORCE line of athletic apparel.

In place of war, bodybuilding offers a rite of passage. Your own body is the battleground, your deltoids a victorious campaign against indolence, your abs a tribute to discipline and strain. How perfectly postmodern, where surface is substance and larger-than-life is life. Like Coriolanus and his battle scars, you too can score points in public by displaying your symbols of suffering. Every muscle is a purple heart. In combat boots and camouflage pants, do-rag, tank-top and the updated armor of muscles, the bodybuilder revels in military symbolism. It's the triumph of Burgess's droogs. Far removed is World War II and Korea and Vietnam, because in the '60s and the Summer of Love a muscular kraut with a buzzcut and a name like Schwarzenegger couldn't get elected dogcatcher in the U. S. of A.

But the new American Adam has no memory. That's the attraction. He is the innocent, unburdened by conscience, doubt, or a sense of shame. In the tradition of Cooper's Natty Bumppo, of Rousseau's Noble Savage, he embodies Samuel Johnson's dictum that "He who makes a beast of himself gets rid of the pain of being a man."[32] Conan the Barbarian in his loin cloth and knee-high leather leggings, the "Barbarian Brothers," identical twin bodybuilding behemoths with leonine Samson manes, both play on the nobility of savagery. So one muscle instructional book is titled "Savage Sets!" So bodybuilder Lee Haney's gym in Atlanta is called "The Animal Kingdom." Pro bodybuilder Mike Christian is billed as "The Iron Warrior," and the muscle magazines sell T-shirts braying "Under This Shirt Lies The Animal!"[33]

The longing is atavistic. It's a primordial return to the time when strength and sex were synonymous for survival of the species. It's the romantic idealization of pre-lapsarian, natural man, untrammeled by thought, by knowledge of good and evil, by, in fact, knowledge. Intellect is held to be effete, essentially feminine and suspect. Better a blank slate, clean and unpolluted, than a mind, filled as it is with vacillation and moral quandary. Rambo is a bimbo is a Gymbo.

So today's yuppies flock to the gym, one and all seeking the myth of the frontier. With the personal trainer's care, they follow blueprints for biceps, all the while reciting homilies of self-reliance and self-determination. Through prescribed diets and methodical exercise routines, protein powder, amino acids, steroids, and a fake tan to highlight his he-ness, the Gymbo turns himself into a modern primitive. It's a case of man using artifice to appear authentically "natural."

It's a paint-by-numbers dream shared by many a baby-boomer as well, as thirtysomethings fade to graying fortysomethings. Not for them the image of savagery, but something else, for as time ticks relentlessly on, the one thing they can't buy with their Beemers and their au pairs and their double disposable income is youth. The muscular body, that picture of eternal adolescence, is their dominant dream, and the gym their nightly launching pad.

It's the ultimate end of the Me generation. "The old alchemical dream," according to Tom Wolfe, "was changing base metals into gold. The new alchemical dream is: changing one's personality — remaking, remodeling, elevating, and polishing one's very self . . . and observing, studying, and doting on it. (ME!)."[34] But writing in 1976, Wolfe didn't know the half of it. How could anyone have known that the baby-boomers would take bodybuilding and make it . . . **moral**. That their '70s personality renovation regimens of Scientology, Synanon, Primal Scream, est and Esalen, would shortly combine with the '70s exercise explosion of skiing, tennis and jogging to create their '80s and now '90s child . . . bodybuilding.

It's not a big jump from the therapist's couch to the personal trainer's bench, and from both comes that choral refrain: "I'm really getting into myself." Recreation comes from the Latin root, *recreare*, meaning to re-create. Through re-creation, one Angelo Siciliano took up dumbbells and changed his name to Charles Atlas. The gym is the latest finishing or night school, where, with the assistance of a nutritionist and a personal trainer, you may apply yourself diligently to "get ahead" and reach your full potential. This regeneration is self-discovery through sweat. Like est, the muscle makeover is another form of breaking down and rebuilding. It offers practical techniques for personal transformation. Every gym member is "a work in progress," busy building self-esteem (which will work only as long as the muscular look is fashionable).

In the language of therapy, personal growth is the goal, where in the name of "self-actualization" ("inside every little man is a big man bustin' to get out"), every training session is an empowerment workshop. "Accessed" by positive thinking, what is sought is proper "alignment," whether spiritual (through the medium of the New Age guru, astrologist or channeler), or physical (through the latest scientific shamans, the chiropractor, Rolfer or personal trainer).

That explains the religiosity of the exercise and the wide-eyed fanaticism of the disciples. The body boosterism of the brethren with attendant fundamentalist fevor ("I'm lifting heavy today. I'm working on my foundation.") is the language of the born-again. It's the early twentieth-century tradition of the muscular Christian, but turned inward. Not toward Christian charity but toward deltoid definition.

The body may be the temple of the Lord, but the gym is the place of worship, and in this church for the secular, one may experience communion (let's lift together), exaltation (the pump), confirmation (the mirror), benediction (the trainer's nod), resurrection (the promise of a new, purer body), ablution (the post-workout shower), redemption (the expiation of sin and guilt through physical frenzy), and even divine selection (genetics — anointed by God). As in any religion, doubt and skepticism, the artist's assets, are the disciple's worst sins.

But cutting the body to fit this year's fashions doesn't end at the gym. It ends at the hospital, where the surgeons of Silicone Valley (not sculptors but stylists) accommodate those seeking "self-improvement" with male boob jobs (pectoral implants with silicone lozenges), calf implants, liposuction (vacuuming fat off the hips, ass, and thighs, with a souped-up Hoover). To those who doubt Susan Bordo, who calls every body both "a cultural form" and "a coercive ideal," surgical augmentation is now termed "correction."[35]

The patients pursue with the physician (make that beautician) the cookie-cutter pattern of the reconstructed body. They're following a dress code in flesh. But muscles, like leather and Levis, like the military uniform, is a loss of individuality. Fascism is sexy because it renders the individual faceless. His urge is to merge in tribalism, to identify himself as a member of a taboo collective. After all, the essence of fashion is that there's more than safety in buying the look and playing the role. There's salvation.

By adopting the slogans ("Tough Times Don't Last. Tough People Do."), the vocabulary ("I'm pumped!"), by mimicking the mannerisms of the subculture, by physically filling the mold, he'll be, for one shining moment, saved. It's the merciful end of free will. There's no need to look at a possibility of choice on the menu or in the mind. Instead, buy *Bodybuilding Lifestyles* or *Shape*, become a walking, talking—actually, lip-synching—cliché. Become a replicant. Add to the three D's of gymspeak ("Discipline, Dedication, Determination") a fourth: Decapitation.

NOTES

[1]Alex Bellos, "Invasion of the Bodybuilders," *Weekend Guardian*, November 3–4, 1990, 14.

[2]Rick Telander, *The Hundred Yard Lie* (New York: Simon & Schuster, 1989), 155.

[3]Arnold Schwarzenegger and Bill Dobbins, *Encyclopedia of Modern Bodybuilding* (New York: Simon & Schuster, 1985), 30.

[4]Julian Schmidt, "This Joker is Wild," *Flex*, January 1991, 123.

[5]Arnold Schwarzenegger and Douglas Kent Hall, *Arnold: The Education of a Bodybuilder* (New York: Simon & Schuster, 1977), 69, 70.

[6]Susan Sontag, "Notes on Camp," *A Susan Sontag Reader* (New York: Farrar, Straus, Giroux, 1982), 116.

[7]Yukio Mishima, *Sun and Steel* (New York: Grove Press, 1980), 48.

[8]Marshall Blonsky, *American Mythologies* (New York: Oxford, 1992), 121.

[9]Jean Genet, *The Thief's Journal* (New York: Grove Press, 1964), 142.

[10]Yukio Mishima, *Sun and Steel*, 23.

[11]Schwarzenegger and Hall, *Arnold*, 16.

[12]*Musclemag International*, February 1993, 263.

[13]David Kopay and Perry Deane Young, *The David Kopay Story* (New York: Donald I. Fine, 1988), 226.

[14]Betsy Israel, "The Muscle Merchant of Venice," *GQ*, March 1991, 244.

[15]Steve Courson & Lee R. Schreiber, *The Steve Courson Story* (Stamford, CT: Longmeadow Press, 1991), 160.

[16]Norman Mailer, "King of the Hill," *Reading the Fights*, eds., Joyce Carol Oates and Daniel Halpern (New York: Henry Holt and Company, 1988), 124.

[17]Paul Solotaroff, "The Power & The Glory," *The Village Voice*, October 29, 1991, 29.

[18]Julian Schmidt, "Rediscovering North America," *Flex*, January 1991, 118.

[19]Hunter S. Thompson, *The Great Shark Hunt* (London: Pan, 1980), 546.

[20]Solotaroff, 156.

[21]Irving Muchnick, "Pimping Iron," *Spy*, June 1991, 57.

[22]*The New York Times*, June 23, 1992, D 18.

[23]Andrew Sullivan, "Muscleheads: Bodybuilding's Bottom Line," *The New Republic*, Sept 15, 1986, 24.

[24]Jeanette Winterson, *The Passion* (New York: Vintage, 1989), 45.

[25]Victor Bockris, *Keith Richards* (New York: Simon & Schuster, 1992), 166, 306.

[26]George Butler, *Arnold Schwarzenegger. A Portrait* (New York: Simon & Schuster, 1990), 34.

[27]1985 NCAA study of 2,040 college athletes, *USA Today*, January 23, 1987, 6C, and *Courson*, 152.

[28]Schwarzenegger and Dobbins, *Encyclopedia of Modern Bodybuilding*, 275, 372.

[29]*Musclemag International*, March 1993, 263.

[30]*Ironman Magazine*, January 1991, 57.

[31]*Musclemag International*, February 1993, 237.

[32]James Boswell, *The Life of Samuel Johnson*, ed. G. B. Hill, rev. L. F. Powell (New York: Oxford University Press, 1934–65), 2, 435., n, 7.

[33]*Musclemag International*, March 1993, 263.

[34]Tom Wolfe, *The Purple Decades* (New York: Farrar, Straus and Giroux, 1984), 277.

[35]Susan Bordo, " 'Material Girl': The Effacements of Postmodern Culture," *The Female Body: Figures, Styles, Speculations*, ed. Laurence Goldstein (Ann Arbor: University of Michigan Press, 1991), 125. Elisabeth Rosenthal, "Cosmetic Surgeons Seek New Frontiers," *The New York Times*, September 24, 1991, C 10.

THE LOST CHILD

Our lives of secrecy, as children.

The secrets never to be uttered, to adults. Even after so long a passage of time we've become adults ourselves.

"Here's something!" one of us said, and snatched it up.

Beneath the rotting pier, at the end of the spit of land called Fox Point, amid muddy sand and beach debris, the torn snapshot, a color Polaroid, lay partly buried.

It was Jean, twelve years old, the oldest among us, who'd found the snapshot and ran out from beneath the pier with it, into daylight, to see it better. There was no sun, the sky was mottled with pearly incandescent cloud. Across Lake Ontario waves were wild, choppy, angry-looking, capped with froth and there was that smell that came with wind from the north — sharp and briny, like wet sand, decaying fish.

"What is it? Let's see — " seeing the expression on Jean's face we crowded around her, but Jean backed off, staring at what she held in her hand, "What is it, what *is it*?"

Jean was a tall, stocky girl whose parents were divorced and whose mother worked in a plastics factory. Her face reddened easily, showing every emotion. Whatever the Polaroid was, it surprised and intrigued her, she stared at it with a look of incredulity, and alarm, and extreme embarrassment. "Something nasty," Jean mumbled, holding the snapshot out of reach, " — never *mind*." Her cheeks were ruddy as if they'd been slapped. Her eyes were damp and narrowed. These were signals to be wary with Jean, she was a big, strong girl, with a quick temper; the kind to lash out with an elbow or a fist if you got too close when she didn't want you close.

Another girl, Bobbie, insisted upon looking, and reluctantly Jean showed it to her, and Bobbie snorted with disbelief, "Jesus," and stood stock still. "What're they doing? — d'you know who it *is?*"

Bobbie and Jean began to giggle, wildly. There was nothing mirthful in their giggling which had a sharp, hurtful sound, like pebbles flung at the underside of the abandoned pier.

The rest of us, three or four of us, including Jean's nine-year-old brother Mickey, clamored to see, too, but were rebuffed, as Bobbie and Jean passed the Polaroid between them, now shrieking with laughter, not wanting to be in possession of the snapshot but not wanting to surrender it to us, either, and this went on for a while, the wind was up and a smell of rain in the air, late August just before Labor Day when there was a quickened sense of urgency among us as if we knew, but how could we have known, that this was the last summer we would be children together quite like this, and farther up the beach, where the boardwalk began, there were young mothers with babies in strollers, there were older kids, familiar faces, there was the risk — but of course this was part, now, of the game — that someone would take note of us, of Jean and Bobbie making such a commotion, and come down, and demand to see, too.

Finally, another girl, Brenda, was allowed to see, for Brenda was Jean's best friend, a red-haired freckled girl with a reliable capacity for surprise, and Brenda too stared, and stared, " — who is it? — oh God," and I pushed forward impatiently, thinking to snatch the Polaroid from them, Brenda cried, not in meanness but in caution, as one stricken with alarm, " — Don't let Junie see!" and so they rebuffed me another time, and my eyes flooded with tears of resentment.

I saw that the three of them would share a secret forever, and I would be one of those, like nine-year-old Mickey, like Sharon Scott who was a little slow, relegated to *not knowing*. Banished to *not included*.

A flame passed over my brain, a terrible feverish need. Yet I could not beg, "Hey c'mon please, — please Jean c'mon," as I'd so often done in the past, for as long as I could remember. I sensed that this was different, for my protection somehow, as Mickey might be protected, and Sharon Scott, who was a little slow, but quick to tears, might be protected; and this startling perception of myself, as in an unexpected mirror or reflecting surface, was disturbing, too, for wasn't Junie the quickest and cleverest of her friends? didn't she get, seemingly without effort, the highest grades in school?

As if here, on the beach, this windy late summer day, the secret Polaroid snapshot hidden from me, school mattered in the slightest.

Sometimes on the boardwalk, down behind the grimy stucco changing rooms for men and women, older boys might call our attention to words scrawled on walls, we'd be urged to see what had been done overnight to posters, for instance the mutilated breasts of a grinning girl in a cowboy hat, or had the curving plume of smoke issuing from her mouth been turned into something tubular and solid, both comic and threatening, and, to me, mysterious — though as always, as in Jean's mumbled words, *something nasty*.

In the older boys' presence, I did not want to know. When the boys laughed in that excited, sniggering way, I did not want to know why.

Something nasty.

Which was how the boys asserted their power over us — the threat of embarrassment, shame.

With my girl friends Jean, Bobbie, Brenda, it was different. My need to know wasn't just curiosity but something stronger I could not have named. *I hate you, and I can't bear not to be one of you.* I rushed at Jean, who had the Polaroid again, and I snatched it out of her fingers, and ran off along the beach with it as they shouted after me, and when I saw they weren't following me I stopped to examine it — peering at it as at one of those puzzles in the children's magazine *Jack and Jill*, where, slyly hidden amid line-drawings of foliage and clouds, were faces, human figures, even animals. *What was this!*

The snapshot had been torn, folded, left out in the wet, dried and baked by the sun. Its Polaroid colors had faded and its images were blurred as in a dream. But it showed, so strangely, to my eyes astoundingly, a frightened little girl of perhaps four in the grip of a man, a naked man, pressed against his belly and groin, and what was she being forced to do, her jaws forced open, her cheeks wet with tears, I could not see, I saw but could not comprehend, staring as my eyes too filled with moisture, shocked, yet puzzled, more puzzled at first than shocked, because incredulous, " — What *is* it?" called out for my friends to hear. Only the naked torso, belly and groin of the man showed, and his fore-arms, his head was cut off so he might have been anyone, any man here at Fox Point, a man with a fatty slack belly covered in dark rippling hairs like fur, muscular forearms like our fathers' covered too in thick dark hairs. The little girl who was a stranger wore a tiny, torn undershirt and no panties; her skin was drained of all color by the Polaroid's flash, and hairless. Her face was partly hidden by the man's belly and hands — big-

knuckled hands, a signet ring on one of the fingers — gripping her
jaws and the back of her head. Her pale hair was matted and dishev-
eled and her eyes narrowed in such pain and terror I crumpled the
snapshot in my hand, and looked away blinking, blind, out at the
lake. Choppy white-capped waves, circling gulls. *What was it!*

My heart was beating strangely. I felt the shock in my body I felt
when I jumped from a risky height, always as a child I jumped to
impress my friends who watched but dared not emulate me, jumping from a lakefront retaining wall down to the beach, jumping
from the roof of our garage, landing hard on my heels, the shock
waves shooting up my body leaving me stunned, giddy.

Jean ran up, flush-faced, scared and angry, "Junie, damn you, I
told you!" and snatched the Polaroid back, and tore it into tiny bits,
and let the wind take them, and I turned and ran, ran and ran until
I was off the beach and far away, frantic to get home to the bungalow my parents rented for August, on a sandy lane lined with similar
bungalows, hard to distinguish one from the other except by the
towels and bathing suits tossed over railings to dry, or a car parked
out front. I didn't know what Jean meant by "I told you!" but I
wished I had not seen what I'd seen.

Something nasty.

I avoided my friends for what seemed like a long time but was
probably a single day, drawn out and seemingly endless as such
summer days are for children, and down at the beach with my
mother and little brother I was quiet, sullen, my mother asked was
something wrong and I said no but don't touch me, and it was so:
my skin smarted as with sunburn or fever. Not wanting to look at
people around me, at men in their bathing suits, my eyes filling with
moisture: no, don't look: I *told* you! Later I wandered off to the
pier, not on top (where you weren't supposed to walk, it was blocked
with a sign DANGER PIER NOT MAINTAINED BY COUNTY)
but beneath, where waves sopped up into the muddy sand, and
there was debris of all kinds, beer cans and bottles and the remains
of fires (though for miles along the beach were signs FIRES FOR-
BIDDEN ON BEACH BY ORDER OF COUNTY SHERIFF'S
DEPT.) and I poked around with a stick unearthing bottle caps,
broken combs, pearly shells, what looked like the charred remains of
snapshots, maybe.

But I found nothing. So I could begin to forget.

Next day, I was back with Jean, Bobbie, Brenda, and Sharon, as if nothing had happened. We never spoke of the Polaroid. We told no one about it. There were many secrets we never told our parents, or any adult, or even an older sister, secrets too certain of us shared with one girl but did not share with the others, for that was what we did, that was the happiness of our lives, such secrets, and the Polaroid Jean had ripped into bits and let the wind take was only one of these secrets, more perishable in fact than the others because it was something nasty of which, even among ourselves, we could not speak; and where a thing is not named, it is soon surrendered to oblivion.

But I remember: looking at the men on the beach for those remaining days of summer, their bodies which were naked except for swim trunks, sometimes the trunks were tight-fitting, you could see the bulge of what was inside, you could sense the weight of it, that secret too, and the fatty-muscular arms, shoulders, torsos, the hard lean muscles of the younger men, the slacker flesh of the older men, some of them deeply tanned, some pale as curdled milk, the arms of some ropy, the legs of some surprisingly thin, and some were near-hairless but most were covered in hairs, kinky-curly, matted or silky or frizzy, there were enormous paunches straining against elastic waistbands to the point of pain, there were chests with muscles hard as armor, chests flabby as melting chicken fat, and I saw with relief that my father was one of the younger men, arriving at the bungalow late Friday afternoon and changing right away into his trunks, just slightly soft at the waist but flat-chested and -bellied, with a thick frizzy swirl of reddish hairs on his torso, belly, legs, and his arms hard and muscular, yes and I saw that he wore no ring on either hand, I saw that right away.

Top: Bruce Springsteen. Photo Neal Preston.
Bottom: Axl Rose. Photo Larry Busacca / Retna, Ltd.

FRED PFEIL

ROCK INCORPORATED: PLUGGING IN TO
AXL AND BRUCE

Those bodies displayed beneath the throbbing lights, those rock stars shrieking and stomping, writhing and wailing away—one Bruce, the other Axl, arguably the two foremost rock superstars of the day, in the U.S. anyhow—what could be more immediately, more intensely True than the sight of either or each of them up there doing his own particular corporeal-musical thing? Why not just go to the videos or fanmag photos, bear down on a few representative shots and paradigmatic poses, read their reality straight off the surface where its charge lies waiting to be picked up and run through us as well?

Here is the basic not-so-simple reason why not: because rock stars, not only *even* but *especially* in their most apparently immediate forms and visages, have a nest of assumptions and histories packed inside them, a complexity the seeming directness of their respective physicalities belies and thus the more effectively insinuates.[1] Or, to put it the other way around, because we are already so primed for those bodies before we even see them, given what we already know, cannot help knowing, of rock & roll as social relations, popular culture, capitalist industry and musical form: because, as that old fascist expert in yearning Martin Heidegger might say, we come to such bodies "so belatedly," no matter how fresh or originary they might feel.

Later on, we will return to belatedness as a motif of at least one of the bodies we will read. What needs to be emphasized here, though, is the resemblance of both the body called Bruce and the other named Axl in the practice of rock & roll to the commodity as described by Marx in the practice of capitalist economic life: both apparently simple things whose sheer, obdurate, naturalized *quiddi-*

tas elides their backstage histories and futures as particular moments within a mammoth ongoing process of production, consumption and unequal exchange; and whose real specificities can only be understood by way of a whole series of general relations and determinations, rising as we narrow in toward the concrete.

Not—not quite—that the rocker's body is itself a commodity. Rather, like the movie-star's body it so resembles, it is precisely that which is permanently withheld from circulation, unapproachable and unpurchaseable except in terms of those products which yield us partial, mediated access to it: the fan-mag interviews and photos, the album, the concert video and of course the live concert itself. Thus the rocker's body, a production yet not a product, stands behind every rock commodity like an unmoved mover, guaranteeing its integrity yet untainted by its sale. On our slow zoom in to close-ups of Axl and Bruce in the flesh, we'll be trying to articulate other background assumptions and definitions: some, like the one just noted, of long standing, rooted in our common sense of "rock"; others, closer in to our imaginary playmates, reflecting newer and more volatile attempts to display, resolve, and/or transmogrify into the stuff of pleasure some more recent social processes and contradictions. But all of them, emerging through the sights and words and music, with something to tell us about how the codes and values and exchanges of sex and gender, race and class, work in this culture—how they trade off and double up and stand in for each other, working difference into domination and domination into difference, keeping us dancing in the dark.

1. Authenticity/History

> "This is *not* about Michael Jackson."
> —Axl Rose, upon accepting the Michael Jackson Video Vanguard award at the 1992 MTV Music Video Awards Program

Questions of what constitutes rock and how to assess its meaning-effects vex all but the most simple-minded and/or hype-ridden accounts of its origins and effects. McClary and Walser, speaking of popular music in general, point out how many more or less purely musical signals are sent and codes evoked by even the most basic pop single, and how impoverished and impressionistic are the languages we use to describe their combinations and effects.[2] (Case in point: how to describe in formalist musical terms the blend of pitch, pulse, emphasis and melisma at work in the young Michael Jackson's first entrance — "uh-*unh*-uh-unh-*UH*" — in that masterpiece of '70s bubble-gum "ABC"?) And Andrew Goodwin reminds us of the exponential surge in complexity and indeterminacy that wells up as soon as we move from a strict musicological analysis to the kinds and combinations of "iconographies stored in popular cultural memory" which any given cut might call up:

> (a) personal imagery deriving from the individual memories associated with the song; (b) images associated purely with the music itself . . ., which may work through either metaphor or metonymy; (c) images of the musicians/performers; (d) visual signifiers deriving from national-popular iconography, perhaps related to geographical associations prompted by the performers [e.g., images of Irishness associated with the Pogues]; and (e) deeply anchored popular cultural signs associated with rock music that often link rock with a mythologized "America" (cars, freeways, beer, beaches, parties).[3]

The polysemousness of pop music thus comes as both blessing and curse to culture critics — including this one, of course — whose readings are licensed and privileges leveled in the same multivalent breath. Yet notwithstanding the sprawling complexity of pop in general, it is still possible to limn out a few of the borderlines and defining traits of the realm of rock that lies within it. A few of these topographical markings are musical in nature, even if their diacritical distinctiveness must shift with the times just to stay in the same dissident relation to the ever-changing practices of pop. If Buddy Holly were alive today, for example, and "Peggy Sue" were a brand-new release, it would probably not be considered rock & roll, given its bouncy beat, teenybop lyric, and Buddy Holly's cheery burping warble. What set it off from other pop music in its time is, however, what still differentially sets off rock from pop in our own: the *relative* centrality and foregroundedness of electric guitar and drums, together with the *relatively* aggressive insistence of the "driving" 4/4 rhythms they make and keep; all that, in combination with the *relative* "rawness" of the R&B-tinged sound it offers its white mainstream audience.

The socio-musical emergence of rock & roll in the '50s and '60s as a fusion of rhythm-and-blues and/or rockabilly with various formal, timbral and structural elements from mainstream pop, is a story that can be and has been told in a variety of ways, each with its own axe to grind: neutrally, as a paradigmatic instance of the interplay of subcultural or, in some accounts, folk practices with mass culture[4]; negatively, as another instance of racist and/or capitalist appropriation and exploitation[5]; and positively, as a romantic narrative of the rise to popularity and acclaim of a music of unquenchable energy, passion and truth, the "music that will set you free," as The Lovin' Spoonful said. This last, of course, is the favored narrative of the music industry itself, from the smallest fanzine and one-band promoter to the upper reaches of Geffen Records and *Rolling Stone*, and for obvious reasons: it helps to sell product while obscuring process, for music consumers and for many an industry insider as well, for whom the myth of rock & roll ennobles what would otherwise be just another way to make a buck. Yet while this triumphalist narrative of rock & roll should hardly be taken as gospel, neither should it be dismissed as sheer mystification. The ideology of rock & roll works — and goes on working, however tenuously — because whatever else it does, it has also, and from its inception, always worked on and within a much larger, ongoing social and ideological project: the social placement and definition of white male youth, from the first of the baby-boomers back in the '50s to the youngest of their sons today.

Once we take rock's romantic ideology in as an aspect of this larger historic project, we can see how its heroic narrative of emergence and triumph actually includes the other, less flattering narratives at least as much as it effaces them. After all, on the one hand rock & roll is a branch or category of popular music; on the other, as a wide variety of critics have argued for years,[6] it has since its inception been co-extensive with a host of other practices used *by* and *on* kids, especially young white guys, to say who they are. So, for example, working on early rock music and '50s mass culture, Harris Freiberg has traced out the complicated dialectic a tune like Elvis's "Hound Dog" has to dance between a free sexuality still at least partly coded "Black," and the scrambling into near incoherence of Big Mama Thornton's country-blues lyrics and smoothing-down of her "raw," throat-tearing vocal style into a sufficiently tamed and whitened product as to be fit for mass consumption. Yet Freiberg goes on to remind us that despite such bowdlerizing and for all the bottom-line repressiveness of many if not most lyrics, early rock was rightly viewed with suspicion and hostility by American cultural and political conservatives, insofar as the "ideology of the beat" it proposed and the "speech of the body" it invited were "not compromised."

Freiberg's account of '50s rock is still more nuanced than my summary here can suggest. But I want to add yet another layer, or possible reading, to that account before moving on to Mark 2 of this brief social history, by suggesting more emphatically than Freiberg does that what is constructed vis-à-vis the compromise formations he explores is not only a space within the music industry for a new kind of product aimed at that new social subject, the "teenager," but also and more specifically the definition of a new version of "teen" (i.e., adolescent, white) *masculinity* as well — a masculinity, moreover, with the well-nigh irresistible attraction of being almost exactly as transgressive as it is normative. So, to return to our example, the new masculinity defined by the white male rocker of the '50s includes, for starters, a different kind of *Whiteness*, one that comes with access to the musical-libidinal resources of Blackness, but unlike Mailer's fantasized hipster-ideal, with no additional risk or requirement to become a "white Negro" oneself;[7] the same domestication of Black country blues styles and idioms Freiberg describes in commercial terms as a prerequisite for mass (re)production here reappears as the comforting sense, for those who get it, that no matter how much friendly shakin' is goin' on there is no doubt as to who is ultimately still in control.

Something of the same is true as well of the new masculinity proposed by '50s rock in terms of gender. David R. Shumway rightly reminds us that for much of white America in the '50s what was most shocking about Elvis was his offering of himself, i.e., his *male* body, as a sexual object for (mainly) *women* to gaze at and enjoy. But this reversal of direction and field in sexual objectification was hedged in a variety of ways; and in any case it never amounted simply to feminization. Rather, in Elvis's person and music the smooth composure of the tepidly hip white male crooner (Perry Como, Dean Martin, Frank Sinatra) split as it erupted into two virtually opposed attitudes perhaps best expressed by the young Elvis's two most characteristic moues — the baby-faced pout, to be held for publicity shots and while singing "But I Can't Help Falling in Love with You," and the sideways sneer for rocking out. If the first suggests a new emotional vulnerability or even, along with songs like "I Can't Help" or "Love Me Tender," a childlike near-subjection to the adored and empowered female love, the open sexuality of the second only appears accompanied by a striking blend of narcissistic arrogance: as his famous hips gyrate, Elvis tosses his head with eyes closed in self-satisfaction, then looks out at the screaming crowd of girls with a gleeful jeer.

"To an unusual degree," Richard Middleton writes, "Presley offered an individual body, unique, untranslatable, outside the familiar cultural framework, exciting and dangerous";[8] and of course we know that body was indeed an affront to white middle-class norms of what masculinity should be. But Middleton also reminds us that the other side of whatever seems to us to be the most uncoded behavior is the very code from which it seems to have escaped, that the "nature" of any "*jouissance* . . . varies in relation to the positioning of the semiotically constructed subject who is 'lost.' " Accordingly, what may strike us now from our position within a moment governed by somewhat different codes is not so much the scandalous invitation issued by the figure of Elvis for young men to open up their constrained bodies and unbind their sexual energies as the lines of power and definition that continue to be drawn between white and Black, men and women, even within the new dispensation. The new masculinity proposed for young white men by the voices and bodies of '50s rock & roll may have been "downwardly mobile" in a variety of ways, but it was hardly an oppositional one even so.

Yet in Mark 2 of the story I want to tell here, the white masculinity proposed by rock & roll does take on a broadly political hue. Or, perhaps more accurately, together with rock it participates in and derives some part of its energy from a widely-shared fantasy of political project. I'm speaking, of course, of the '60s (meaning, as we usually do, mainly the years between 1966 and 1974), when rock & roll was taken to be in cultural practice what the so-called "youth movement" was perceived to be in politics: to fans and detractors alike, an organic expression of a generation of white American youth whose size, affluence, and influence in political and buying power alike were unprecedented. For these "baby-boomers," the idioms and energies appropriated from Black music, together with the sexual flaunting of bourgeois norms, seemed "naturally" affiliated with sympathies for Blacks and other oppressed people at home and abroad, and a hostility toward the corporate boardroom, the military-industrial complex, and the State: what brought rock and white youth movement politics together was their mutual opposition to everything "straight."

At this moment, then, rock & roll took on the same sort of resonance for and relationship to its social audience of white baby-boomers that the English novel did for its bourgeoisie a century and a half or so earlier: so much so that we might speak of it as the equivalent of the earlier form's moment of "organic realism." At the same time, fueled by industry hype, the consensual definition of rock stretched to the widest limit of its loose unity, ranging from the extended obbligato figurations of blues-based psychedelic music (e.g., Cream or Jefferson Airplane) across now-traditional rock forms (Credence Clearwater Revival) to include a variety of eclectic transactions with older idioms of popular music (the Beatles and the music-hall sing-along tune). It even briefly stretched to include a few women as *bona fide* rockers — Grace Slick and Janis Joplin — and, along its most countercultural edge, one African-American, Jimi Hendrix, as crossover flower child. Yet the body to be found at the epicenter of the moment characterized in our romantic narrative as *the* Triumph of Rock & Roll, is, inevitably, still that of a white man, Mick Jagger, lead singer of The Rolling Stones.

The Stones' music, especially in the years 1968–72, played across the spectrum we have just described, yet all the while continued to develop and refine its appropriated home in R&B into an edgier, grungier yet more amped-up sound that even today serves as the North Star of Rock. Moreover, on an album like *Beggars' Banquet*, the Stones' bad attitude slid easily from solidarity with the oppressed ("The Salt of the Earth") to a gleeful Nietzschean identification with power ("Sympathy for the Devil"). But the clincher here is, of course, the way Jagger's body looked, sounded and performed throughout the late '60s and into the '70s: doing "Sympathy" in his American flag suit and cape, prancing through "Jumpin' Jack Flash" or lashing the mike cord like a whip for "Gimme Shelter," wrapping his fat lips around the mike for the verses of "Satisfaction" then snarling out the choruses, as his skinny hips kept jerking and pumping the entire time. Just as the Stones consolidated rock's paradigmatic sound, Jagger's body re-enacted and extended its Mark 1 version of white masculinity. His pasty-white Britishness gave him license to steal stage moves from soul stars like James Brown and their reviews more brazenly than any '50s rocker ripped off any Black R&B performer; he could do all the blues dips, growls and slides he liked, knock off any number of — usually uncredited — Robert Johnson tunes, since his every attempt to do a Black English drawl (the way he does his "my's," say, in "Under My Thumb") was doomed to succeed exactly as much as it failed. Moreover, like many a hippie's or New Left activist's, Jagger's lissome frame appeared before us not only fully sexualized, but in marked distinction from — indeed, virtual opposition to — that fully armored body-image of (especially) working-class masculinity whose "muscle tensions, posture, . . . feel and texture" traditionally enforces both a hierarchical order within masculinity and the domination of women, by "allowing belief in the superiority of men, and the oppressive practices that flow from it, to be sustained by men who in other respects have very little power."[9] But, as with the misogynous New Left men so brilliantly anatomized in Dorothy Dinnerstein's *The Mermaid and the Minotaur*, the counterweight to all Mick's dabbling in androgynous and/or femininine qualities and imagery was a taunting sexualized viciousness toward women in the songs themselves, from "Under My Thumb" to the notorious *Black and Blue* album and slogan (the battered woman on the billboard proclaiming "I'm Black and Blue from the Rolling Stones and I love it!") and many stops in between.

In a pair of valuable essays on rock, sexual identity and commercialism whose narrative tracks run close to mine here, Jon Savage and Mary Harron both maintain that in the '70s the radical impulses and energies that fueled rock culture and the youth movements of the 1960s hit the skids, as the murky left-libertarianism of the latter evaporated into so many lifestyle choices, and "artists and fans who wanted to express themselves rather than simply be entertained" turned into a pack of consumers to be manipulated by "record companies . . . making their biggest profits ever by *regulating* the urge to be different that had once given rock music its reason to live."[10] Yet, according to Savage, the "consumer society based on the teenage sensibility" which survives "is still dominated by that brief but explosive period in the mid-sixties whose implications (and detritus) live with us still."[11] But for all their valuable attempts to take stock of commercial motives (Harron) and the confusion of political commitment and consumerist lifestyle (Savage), such accounts are distorted by their complicity with the very romanticism they seek to resist.

After all, it is not so much that rock & roll lost its soul in the '70s and '80s as that various forms of rock & roll practice, and various audiences, claimed they had it and the others didn't; not so much that the music industry once had to run as fast as it could to keep up with rock "authenticity" but now needs only pump out its simulacra, as that the "urge to be different" has itself become differentiated within rock & roll and so demands further product differentiation in turn.

The specific historical point here may be extrapolated into something of a categorical observation on what the social project of rock "authenticity" has been about from the get-go. Rock critics have generally agreed that "[t]he rock aesthetic depends, crucially, on an argument about authenticity";[12] and even that this "myth of authenticity" is the spinning flywheel of the rock imagination, Maxwell's Demon of the industry, insofar as the "desire for the original and the authentic exists alongside the recognition that there can never be such a thing."[13] But no one, so far as I know, has pointed out just how thoroughly this desire for a break with commercial culture and a disavowal of the commodity status of rock — to be opposed to "pop" from within, by dint of an "organic" relationship with the music, its traditions and its audience — is imbricated with the desire to construct, maintain and emulate an alternative white masculinity. Rock, Harron writes, "wants deep emotion and catharsis and truth . . . has a religious element that pop does not . . . believes in originality and self-expression in defiance of crass commercialism."[14] But all these terms, true enough in themselves, read as an allegory of racial and sexual positioning as well. Decoded in this way, what rock authenticity means is not just freedom from commerce and opposition to all straight authority combined with deep vocational allegiance to the music, but being a free agent with ready access to the resources of femininity and Blackness yet no obligations to either women or Blacks.

Rock, then, is a cultural practice which defines itself — musically, socially, and perhaps most of all, physically — in distinction from Blackness, opposition to official authority and mainstream rectitude, and a combination of difference and charged opposition to women. The coexistence and historical development of these factors is both cause and effect of the fact that at any given moment almost all rock stars are white men; or, to put it the other way around, why so little music by women or non-white bands (with, generally, single exceptions at best — today, Living Colour and Los Lobos) is ever considered rock, by either promoters, critics, fans, or for that matter the bands themselves; why the most Michael Jackson can ever aspire to is the self-proclaimed title "The King of Pop"; and why it is so important for so many reasons for Axl Rose to insist that his band's award for best new video is "not about Michael Jackson" at all.

2. The "Get in the Ring" Tour: Bodies and Masculinities

When in the '70s and '80s contending rock bands, genres, and audiences vied for rock lineage and natural title, what was then at stake in the opposition of their musical idioms, mythical histories, and social behaviors was not a merely musical issue, much less just a matter of marketing and profits. The question of who is the hardest, realest rocker will also, and perhaps above all, be a matter of which alternative white masculinity is to be affirmed and approved above all other options. And the place where such choices show up in their most condensed and visible form is the rocker's body itself: the figure in which the polysemousness of rock music and its claims to authenticity find their anchor and *omphalos*.

Problem is, though, the closer we approach such nodal figures, the more seductive their siren songs of authenticity tend to become. How else understand no less astute a commentator than Simon Frith falling prey to the authenticity trope — or, more likely, of the whole complex of rock meanings and effects known as Bruce Springsteen — when he tries to make the two into a genre he seems to think, and want us to think, was there the whole time? An "interesting way of approaching genres," writes Frith,

> is to classify them according to their ideological effects, the way they sell themselves as art, community or emotion. There is, at present, for example, clearly a form of rock we call 'authentic.' It is represented by Bruce Springsteen and defines itself according to the rock aesthetic of authenticity. . . . The whole point of this genre is to develop musical conventions which are, in themselves, measures of 'truth.' As listeners we are drawn into a certain sort of reality; this is what it is like to live in America, this is what it is like to love or hurt. [15]

Here, in the slippage between rock in general and one rock star in particular, the whole conceptual level of genre is actually elided. Nor is this the only place in Frith's *oeuvre* where he lets his categories slide for Bruce's sake. In an essay-review of the live box-set issue, *Bruce Springsteen and the E Street Band Live*, ominously entitled "The Real Thing — Bruce Springsteen," Frith tells us that "what matters in this post-modern era is not whether Bruce Springsteen *is* the real, but how he sustains the belief that there are somehow, somewhere, real things to *be*."[16]

What's wrong — astonishingly wrong, really — with such pronouncements is not only that it is of course possible to think in much more specific generic terms about the kind of music Springsteen makes than Frith is willing to acknowledge, but that there are any number of other rock stars and bands working other idioms in such a way as to sustain "the belief that there are somehow, somewhere, real things to be" — albeit for other rock audiences of whose existence Frith is momentarily unaware. Perhaps foremost among these other audiences in the '70s and '80s, as Guns N' Roses' shot to the top of the charts has made so plain, is that for heavy metal. And just because Axl Rose sustains the belief there are real things to be in a way that's different from Bruce's doesn't make Axl's "Real" any more or less constructed than the Boss's; it simply means that there are two different *constructions* here, of the Real, of rock authenticity, and of alternative "wild" white-guy masculinity, one that went supernova back in 85–86, and the other on its heels at the cusp of the '80s just past, a timing sequence that suggests something happening out in the land around the place and image of white guys, something legible in the contrast of these stars.

Genre in rock is in fact nothing more than the way such differences — in claims for authenticity, definitions of the real, visions of masculinity, and audiences willing to swallow or at least enjoy them all — group themselves around a given sound and all its associations, inherited and constructed; and it exists in roughly the same co-constructive relationship with the figure of the rock star as film genre does to the movie star. In both cases, the figure of the star condenses "values felt to be under threat or in flux at a particular moment in time,"[17] and does so from a peculiarly intermediary position between the "personal" — the star's "offstage personality" and "private life" given to us through an array of interviews on tv, in magazines, etc. — and the generic pool of meanings and values with which their performances are associated. What most distinguishes rock from film culture in this respect is, however, the consistency and coherence which rock fans expect from their stars in terms of just this relationship between rock genre and "offstage" personality profile. In the late 1940s and early '50s, for example, Humphrey Bogart's star image is a contrapuntal construction: existential tough-guy loner on the generic side thanks to *Casablanca* and *film noir*, happy family man with loving wife Lauren Bacall in private life. Rock performers, on the other hand, tend to pay a price for such inconsistencies — as heavy metal's Ozzy Osbourne found out when he went clean and sober, and as Bruce himself, the former New Jersey rocker now happily ensconced in his Beverly Hills mansion with his lovely wife and kids, may be learning from the slump in sales receipts for the two albums he put out last year.

Such surmises, though, whatever they are worth, may be found in any music or entertainment guide that covers rock; and in any case, I'd rather ponder the more interesting possibility that what those disappointing sales figures mean, combined with the monster success of GN'R, is that Bruce's aureatic power as a rock star is fading as Axl's (at least up to the close of '92) is blazing ever brighter. But to explore this possibility, we'll have to shuttle back and forth between star image and rock genre for both Bruce and Axl without either buying or dismissing either's claim to authenticity — and repeatedly, inevitably, find ourselves stumbling over their bodies as we do.

Axl and heavy metal, then, Bruce and — and what? The problem of locating Springsteen generically is an interesting and complicated one, partly because the generic claims he and his music make have always been so syncretic, and partly because of the way those claims have accreted and altered over time. The through-line, though, is a mythologized biography dwelling on, and so reinforcing, a pre-given set of associations in rock culture: the white working-class kid from a working-class family in a blue-collar town in New Jersey, no less, who grows up first loving then playing rock & roll, and pays his dues by playing it year after year in his own area, building a following among kids like him, playing the joints and developing a name. Eventually, thanks to his devotion to the music/his culture/the kids, this kid miraculously gets signed by the most prestigious producer not only at Columbia but generally in '60s rock, the guy who signed Dylan for crying out loud. But even then he just keeps on putting in his time, working on his albums but still giving everything he's got up on stage, putting himself and the music out there on the line until eventually, in 1984, he puts out this album and goes on this tour, and *everybody* gets it, *everybody* identifies, but even that doesn't change him: he's still the same Bruce, the same hard-rockin' working-class guy.[18]

The basic image, then, through which the Bruce's authenticity-effect is secured is that of unbroken organic affiliation and continuity: Bruce = rock & roll = the sound of passion, excitement, and rebellion in industrial working-class life. Thus too, of course, Bruce's own physical image, even off-stage, in jeans and sleeveless t-shirt with a day's growth of stubble on his face, not to mention the guy with his back to us and his ballcap in his back pocket on the front of *Born in the U.S.A.* But before going on to explore this image further, it's worth pointing out just how gradually and, at least at first, uncertainly it was built up over the course of Bruce's recording career. Take, for example, the earliest and most "organic" performance collected in *Bruce Springsteen: Video Anthology 1978–1987*: Bruce and his E Street Band rocking out on "Rosalita" in what looks vaguely like a mid-sized auditorium, with the crowd so near and the security so lax that through much of the performance he is assailed by adoring young women leaping up onto the stage. Here, we seem to be watching a Bruce before superstardom, back when his fame was still mainly regional, not that far from the days of Asbury Park; yet even here, already here, we see the distinguishing marks of his later live performances. The joyful and capricious interactions with the other members of the band, including and especially Black saxophonist Clarence Clemons, the "Big Man," filling stage left to Bruce's stage right; the playful yet sincere, parodic yet enthusiastic rock moves of aiming the guitar neck out at the crowd as the riff is "fired off," of stalking the stage or dashing across it to skid to his knees as the song's excitement mounts, of tossing himself up back-down on the lid of the piano in the sheer delight of his own guitar riffs: all these gestures and behaviors testify not only to the raw excitement and ecstatic pleasure of the music, but, combined with Bruce's near constant eye-contact with his audience and eager smile (except when he is singing — that, as we shall see, is something else), also to his need to offer these same pleasures out to his audience, to include them in — his desire, in short, to *please*.

So runs the now-familiar rhetoric of joyful populist sincerity in the Springsteen performance. Yet at least as interesting and significant as the continuity of this behavioral communication are the disjunctive elements in Springsteen's image at this point. Disjunctive, that is, with the more emphatically blue-collar imagery that will eventually become official, even regulative, aspects of Bruceness once he goes mega: for this earlier Bruce is a guy with a smooth face, tousled longish curly hair, some kind of a silk or polyester shirt unbuttoned to the waist underneath a box-shouldered *sportcoat*, no less — Bruce actually *dressed up*. This dressed-up quality, ironically enough, may supply further warrant for the organic nature of Bruce's relationship with working-class milieux and audiences at this point, for those who know how much such folks tend to appreciate the performer who suits up a little for them. Moreover, such attire harks back to the time and image of such '50s "dreamboats" as Fabian, Frankie Avalon, and the "pop"-ularized Presley himself, all stars plucked from white working-class backgrounds and molded into visual and musical shapes designed to attract young white working-class women most of all.

This retro image appears more explicitly in the live performance that follows "Rosalita" on the video anthology, a version of "The River" Bruce delivers decked out in a baby-blue sportcoat with his hair in a d.a.'d pompadour. But here it is refined, complicated, and updated even as it is emphasized by the rapt attentiveness with which the camera holds Bruce in closeup through the song, except for a few slow zooms in and out. This still concentration, along with the quiet intensity of Bruce's delivery, not only helps pin our sense of Bruce's sincerity to the lyrics' narrative of male working-class experience ("For my nineteenth birthday, I got a union card and a wedding coat") and its dissatisfactions ("Is a dream a lie if it don't come true / Or is it something worse?"), but invites us to regard those words as somehow more artful and more deeply true than the usual rock lyric; just as Bruce's curly locks in the "Rosalita" video and the *Born to Run* record cover, backed of course by his occasional Dylanesque use of the mouth harp, are conversely meant to say "Rock *Poet*" to us.

This image of Springsteen as working-class *artist* will later on in his career be deemphasized but never revoked. (And if one knows, or remembers, the story of how Bruce Springsteen was introduced as "the next Dylan" to John Hammond, the man who first signed him for Columbia, so much the better.) Even for those whose fandom began twelve years later, when *Born in the U.S.A.* hit the racks, its faint yet precious penumbra of cultural cachet stands behind and backs the later image as swaggering, solidly muscled working-class rocker, legitimating backdrop for what the foreground seems to authenticate. In this sense the packed lines and home-grown metaphors in Springsteen's lyrics and the raspy clenched coarseness of his singing voice from the beginning complement and justify one another, yet together serve as well still another function: that of obscuring the dubious (from a rock perspective, that is) genealogies of many of the musical idioms Springsteen has tapped for his songs. Of the two most famous songs from what we can now call the "early" period of Springsteen's fame, for example, "Rosalita" stripped of Springsteen's gritty delivery sounds more like "Only in America" or some similar piece of mid-60s pop by a group like Jay and the Americans than any rock & roll; while the overwrought "epic" structure of "Born to Run," minus the edge of the electric guitars and Bruce's voice, seems suspiciously close to the near-forgotten pop-pretensions of Richard Harris's "MacArthur Park."

Something of the same "stirring" film-soundtrack sonority runs through "Born in the U.S.A." as well, in a similar pattern of instrumental repetition of the song's main phrase as the lead-in to each verse. Here again, the trick is to ennoble what the voice authenticates via the soundtrack sound's marriage to the gritty shout—so "close to the heart" and "true to life" it is hardly even singing, one might feel—of Bruce's monotonously emphatic stamping out of the lyrics, a "singing" which functions in turn as a metonymy for the monotonous oppression of male working-class life the lyrics narrate from hometown to Vietnam and back. But before delving any further into this particular song and its associated body-image, I want to close off this no doubt incomplete tour of musical idioms by noting the regular, indeed well-nigh constitutive presence in much of Springsteen's output of yet one more idiomatic strand, i.e., that of rockabilly and country-western. You can at times hear in Bruce— say, in a song like *Tunnel of Love*'s "Spare Parts"—a little Chuck Berry; but Chuck Berry himself, of course, has his own complicated relationship to white rockabilly sound. At any rate, the main point here is how relatively little Bruce's music owes to Black-centered blues and R&B, how much to the traditionally white idioms of country blues and ballads. Such influences show up practically everywhere in Bruce's music: in the western Frankie Laine or Jimmie Rodgers-style yodelling he trails off the end of a song like "I'm on

Fire"; in the ballad structure of "Spare Parts" and other songs; in the pulse of the rhythm, timbre and drawl of his voice in a first-person love-trouble tune like "One Step Up," to name only a few.

The "Whiteness" of these musical influences contributes to the construction of Bruce's image in a variety of ways, even as they too are inflected by other elements of the Springsteen complex. Circumscribed and to some degree masked by Bruce's "tougher-than-the-rest" voice, and elevated sonically, visually, and/or verbally by the various strategies of ennoblement I have described above, they nonetheless function to *dis*-affiliate Springsteen's rocking from rock's traditionally uneasy, energetic, and exploitative relationship with "Blackness." At the same time, and as part of the same process, they help to reconnect the notion of rock and rock authenticity to the class signifier to which they were first attached in Mark 1 of our narrative: the white *working-class* rocker, albeit here one shorn of any musical attachment to Blacks. In so doing, moreover, we might say the image of this ennobled yet class-specific rocker simply leaps back over and "forgets" the '60s moment in rock history when rock largely lost its class accents to become the music of "its" generation, i.e., of college- and draft-age baby-boomers as volatile political subjects and target-rich consumer group: a moment when, as we have seen, rock masculinity draws closer to "femininity" and "Blackness" alike while remaining hostilely or at least pre-eminently distinct from each.

Nor are these elements the only ones lost in this great leap backward: for there is, after all, the effect of the leap itself to take into account as well. At a moment in the Reagan '80s characterized by the decline of traditional manufacturing sectors and the loss of manufacturing jobs, Bruce's reconstruction of the rocker as organic white working-class hero might — on the surface, as it were — seem a potentially volatile and energetic figure capable of condensing and reflecting, if not actually galvanizing, a progressive class-based political will. Yet as all but Bruce's most indefatigable boosters have acknowledged, Bruce has been "read" as a progressive left-liberal figure mainly if not exclusively by intellectual and/or professional baby-boomers who've retained some vestige of radicalism from the '60s. Otherwise, he has proved notoriously enjoyable, not only but especially in his most explicitly proletarian poses in *Born in the U.S.A.*, by a predominantly Reaganite generation of middle-class white youth, and even appropriable, in the '84 campaign, by Reagan himself.[19]

How then to explain this lack of danger or threat in Bruce's white working-class image, especially given the "organic" linkage (re)articulated between that image and the discontents his songs explicitly name? For starters, I want to say it has something to do with the sheer overdetermined "pastness" — or "belatedness" as I referred to it earlier — of the working-class image constructed in Springsteen's music and words. So many of those songs themselves — "Atlantic City," "Glory Days," and "My Hometown," to name only a few — as well as the video clips that accompany them, speak of industrial working-class life and its entertainments in the past tense, as it were. These themes of disappearance and attenuation, moreover, are both complicated and, at least partially, cancelled out when put alongside songs like "The River" that balladize the frustrations of working-class life *with* a job, or "Born to Run," which dreams of escape from that life. But the confusion we might feel as to whether blue-collar white working-class life and masculinity are worth saving, whether we should mourn or celebrate their passing away, is obviated both by the aestheticizing strategies we have spoken of above, and by the sanitizing "back-to-the-future" jump back over the '60s Springsteen's rock makes in terms of the idioms it most commonly draws from. The way Springsteen works in the mid-80s is thus the opposite of how Harris Freiberg tells us Elvis and Chuck Berry worked in the 1950s. In their cases, the pulse and energy and provenance of the musical idiom, combined with the sight of the rocker, belied and overcame the conservative containment strategies embedded in the songs' lyrics; in the case of Bruce, thanks to both the whiteness and the belatedness of the musical idioms involved, it is the other way around.

Bruce, then, could be massively enjoyed as working-class hero precisely insofar as the working-class life he portrayed came across as aesthetically and historically distanced from the lives of those taking him in as an *authentic artifact*. Even the nickname "The Boss," affixed to him at that moment of his greatest success, bespeaks this sense of distance, insofar as underneath its obvious implication that Springsteen is the champion of rock & roll lies the pleasant reminder his star image offers its audience of an earlier moment in industrial culture when there were, directly above your head, *visible* bosses owning and running the plant; only that moment is so far gone and so fuzzy that a white guy dressed sort of like a worker sort of makes you think of that. By the same token, Bruce's claim to be "Tougher Than the Rest," in the song of that title (where its meaning is, basically, more capable of a mature, responsible, hetero relationship) can even take on a vaguely progressive hue for those with liberal gender politics without quite losing that piquant yet residual *frisson* of white working-class swagger—just, and just as easily, as what's left of that swagger can regardless of the lyrics be folded into the reactionary flagwaving on which so many Reaganites battened, young and old. For that matter, moreover, the Bruce body that showed up in '84—that scruffy-whiskered, sideburned, thickly-muscled bare-armed one in jeans jacket or a sleeveless T or both— also fed in to the climate of Reaganite reaction simply by appearing, on the album cover, in concert, and on MTV, against the background of the flag. For as Connell reminds us, such images are already conjoined in patriarchal reaction, insofar as "working-class milieux that emphasize physical toughness" have long since come to function within the industrialized world as a crucial ally of male dominance in the upper reaches of the economy and the State.

Yet now, returning from all these histories and determinations to this parodic paradigm of the heavy-duty white male worker, this body-become-superstar, it is time to note one final respect in which the meanings of Springsteen—virtually all the meanings, reactionary as well as progressive—are held in by that body's performative behavior, by the extent to which this Bruce's singing and movement speak of energies *confined*. Here again, the *locus classicus* is probably the concert footage from "Born in the U.S.A.," though other examples from the same period are not hard to find. Watch the way he delivers the song, starting with the way his head and shoulders jolt in time with the rimshots squarely keeping up the hard 4/4 beat. The camera gives us much of his singing in close-up—the intensity effect, remember?—yet there is something special and specific about the rigid quivering of that face as it shouts out the lyrics, about the tightness with which the eyes are clamped shut as the head bends down and the right arm stiffens in a clenched fist salute. Or think how, in the video-clip of his cover of Edwin Starr's "War" (coincidentally, probably the "Blackest" song in his repertoire), the hard-working bicep-bulging body in black vest over a sleeveless red T is over and over so heavily taken by the "woah-oah-oah-oah"'s of the choruses that they bunch him up and bend him over like a man with some serious abdominal pain. And otherwise in both clips the body basically stays still and stiff: no wiggling or thrusting here from inside those jeans; nothing more than the hammerlike heel of the right boot clumping out the beat.

For me at least, in the context of all Bruce's other meaning-effects and in conjunction with his white worker image, such rock & roll behavior glimmers with resonance. For starters, it insists that he ain't anywhere *close* to being Black: which, together with how rigidly *straight* it also appears, helps a lot to balance off or mitigate the effect of having an actual Black man up there to play off of, and sometimes even flirt with, on the front of the stage.[20] Moreover, the power of the burly white working-class signifier is at one and the same time made available *to* young and yuppie Reaganite economic reactionaries *and* "gender progressives" (if you'll pardon the phrase) and safe *for* both groups by the visible bottling up and strained containment of its potentially alarming force for class mobilization and/or oppression of women, good and/or ill. The constricted self-binding of rock energy in "The Boss's" performances thus bespeaks neither aggression nor rebellion, but *ressentiment* in its classic Nietzschean sense, as "impotent hatred, envy, repressed feelings of revenge, the inability to act out antagonistic impulses in open conflict";[21] the degree to which that pain and anger and sheer energy are held in, squared off, bottled up — exactly as much, we might say, as his body is built up — is part and parcel of the way, in other aspects of Bruce's music and beyond it, a certain kind of white working-class masculinity associated with Fordist regimes of mass production and capital accumulation, is being rendered artifactual. Bruce's worker's body circa 1984–86 pins down and neutralizes all the other meanings in his music by becoming, finally, an object of nostalgia, a social emotion suitably defined for us by the great American socialist poet Thomas McGrath as "failed dynamite."

With the appearance of Axl Rose, though, and in accordance with changing times as well as musical idiom, the mythic narrative departs from those reassuring continuities with which the story of Springsteen's "authenticity" is invested. What's real about Axl is founded not in continuities but in breaks, in both senses of the term: not being a good crowd-pleasing boy even in rebellion, like Bruce, but being offensive even — or especially — in success.

To understand the viability of Axl's particular kind of story and body, though, requires us to review the particular dynamic of authenticity that story and body must engage. As Axl himself has described it for *Rolling Stone*, the "basic root" of the Guns N' Roses' music "is hard rock, a bit heavier than the Stones, more in a vein like Aerosmith, Draw-the-Line type stuff"; and the formulation, though circumlocutory, is an accurate one. The term Rose's description of GN'R's sociomusical practice walks around is, of course, heavy metal, mutated offshoot of '60s rock; so we need to turn to where that sound comes from, who it reaches, what body images it calls for and calls up, and what all that has tended historically to mean.

Heavy metal, not at all coincidentally, picks up at the tail-end of the moment Bruce's music leaves out, i.e., with the rock of the late '60s.[22] Both culturally and musically, it derives from "acid" or psychedelic rock of the late '60s and the white boomer-based counterculture that claimed that music as its own. Bands like The Jimi Hendrix Experience, Big Brother and the Holding Company, and, perhaps most influentially, Cream, used a base provided by Black blues, especially the industrialized, electrified "Chicago" sound of Muddy Waters, Willie Dixon and B.B. King, as launching pad for ever more extended, free-form guitar improvisations, and similarly emphasized the instrumental-expressive qualities of the voice over its tune-carrying, lyric-delivering capability. Led Zeppelin, widely considered the premier heavy metal band, was in the early '70s one of the first to inflect this mix in a "heavier" direction, by mixing a miked-up drum kit and bass drum — metal's so-called "bottom sound" — into a thicker, louder, and more steady-rocking impasto of boogeying guitars lending low-pitched blues figures an insistence both monotonous and menacing. Likewise, extended guitar solos became yet more aggressively chromatic, at points of maximum intensity crossing over from musical to acoustic event to express both the guitarist's artistry and deep emotion, just as the abrupt movement of the singer's vocals from tender lyricism to gruff roars or falsetto screams suggested equally arbitrary shifts from the "soft" emotions of love and sorrow to the sharp edges of anger, fear, and pain.

Such musical developments coincide and, for most commentators, are correlated with the large-scale social and cultural shifts in the rock audience sketched out in the first part of this essay. As the white youth movements of the '60s foundered on their own contradictions, and the counterculture broke into a scattering of life-style options and fads, heavy metal became the homeboy sound, in Deena Weinstein's words, "where lower-middle-class and working-class whites were more likely to be found . . . in the large cities of the American Midwest, as well as in medium-sized cities and blue-collar suburbs,"[23] and so inflected the gender and generational connotations of '60s rock with fresh accents of uncertainty and rage. Metal's attitude problem, Weinstein argues, is a function of the downward mobility young white lower-class and/or working-class men have suffered in the '70s and '80s, as their sense of racial and gender superiority, even and perhaps especially *within* what was left of '60s youth culture, has come under assault by women, Black and other non-white people seeking power, justice and redress, at the same time as their economic prospects, at the end of the Fordist era of mass production and in the age of Reagan, have dried up and blown away.

Thus the complicated circuitry of politics and pleasure involved in finding this music "real" and using it to authenticate and legitimate your own life. Take what Weinstein calls "the essential sonic element in heavy metal" — "power, expressed as sheer volume," together with the regular rhythmic forward snapping of head ("headbanging") and upraised arm that are the classic metalhead audience's response to that power's exhibition in live performance. One common enough reading of such behaviors would have it that the metalheads' actions constitute a near-straightforward protofascist identification with white male power in its most nakedly direct and violent forms. But surely this is too univalent and reductive. More likely, such identifications are only one moment of a much more mobile response, in which the sonic power of the music oscillates among various guises and affective relationships to the metal fan: as oppositional or subversive power with which the metalhead identifies; as hegemonic authorized power against which his responses beat their oppositional time; as an overwhelming life force he joins, and as an inexorably destructive, apocalyptic fury he both welcomes and fears, to name only the most likely alternative possibilities. Of course it matters that the members of the band putting out that deafening sound and swathed in an equally enormous spectacle of smoke and light are the same sex and color as yourself, wear the same regalia and sport the same long hair — or, for that matter, like Alice Cooper or Kiss, two of the longest running and most successful, look and act even more socially out of it than you are, and celebrate the fact. Otherwise, though, the fan's response to performance and scene is as multiform and multivalent as is any enjoying subject's dazed and blurry decoding of an experience whose foremost effect is simply to overwhelm — any experience, that is, of the romantic sublime.

Along with this multivalence toward a multiply defined power, moreover, the genre of metal as a set of rock & roll practices from production to reception and back has tended to insist on an equally definitive set of exclusions and negations. Women as a group tend to be marginalized by the deliberately aggressive and/or ugly loud sound of metal, and are evoked in metal songs mainly as either straightforward sex objects, "bitches," or some combination of both. And the portentous *Sturm und Drang* into which metal converts its blues figurations stiffens and bleaches the Blackness out of them, thus helping to produce heavy metal as, in effect, the equivalent of rap for downscale young white men. Finally, in spite of the very long and often teased-up hair, and what Weinstein describes as "the S&M paraphernalia of segments of the gay subculture" — or perhaps just as accurately, because of it — the practice of metal hardly commends any softening or femininization as part of the alternate "wild" masculinity it models, much less any blurring or breakdown in the borderline separating gay from straight. Such distinguishing practices seem designed instead to increase and emphasize the distance of metal music, bands, and fans from the straight world, while reinforcing what Eve Sedgwick has taught us to call a strictly "homosocial" fraternity of defiant, socially and politically incorrect rejects for whom the social stigmatization of being "out of it" culturally, economically, and politically has been rendered via metal a heroic, even transcendent fate.[24]

Now, though, before these generalizations congeal any further, they ought to be quickened with a more detailed sense of metal history. First, it's important to note what every metalhead knows and practically every metal-hater doesn't, i.e., that all metal bands are not and have never been the same. Nor are the differences between, say, Aerosmith, Motley Crue and Metallica merely sonic and/or musical in nature (even though they are always also that); there are also, within the general outline and description, important distinctions in temperament and emphasis. Aerosmith blends some Stones into the standard metal mix, not only in terms of its relatively bright and polished sound or the visual homage Steve Tyler's face, coiffure and wardrobe render to Mick, but in the band's ongoing preoccupation — expressed in video clips and interviews as well as, of course, the songs themselves — with specifically sexual (though always heterosexual) forms of naughtiness and transgression. Motley Crue, coifed in teased hair and semi-clothed in black leather, gives us a rougher, more classically metal sound, and trades in a squarely conventionalized language of social transgression and apocalypse; thus one of its signature songs, "Dr. Feelgood," trades away all allusions to good sex and/or Blackness in general and Aretha in particular in favor of a jeering vocal and a manic driving energy. And Metallica combines some of the thickest bottom sound and most gravelly vocals in all metal with an attitude compounded of equal parts of its most romantically despairing self-exaltation and the prin- cipled anarchist suspicion associated with its more culturally upscale cousin, hard core.

Moreover, as metal's audience has grown in the '80s, it and metal have further diversified as well. Thanks in no small part to the influence of MTV, which in the first part of the decade gave it very extensive coverage, one of metal's edges has softened its sound and look and moved toward the mainstream and a more female audi- ence (e.g., Jon Bon Jovi); while another, in response to this dilution, has hardened its sound, quickened its tempos and borrowed from hardcore to come up with an altogether more hostile and nihilistic mix (e.g., Anthrax or Suicidal Tendencies). Toward the end of the decade, then, within and across this diversified field, Guns N' Roses will become superstars in terms of both range and presumption. The band's range extends from the "power ballads" of so-called "lite metal," defined by Weinstein as "songs with just enough metal sound (the bass) to be heard as metal, but not so much . . . that they will be detested by those who are turned off by traditional heavy metal music"[25] (GN'R's hit "Yesterdays" is a good example here) all the way out to the distended Moody-Blues-style shlock of "November Rain." Likewise, along metal's harder shores they can shift from the classic hysteria of "Welcome to the Jungle" and paranoia of "Out ta Get Me" on the band's debut album *Appetite for Destruction* (1987), to the manic thrash rhythms and energies of "So Fine" on *Use Your Illusion II* (1991). And their level of presumption is already sug- gested by Axl's choice of "hard rock" rather than "heavy metal" to describe this range, a rhetorical power play whose implicit aim is to redefine the broader field of rock on terms favorable to declaring GN'R Heavyweight Champion of it. (Their recently completed

World Tour, and one of *Use Your Illusion's* tracks, is titled "Get in the Ring.")

But this struggle over the signifier of rock is hardly the limit, or even the most decisive instance, of GN'R's audacity, which also extends to the speed and manner in which they broke themselves, and were broken, as a "national" act in the first place. The dues-paying component of most rock mythologies has traditionally been more sternly required in the province of metal than in any other genre of rock, given the stigmatized outsider status of the classic metal fan. Yet far from touring for years to build credibility and a following, Guns N' Roses was signed to Geffen Records in 1986 a mere nine months or so after its formation, by a guy who'd been brought in from Elektra expressly to bring Geffen its own version of Motley Crue. The following year the band's first LP, *Appetite for Destruction*, was released, and chalked up steady but not earthshaking sales (it took ten months to crack *Billboard's* Top 100), until such time as the video clip for "Welcome to the Jungle" was released and played extensively on MTV. And the rest, as they say, is history: today, at some 17 million sales worldwide, *Appetite* is the best-selling debut album of all time, while Geffen has let it be known that as part of its strategy for marketing the double album *Use Your Illusion* I and II, it intends to stretch out its release of singles from the album over a three-year period, 1991–94.

The full eccentricity of such a narrative from that conventionally requisite to metal-band success lies, moreover, not just in these details themselves but in their dissemination as part of the GN'R mystique.[26] The massive anonymous crowds of GN'R's first full length live performance video, "Paradise City," are there to make a point virtually the opposite of that made in the footage of Bruce doing "Rosalita": here it's not about the moment of intimate regional renown, but about what a monster band they are right off the gun. Such a freely confessed market strategy dovetails nicely with lead singer Axl Rose's unabashed interest in making money and achieving commercial success — as in the first of his *two* interviews in *Rolling Stone*, the one attendant on the runaway success of *Appetite* in which he counsels "any kid in high school" no matter "what else you're gonna do," to "take business classes," and proudly asserts that in the making of *Appetite*, "Everything was directed at trying to achieve the sales without sacrificing the credibility of our music. . . ."[27]

There are a couple of important points to make about how such an avowedly complicit hustle gets squared with — and thereby redefines — the cardinal rock & roll value of authenticity, both of them relevant to the way we take in Axl's body and the meanings we take out of it. But on our way to them it is worth pausing to note a contradiction around Bruce's body-image and its exchange-value usefulness which stands in direct opposition to Axl's stance. This contradiction is suggested by a possibly apocryphal bit of Spring-steenia: the story goes that a spokesman for Levi's, asked whether the company had tried to engage Springsteen's services for its ads, replied that he could not imagine how Bruce could help them any more than he already was. Thanks to his intransigent refusal to compromise or cash in his authentically burly working-class mascu-linity, in other words, it is with Bruce as with the sailors and/or longshoremen on the tags attached to those Dockers pants marketed to mid-level professional-managerial-class boomers like myself. In these images, drawn and colored in a faux-thirties style for the nos-talgia of the thing, the working man is invariably depicted as an idler whose strapping shape and proletarian style draw the erotic gaze of the swanky well-dressed woman being drawn past him on the dock or at the train station by the oblivious dun-suited upper-class man to whose arm she is attached. Obviously enough, the allure of the workman for the woman in the illustration, and for us, is inextricable from the purity and unbridgeability of his distance from her, from us, and from the system of gazes to which he is nonetheless linked; just as that relay of gazes, the woman's exposed and ours hidden, creates the space of a new desire for, and a new definition of, an intermediary masculinity in between the stiff orthodoxy of the empowered normative ruling class male and the superseded roughhewn worker — the space of the sensitive yet still sort-of-rough guy who buys and wears Dockers and appreciates Bruce.

If the very distance the Bruce-image seems to take from commerce and commodification thus only serves to render it more serviceable to both, the complicity displayed by Axl and GN'R follows out a perverse counterlogic whereby one is exactly as much "*in*" as "out of it," and the only meaning left for authenticity involves flaunting just how unapologetically dirty you are. Such repositioning and such shocking pleasure are in fact exactly what happens and matters in the video clip of "Welcome to the Jungle," widely considered to have launched *Appetite*'s flight to the stratosphere of sales and GN'R's ascension to rock superstars. Musically, the song is a classic metal blues-boogie graced by one of Axl's most extensive displays of hysterically shifting chops, from a grated snarl through most of the verses, to high rips and overwrought stutters on every chorus, and falsetto taunting through the instrumental bridge. Lyrically and dramatically, as the title suggests, it's a celebration — ironic, oppositional, and straightforwardly sincere, like most of metal's evocations of power — of the contemporary social landscape as a terrain of utter savagery: "Welcome to the jungle, it gets worse here every day. . . . You can get anything you want, but you better not take it from me. . . . I'm gonna watch you bleed/scream," etc. What the video clip does is wrap a basic before-and-after narrative around this sadomasochistic circuitry, a narrative both punctuated and punctured by the performing Axl at its center. As the video (but not the song) begins, the first Axl we see is the ballcapped hayseed chewing a stalk of green wheat as he steps off the bus onto the mean streets of the city. There he gawks at the figure of a passing woman, then turns his dazed and overstimulated gaze to a display window full of tvs all broadcasting an extreme close-up of You-Know-Who snarling and writhing with a leather strap across his head. At this point the song's blues-bottom figure kicks in, as the video straight-cuts from this tv image to the figure of yet another Axl, this one wearing virtually the same expression in performance on stage, switching thin hips poured into tight black leathers and sporting a nimbus of teased blonde hair as he tears into the opening verse.

There are more Axls waiting for us in the remainder of the clip: a very glammed-up one in the first instrumental break, shown watching a group of tvs in a softly-lit peach-colored living room together with a few other men and/or women as sexually ambiguous as himself (this, by the way, following the only verse that explicitly addresses the subject of the song's taunting appeal as a "very sexy *girl* [my emphasis] . . . very hard to please"); a straight-haired pre- or post-decadent Axl strapped to a chair à la *Clockwork Orange* in the second break and forced to watch two banks of four tvs apiece pulsing out the same images of riot, police and military repression, and lush female bodies on display as the last Axl was watching in the living room; and finally, at the song's end, a near-version of Axl-on-stage back out on the street shaking his head in sad disgust at the display window's stacked close-ups of the televised tortured Axl we started with, and walking away. But the video's main image is clearly that of the demiurge who both generates and grows out of all the others, the Axl that delivers the song. In a Springsteen clip — say, "Glory Days" — that plays with narrative as much as this one does, the Springsteen performing the song up on the cramped stage with his bar-band is continuous with all the other Bruces we see in the course of the video, first practicing his own pitching, then finally tossing a few to his own kid: wherever the performing Bruce belongs temporally, however we order him into the narrative, the point is he fits. But the relationship of the performing Axl to the proto-narrative suggested by the "Welcome" video is by no means so smoothly accommodating. Alternately taunting and whimpering, strutting and collapsing, his long hair, bangles and tattoos at one and the same time both placing him monstrously beyond any system of pleasure and repression and positing him, effeminized, overin-scribed and abased, at the bottom of its vortex, this performing body reflects, exceeds, screams back at, submits to and masters every other image in the video, including and especially any and all other images of himself.

The struggle, then, to make GN'R's metal-based rock into the definition of Rock is thus condensable into the struggle to posit Axl as the figure of a new (or newly modulated) wild rocking masculin-ity, to move beyond merely serving as an organic figure for other young, culturally and economically subordinate white men; and, conversely, the task of this redefinition overlaps with that of remak-ing rock authenticity itself. Axl may be a kid from a downscale family in a small Rustbelt city on the skids, and may advertise that fact when he plays his Indiana hometown: "I know what the fuck's goin' on out here and this band's one of the only things these kids got."[28] But the more distinctive stage behavior of GN'R is not identi-fication with the audience but suspicion, hostility, and even con-tempt for it, manifested in a wide array of notorious behaviors: short sets and chronic lateness; abrupt cancellations whenever Axl's throat is giving him trouble; Axl's walking off the stage if the techni-cal arrangements or security is not up to scratch; or even, in one famous case, Axl's jumping offstage and, still resplendent in white feather boa, personally smacking up one unruly fan. We began our exploration of Bruce on stage by noting how he aimed to please; here, as Axl's mid-concert sermon to the crowd in New Orleans demonstrates, it's a question of the fans being worthy of the gift.

O.K.? How much did you pay for this show? . . . I'll tell you what
I'll do—I'll pay you back because this just isn't going to work. It's
hard to be up here giving like this with all you people sitting there
taking a f---ing nap. Yeah, yeah, I know, there he goes begging for
attention again. My therapist always says, 'You crave attention.'
And I go, 'No s---'[29]

Such displays of narcissistic need and aggression are, moreover,
consistent with another aspect of the band's mythical profile we
have left unmentioned till now: their advanced reputation, even
among other metal-based bands, for dissipation in general and
heavy drug and alcohol use in particular. According to this heavily
promoted legend, most of GN'R's advance on their first album went
out to the L.A. street to service old debts and score new stuff; heroin
addiction cost GN'R's first drummer his job eventually, and conspicuous consumption of smack is even said to have strained relations
between Axl and his half-black lead guitarist Slash.[30] Such well-
circulated stories, together with tales of wrecked hotel rooms and
casual sex, and the virtually obligatory presence of some Jack Dan-
iels, Jim Beam, or at least a Bud in the hand in every fan-mag photo,
provide further evidence of GN'R's poor impulse control in such a
way as to redefine and legitimate their leap over the dues-paying
moment. Not for these boys the hard work of establishing a presence, connecting with the audience, coming up slow; these boys are
way too greedy, bored and pissed off for that.

Such fables and photos of advanced dissipation, along with the
tales of stage misbehavior and performance breakdown, thus serve
to counterweight as well as justify the band's commercial success,
reassuring us that their complicity with the Powers That Be does not
constitute acceptance, you can have a career and be a Bad Boy after
all: this arguably a message whose comfort is at least equal to that
given off by Bruce to those going or staying upscale in "post-
industrial" post-working class America, albeit quite different in
kind. So also with GN'R's and Axl's easy avowal of degrees of
homophobia, racism, and xenophobia which even most metal bands
and their fans keep under wraps, not to mention near-parodic levels
of misogyny in others (e.g., "Back Off Bitch"). When asked to com-
ment on the open expression of the first set of thuggish attitudes in a
song called "One in a Million," Axl's reply provides a beautiful
instance of the dissolution of any sense of difference or community

in an ocean of undifferentiated self. "The thing with 'One in a Million' " he said, "is, basically, we're all one in a million, we're all here on this earth. We're one fish in a sea. Let's quit fucking with each other, fucking with me."[31]

If, as we saw, Bruce's contained and emblematically working-class body was racked and choked by the classically oedipal-neurotic reactions of guilt, disappointment, and dreams of escape, Axl's bareskinned, lissome, nakedly exposed, multiply-tattooed body *acts out* its rebel masculinity and rock authenticity as a fitful, flailing rage. Rock's newest wild white boy is, as he likes to tell us himself nowadays, the offspring of a dysfunctional family; and up there on stage he behaves as if he were, literally, still in one, the way he stalks obliviously past the other band members' widely scattered positions, or randomly dashes from ramp to ramp or wing to wing, or stands stage center leaning forward from the waist, staring blankly past the crowd as his voice shrieks intensity and his outstretched stiffened arm quivers in disjunct convulsion, his actions and gestures as alienated from whatever song he may be singing as he is from both his audience and the rest of his band, each of them in his own particular trance: no community here, neither onstage nor beyond it, only one damaged fish in the sea. Likewise, while Bruce appears even off-stage in the same working-guy t-shirts and jeans, seamlessly continuous with his history and himself, the clothing signifiers pinned to Axl's chronically unstable self keep altering their random concatenations throughout his show in the "Get in the Ring" tour: from tartan skirt to spandex shorts, buckskins to frogged and epauletted officer's coat, a t-shirt with Manson's image to one reading NOBODY KNOWS I'M A LESBIAN. This is rock authenticity as pure pre-oedipal fury and appetite, "wild" masculinity in the unbounded and amoral form of what Lacan wittily called the "l'hommelette," the body that eats and rages, whines and snarls, grabs and flails; the loose-limbed asexual body whose pronounced racism, homophobia, misogyny are only so many paranoid reflexes of its unbounded narcissistic self; perhaps above all the unproductive, overinscribed, spastic body that, although complicit, is nonetheless scandalously unavailable to appropriation because it *doesn't work*.

3. The Kids Might Be All Right; or, Masculinities In Bloom

Obviously, I have not written this piece to plump for either Axl's or Bruce's version of rock masculinity. Rather, I have tried to show how each carries complex messages of racial and sexual differentiation; how Bruce's moral authenticity is part and parcel of the nostalgia that contains it, how Axl's sincere instability, complicity, and snarling viciousness are one and the same; and how their rock bodies deliver all these messages in each case. On the other hand, though, I am also very far from arguing that the commodification of whatever synaesthetic body-center cluster of sounds, words, and images constitutes rock & roll at any given moment must be in and of itself the sign the fix is in *re* white straight masculinity or anything else, given the ongoing power of popular music to condense, idealize and disseminate new models of being and behaving far beyond their initial moment, site, and audience, together with the industry's hard-wired hunger for dissent. So, rather than argue for one body over the other, the artifact of modernity or the postmodern basket case, as incarnation of a white straight masculinity worth pursuit and affirmation, I want to end here with an evocation of a rock masculinity—that is to say, still virtually by definition, of a white straight masculinity—that seems to me to have more potential than either Bruce's or Axl's, to hint at something more and something else.

You can see it, or I hope you can, in the video clip of "In Bloom" performed by Nirvana, the flannel-shirted, tattered-jeaned all white-male group from Seattle whose "grunge" album (think a dirgelike fusion of punk and metal, those of you who haven't heard it) to everyone's astonishment went platinum last year. The clip ironizes that fame and takes a Brechtian distance on MTV and rock bodies alike, by referring to a moment in rock history that prefigures both their presents. It opens with a shot of another, older tv set on which an Ed Sullivan-style host, in grainy early-60s black-and-white, has just come back on camera at the end of a performance by the unseen but "world famous Dancing Poodles" to introduce "three fine young men from Seattle . . . thoroughly all right and decent fellows" to the screaming crowd. The basic through-line of the rest of the video consists of cross-cuts from this bland-faced band, a time-warped Nirvana in matching striped sport coats and Beatle-length hair duly combed down and back, cheerfully bobbing as they strum their instruments and "sing" slightly out-of-synch, and group shots of a hysterically wrought-up, shrieking crowd of mainly junior-high girls circa 1963—only every so often, especially around the chorus, something happens like a reception problem, or swishpan, or both, and we get instead an image of the same band on the same set but looking quite different and hardly playing the same song at all. Instead, as the chorus thuds blearily, drearily along—

> He's the one
> who knows all our pretty songs
> and he likes to sing along
> and he likes to show his gun
> but he
> knows not what it means
> knows not what it means

—the band members lurch around in the frocks they're wearing now, at one moment pushing over the flats of arches that framed them, at another haplessly watching the drum-set topple down. Lead singer Kurt Cobain tries a couple of goony airplane spins with arms outstretched; engages in a mock duel during the instrumental bridge with his co-guitarist, who falls to his knees and leans back in his dress as Cobain shuffles astraddle him with his guitar; tries whipping his guitar by its strap around his waist only to have it slip and fly offstage; and mimes a moment of great intensity by hobbling forward with his knees held tight together and his hands crushing his dress against his groin, as if suffering from either menstrual pain or a kick in the nuts. And all the while we keep cutting away to that screaming audience, swishing back to that straight band of really decent guys, till the song is done, and the host comes back out to shake their hands and declare, through the girls' screams, that these guys are "gonna be *really big stars.*"

What this clip's about for me has more to do with the rock masculinities it mocks and refuses than with any it might be said to recommend. I appreciate the way it posits the band's anarchist shenanigans as the end of a line that began with the hysterical sexualization and careful counter-regulation of the white male rocker's body; and I like the way they wear and use those dresses, not to increase and ambiguate their sexual allure, but to include gender breakdown as part of the confusion and revolt they recommend. These are male bodies that refuse to be sexually fetishized, but not in the usual way: not by being too stiff, too drably or officially suited, too repressed and covered up. And when in their dresses they mimic the homosocial moment of "cock-rock" communion through dueling guitars, it cracks me up.

Last but not least, I like the way all these dissident behaviors are explicitly linked by the lyrics I have quoted with a sneering refusal of a conventional identificatory alliance between white male band and white male fan, an alliance in which knowing the words to the songs is felt to be equivalent to having and showing a gun, a possession that's about phallic mastery. Such a refusal both makes and marks a break with all those other rock masculinities we have seen which pay the price of difference from hegemonic masculinity with the coin of emphatic "Whiteness" and/or hyper-hetero-misogyny. If the mutation in this rock tradition named Bruce finally signifies the depletion and vacuousness of his white working-guy image, as well as of the class-centered, racist-masculinist left-populism that once buoyed that image up, and the counter-image of unbound Axl, extension of this tradition, warns us against embracing a newer psycho-politics of dispersion and desiring-flow, Nirvana's ability to hold on to its insistent bored anger while individually and collectively "refusing to be a man"[32] hints at a politics and definition of white men that just might be a big improvement over what we've made and got so far, within rock and outside it — not to mention a bunch of kids out there that, with some luck and some tough coalition-building, still might just be all right.

Postscript: On the other hand, today — that is, in June 1994, as I add these words — the fact of Cobain's recent suicide seems to symbolize and augur the terrible difficulty of sustaining such a counter-logic from within the mainstream, in the face of commodity culture's apparently limitless power to deflect and absorb. At least for those of us to whom Nirvana and Cobain suggested the possibility that the conventional romantic-resistance effects built in to rock & roll could be deconstructed from within, via the right blend of rage and abjection, the death of this explicitly antimasculinist, antihomophobic 27-year-old *lumpenprole* carries a special chill, here in the middle of what was supposed to be the beginning of the end of the Reagan-Bush time, when there is still far too little peace or justice or even decent-paying work around. The "star-text" Cobain incarnated brought many of us a jolt of hope and joyful recognition, by articulating that old radical-individualist resistance with a freely admitted self-loathing, complicating the arrogantly assertive desire to break on through with the vulnerably self-effacing urge to nod out. The suicide that now short-circuits that text brings us the arguably even more salutary message that performances like his are an almost impossibly hard act to pull off all by yourself — even, perhaps especially, when that ever more isolated and commodified performance becomes, despite your best intentions, only an act . . .

ACKNOWLEDGMENTS

Thanks for help to Ann Augustine, Barbara Benedict, Andrew Goodwin, David McMurray, Mark Miller, Laura Rice, Rob Sayre, Michael Seavers, and Ted Swedenburg; and special thanks to Peter Copek and the Center for the Humanities at Oregon State University, for the time and the fellowship.

NOTES

[1]For further elaboration of this point, see Lawrence Grossberg, "Teaching the Popular," in Cary Nelson, ed., *Theory in the Classroom* (Champaign-Urbana, IL: University of Illinois Press, 1986), 177–200.

[2]Susan McClary and Robert Walser, "Start Making Sense! Musicology Wrestles with Rock," in Simon Frith and Andrew Goodwin, eds., *On Record: Rock, Pop, and the Written Word* (New York: Pantheon Books, 1990), 277–292.

[3]Andrew Goodwin, *Dancing in the Distraction Factory: Music Television and Popular Culture* (Minneapolis: University of Minnesota Press, 1992), 56.

[4]Such neutrality at its best — that is, as the result of a complicated dialectical balancing act of contradictory determinations — characterizes Harris Freiberg's "Hang Up My Rock & Roll Shoes," lecture delivered at the Center for the Humanities, Wesleyan University, Middletown, Connecticut, November 15, 1992.

[5]See, for example, Nelson George, *The Death of Rhythm & Blues* (New York: Pantheon Books, 1988).

[6]For a relatively early but still cogent version of this general argument, see Simon Frith, *Sound Effects: Youth, Leisure, and the Politics of Rock 'n' Roll* (New York: Pantheon Books, 1981); and for a smart piece on rock *as* a set of practices, see David R. Shumway, "Rock & Roll as a Cultural Practice," *South Atlantic Quarterly* 90, 4 (Fall 1991), 753–69.

[7]"The White Negro," in Norman Mailer, *Advertisements for Myself* (New York: G. P. Putnam's Sons, 1959), 337–358.

[8]Richard Middleton, *Studying Popular Music* (Philadelphia: Milton Keynes, 1990), 263. The next quotation is on p. 266.

[9]See R. W. Connell, *Gender and Power: Society, the Person and Sexual Politics* (Stanford: Stanford University Press, 85.

[10]Mary Harron, "McRock: Pop as a Commodity," in Simon Frith, ed., *Facing the Music* (New York: Pantheon Books, 1988), 193.

[11]Jon Savage, "The Enemy Within: Sex, Rock and Identity," in Frith, ed., *Facing the Music*, 163.

[12]Simon Frith, "Towards an aesthetic of popular music," in Richard Leppert and Susan McClary, eds., *Music and Society: the politics of composition, performance and reception* (New York: Cambridge University Press, 1987), 136.

[13]Steve Connor, "The Flag on the Road: Bruce Springsteen and the Live," *New Formations* 3 (Winter 1987), 134.

[14]Harron, 210.

[15]Frith, "Towards an aesthetic of popular music," 147.

[16]*Music for Pleasure* (New York: Routledge, Chapman and Hall, 1988), 95.

[17]Christine Gledhill, "Signs of Melodrama," in Gledhill, ed., *Stardom: Industry of Desire* (New York: Routledge, 1991), 217.

[18]For the fullest elaboration of this perspective and mythic narrative, see Dave Marsh's adulatory *Glory Days: Bruce Springsteen in the 1980s* (New York: Pantheon Books, 1987).

[19]In the waning days of his crushingly successful reelection campaign and, it must be said, in perfect ignorance of the content of Springsteen's songs, Reagan saluted the "American spirit" of Springsteen's music for whatever the evocation might yield in the way of a few extra votes.

[20]In "Sexual Mobilities in Bruce Springsteen: Performance as Commentary," *South Atlantic Quarterly* 90, 4 (Fall 1991), 833–854, Martha Nell Smith argues that Springsteen in performance often flirts with and even at times transgresses the boundaries of conventional masculinity and heterosexuality. "Homoeroticism permeates his performances," she claims, "assumption of the feminine is one of his repeated artistic maneuvers, and, though he writes and sings about Adam, he finally seems much more like Eve in his approach to knowledge" (849). But I would argue both that such flirtations and provocations are far less frequent than Smith suggests, and, more importantly, that the emphatically masculine, heterosexual signal Bruce's image sends out is so strong and insistent as to render such potentially transgressive divergences practically unnoticeable even when they do occur.

[21]Lewis Coser, Introduction to Max Scheler, *Ressentiment* (New York: Free Press, 1961), 21.

[22]Here and below, my account of heavy metal is much indebted to Deena Weinstein, *Heavy Metal: A Cultural Sociology* (New York: Lexington Books, 1991). In addition, see Grossberg's comments on heavy metal in "Teaching the Popular"; Will Straw's "Characterizing Rock Music Culture: The Case of Heavy Metal," in Frith and Goodwin, eds., *On Record*, 97–110; and Dan Rubey's gloss on metal music and music videos in "Voguing at the Carnival: Desire and Pleasure on MTV," *South Atlantic Quarterly* 90, 4 (Fall 1991), 879–884.

[23]Weinstein, 118.

[24]The word "homosocial" as a concept contiguous to yet diacritically distinct from, and often opposed to, "homosexual," comes to us from Eve Sedgwick's *Between Men: English Literature and Male Homosocial Desire* (New York: Columbia University Press, 1985).

[25]Weinstein, 46–47.

[26]Most of the story I've just told above, for example, is taken from Daniel Sugerman, *Appetite for Destruction: The Days of Guns N' Roses* (New York: St. Martin's Press, 1991), a bio-band quickie knocked out in time to catch the upswell of the release of *Use Your Illusion* I and II in spring 1991. The exception is the detail concerning Geffen's plan to "time-release" the singles from those two albums; that is taken from Deborah Frost's "Wimps 'R Us," in *The Village Voice*, October 1, 1991,

77–78 — though presumably it comes originally from a Geffen press release designed to fuel the hype.

[27]Del James, "Axl Rose: The Rolling Stone Interview," in *Rolling Stone*, August 10, 1989, 44.

[28]Quoted in Dean Kuipers, "Guns N' Neurosis," *Spin*, October 1991, 74.

[29]Quoted in Jeanne Marie Laskas, "On the Road with Guns N' Roses," *Life*, December 1, 1992, 108.

[30]Again, it is symptomatic that I have been able to collect these stories from the Sugarman band-bio mentioned above, as well as such fan-mags as the "special collector's item" issue of *Wow!* for Summer 1991, devoted to Guns N' Roses and Skid Row, and complete with "backstage exclusives" and an even more special section: "The 'Lost' Interviews 1987–89: Guns N' Roses' Wildest Tour Stories!"

[31]Quoted in James, 44. And James also recites the relevant lines from "One in a Million": "Police and niggers, that's right / Get outta my way / Don't need to buy none / Of your gold chains today"; and the following verse, "Immigrants and faggots / They make no sense to me / They come to our country / And think they'll do as they please / Like start some mini-Iran or spread some fuckin' disease."

[32]The phrase in quotes is a rip-off of the title of Dworkinite feminist John Stoltenberg's latest book, *Refusing to Be a Man: Essays on Sex and Justice* (New York: Signet/New American Library, 1990) — though I think it safe to say that Stoltenberg is far too suspicious of any physical or sensory pleasure or license, especially any enjoyed or enjoyable by actually existing men, to approve of Nirvana's antics here.

RUTH BEHAR

FOR MY SON GABRIEL WHO MUST ONE DAY BECOME A MAN

> . . . *our sons must become men — such men*
> *as we hope our daughters, born and unborn,*
> *will be pleased to live among. Our sons will*
> *not grow into women. Their way is more dif-*
> *ficult than that of our daughters, for they*
> *must move away from us, without us. Hope-*
> *fully, our sons have what they have learned*
> *from us, and a howness to forge it into their*
> *own image.*
>
> — Audre Lorde, "Man Child,"
> from *Sister Outsider*

I wanted a son. Most women I know want a daughter. But I didn't. I wanted a son. Male body and all. And I had you.

I see myself in you so completely. I know you have your father's baby fine blond hair and your father's lanky body, the kind of body stretching toward heaven that El Greco liked to paint. That makes people who don't know any better think you're a replica of your father. But you have my eyes, my lips, and my hands. Our thumbs match exactly; they have since you were born. You came out of my body. I tell you that a lot. And your body remembers my body. When you come into our bed in the morning, you reach for me, you put your hand in mine, thumb to thumb.

One day, as if you've had a taste of the apple, you gain the knowledge that you can strip the grass skirt and bathing suit off your Hawaiian Barbie, the only female doll you have amid an overpopulation of muscle-heavy male action figures. Look, you say, pointing to the breasts. Look, you say, pointing again, a vagina. And you take that naked Barbie into the bath with you. I watch you pulling her around by her long dark hair. Be gentle, I say. For my sake, okay? And you look at me with those eyes of yours that are so like mine, as if this is something you will remember. Without a word, you release her and let her float.

It is to you I am telling the family stories about the journeys that brought us here. How your great-grandparents left Russia and Poland and Turkey to find their America in Cuba and then how we left behind that promised land and went to New York and how that led to your Mami going to study in Connecticut and crossing paths with your Daddy, an exile from Texas, whose family remembers they came on the Mayflower by drinking milk with every meal. I want Spanish words to flow from your mouth like sugar from the cane, but you are not to forget that as Jews we have not stopped waiting.

This last Erev Yom Kippur, you sat on my lap, anger charging your heart. Your dignity had been offended and you declared that you wished one of your Ninja Turtle action figures would go poke the mean lady in the back row who had ordered you to stop playing your game. The room was crowded and there was not much for a little boy to do, so you slid down onto the floor and, with my jacket underneath your body like a motorized lily pad, you managed to travel under the seats for several rows, appearing between people's legs like a frog just leapt from a pond. Most people welcomed your six-year-old boyishness, but not that sullen lady who wanted you to know it was a holy night, the beginning of a long twenty-four hours of fasting and remembering of sins.

As I hold you, stroking your back slowly to calm the fury from your body, which I love more than my own body, you suddenly ask me, What's more important, the yarmulkas, the prayer shawls, or the books? I immediately say, the books. Because everything is written there. You shake your head, smile, and answer soberly, You know what I think is most important? The prayers. . . . In case the books get lost. . . .

ALAN SOLDOFSKY

THIRTEEN

Tell me why this hair grows out of my face,
my stupid face with its big nose
and volcanic skin breaking out in moon-size craters.
Who asked me if I wanted all this fuzz
above my lip where the skin is so shy
it blinks at the razor?

And what about the tangled vines under my arms
that mat with sweat. How I am supposed
to hide those from the smooth-faced girls?
And what should I do about the shaggy flower
that blooms around my balls,
or my secret risings and fallings?

It's difficult to conceive of myself as manly.
A man is the growl under the hood of a car,
or the snarling look of a semi
coming toward you on a two-lane road.
But I suppose, someday, I'll get barrel-chested
and bald, and eat my steaks well-done always.

I guess when I'm older my eyebrows will
bush together, like two explorers shaking hands
on an iceberg at the top of the world,
and hair will bristle out of my nostrils
and swarm from my ear lobes
like loose barbed-wire.

My chest will become a forest of creepers and stinging nettles,
of milky head thistles and steely burs.
My shoulders a snarl of thorns and foxtails.
Someday, I'll be completely covered over
unable at last to even feel my flesh.

IF IT WAS YOU INSTEAD OF ME

I had never seen a penis as large as his, and I stared, mesmerized by its buoyant, almost jovial swing from leg to leg as he walked dripping wet from the showers to his locker. The testicles swung in their long, loose sack. The shaft was rolled with veins, like it had been wrapped with flesh-colored leaves. The greyish-purple head bounced happily between Macowski's strides, as if saying "Hello, foot. Hello, foot." There was springy power in it, a living heft, a rubbery weight or force that was hypnotic. When he stopped in front of me, I didn't even notice.

"What the fuck you smilin' at?"

Looking up, I saw the right corner of Macowski's mouth turning down. He had a pink scar, hard and shiny as wax. It pulled the left side of his mouth into a tight little line that didn't move, so that he seemed only half mad, or half happy. Greg Macowski weighed one hundred seventy-seven and one-half pounds, but looked as if he were wearing another thirty. All muscle and tight skin, he had been starving himself for days on lime Jell-o and Juicy Fruit gum to make weight, and it made him mean. Earlier, wrestling Lake Central, he pinned his man in two minutes. It was loud in the stands. People banged their feet on the wooden bleachers, chanted his name.

No one chanted my name. There was a smattering of applause— my mom and dad and sister—, the ruffle of programs, and the slide of ice in paper cups. I won on a six to five decision, doing just enough to win, which was my strategy. Because I weighed one hundred thirty-four pounds and was wrestling up two weight classes, I had to wear my opponents down, stalling when I was on the bottom, riding when I was on top. I had to second guess the referee, waiting for that last moment before he would call me for stalling, and then throw a sit-out spin for a reversal, and, if I was lucky, a quick guillotine or a stack-up for some nearfall points.

Unfortunately, it was a strategy that bored audiences. It stopped team momentum. My matches were long and torturous to watch. It wasn't enough just to win; there was a certain way to do it. Walking off the mat, the words "nice job" coming from a teammate meant, "Get out of my face."

Coach hated me. At least once a week he brought someone up — often the same guy over and over — from the frosh and junior varsity teams to challenge my position. Long, gangly freshmen who tripped over their toes; guys who slapped and finger jabbed me like I was a piece of cookie dough. But always, in my slow, methodical way, I beat them.

Coach talked a lot about how a team needed an *esprit de corps* to win consistently. "You need hunger!" he would shout during one of his after-practice pep talks, "You all need to row in the same direction." I would shake my head waiting for the little steel balls of meaning to roll into the clown's eyes, nose and mouth; but it wasn't until late in the season that it dawned on me that what coach wanted was a team of Greg Macowskis.

Water beaded down his body into little pools that darkened the cement around his feet. "I said, what the fuck you smilin' at?"

Everyone stopped dressing, all eyes on the naked shapes of Mac and me. As always after a meet, coach sat on the desk in his office. He was lacing up a pair of shoes with new strings, smiling because he heard everything through the open doorway. He wore one of those shiny, nylon sweatsuits. A gold whistle dangled under his chin. Whenever he turned his head toward the door, I could see his little bald spot rotate into view like a land mass on a globe.

"What are you, Keiser, queer?"

"Mac, maybe he likes you."

"Oh yeah!" said Mac, taking the bait. "Is that right dicklick? Well, why don't you show me how much you like me!" He grabbed his penis with one hand, gave it a shake. "Come on, sweetheart, I'm ready!"

I sat there, big-eyed, staring at Macowski. Mountainous, fearsome, articulate, Polish Mac. The adrenalin surged, tingling my fingers and toes. I felt the lockers behind me, Mac in front of me, the rest of the team crowding my shoulders. What had happened? Was it the meet? But I won! I had been winning all season!

"Back off, shithead," I said, standing up.

Then he hit me. Three times actually. The first stunned me — a left hook that caught the corner of my eye. I didn't fall though, and I think it unsettled him, his eyebrows gave a little hitch. Then came a right, with only a slight pause after it burst my lip, so he could balance himself for the next swing. Then, like a hammer, he threw his body in the other direction, behind another left. It was over in a matter of seconds. My hands covered my face to keep it together. Blood salted my mouth. There was no pain, but my knees gave out.

I remember wishing I had done something. I felt so weak, so humiliated lying there, beaten by a naked man. But it was obvious I couldn't do anything. He was twice my size. Twice my neck. Twice my wrist. As always, I came up short in comparison to the cages others lived in — my body stood somewhere between awe and terror of its passage from day to day.

In 1975, the year I entered high school, I was physically coordinated and had lifted weights since seventh grade. Gaining a spot on the wrestling team wasn't that difficult. Most freshmen, however, sought out the smaller, less selective, nervous gatherings created solely to increase the chances of its members surviving the next four years. They met once a week after school and always in the same empty classroom. They built agendas, elected officers, designed club jackets.

I remember one group in particular. We were running the hallways before practice. On the third floor, in a classroom facing Joliet Street, were seven guys in button-down shirts and perma-pressed pants sitting behind a closed circle of desks. Their heads were bowed as if in prayer. Boyd Owens and I passed the classroom eight or nine times trying to figure out what they were doing, until finally we decided to stop in on the next pass.

We came into the classroom, panting like wolves, and sat down behind their group. A large, complex mathematical equation spread over the chalkboard. Papers, pencils, and notebooks cluttered their desks. They didn't say anything and only moved to look down or at each other for help. After five minutes of frightened silence, one of them stood up, faced Boyd and me, and said, "Would you please leave us alone." He spoke slowly, a slight tremor in his voice; the point of his finger and the nod of his head to show us the door were measured, like all at once he knew just how to handle us or just how far his body could take him in a fight.

From the first day of high school, I was shy, self-conscious and unapproachable. The fact that I was a wrestler, a letterman to boot, never guaranteed that I wouldn't blush, stammer, or look at my feet when speaking to someone new. Day after day I ate lunch at a table with six empty seats then milled around the hallways until the bell rang. Dates were impossible. My picture was never taken for the yearbook.

During wrestling's off season, I hung out at the public library after school, waiting for my father to pick me up. He worked in Gary—an engineer for Clark Controls—and was usually late, so that by my junior year I knew the major rivers, mountain ranges, seas, lakes, populations, and exports of all the countries of the world. I read books on art and history, too. The Napoleonic Wars and the Greek conquest of Asia Minor were favorites. But the Great Depression was my passion, for my father was born in 1930, one in a family of twelve, and he would often reminisce on the long drive home. He spoke fondly of poverty, as though it, and not me, were sitting next to him. We drove into the dusk, the Pontiac humming under our feet, the sky a narrow ribbon of blue no bigger than a wrist. Tiny yellow squares of light appeared in distant houses. After a while, I could just make out the outline of his nose, forehead and chin in the glow of the dashboard. "Oranges!" he would say. "And a new pair of shoes for Christmas."

Because of him I joined the wrestling team. He thought I moped around too much at home. "Do something," he would say flatly from behind his newspaper, tired, I suppose, of hearing me pace from room to room. The question was what to do? Sometime, somewhere, in a little book, the princes and princesses of Crown Point High School had written my name, and next to it, the word *loner*. It fit. The kids I admired possessed a social confidence which allowed them to move easily among friends and strangers. I, on the other hand, couldn't reach beyond my circle of fears and self-inflicted inadequacies. At best I possessed a physical consciousness. I was strong for my size, pliant, and had a quick motor memory. When I sat down and tallied up the positives and negatives of my character, wrestling seemed to suit me. It was a loner sport, unlike football, where you worked in concert with ten other guys. To win you had to balance strategy with strength and persist between them. The odds were never stacked in anyone's favor. From the moment the referee blew his whistle and the match began, you knew you were struggling against someone of equal weight, height and determination. Wrestling was two guys on a mat. One on one.

I quit the team the day after the fight. I wanted revenge. A revenge truly destructive in its scope, something really satisfying in its menace, and its ability to leave bodies strewn in the hallways.

I began tailing Macowski, watching him as he went to and from class; to the woods behind school, where he smoked joints, one after the other, with his buddies; to bars where I would have to wait outside in my car, fantasizing. Yes: I would confront him, call him a "Fucking Polack," then throw a punch that would lift him off his barstool and shrivel that huge thing in his pants.

I was in awe of his girlfriend and, perhaps, even feared for her. "How?" I would ask myself, thinking of Mac's dick swinging in front of me. But he was gentle with her. I watched them once at a park. He would brush the hair from her face with his hand, moving his lips on her ear, saying, I imagine, the things I would not—could not—say to a woman until years later. Then she would smile and hold his hand as though it were her future.

Macowski was a "Lake Rat." He lived with his drunken father in a junked house that seemed to be sliding nearer and nearer to the black water of Cedar Lake. Trouble rose from its oily surface, voicing its anger over the roar of motorcycles and police sirens. Mac had a black biker's jacket with the picture of a rat, a toothpick in its teeth, embroidered on the back. But he never wore it to school. He rode a used Harley-Davidson and worked at a garage on the weekends. A leather wallet stuck out of the pocket of his bluejeans, a silver chain linking it to a beltloop. He was a good-looking kid with shiny black hair, a square chin and a sharp, straight nose. But everyone knew a Lake Rat was a Lake Rat forever. What was wrestling to Mac?

To keep tabs on him, I ditched classes for entire days. I stopped reading in the library. But after a while, it was clear that I would never confront Macowski, that I would never hurt him. Revenge seemed unimportant. Instead, I sat on the small hill behind my house, stoned, watching the smoke clouds roll south out of Gary. Lying on my back with a blue bowl of sky above me, all I wanted was out.

In February, three months after the fight, Mr. Brist, the assistant principal, counted up forty-five truancies in one class and expelled me from Crown Point High School. My mother yelled and then threw up her hands; my father took off work to try to change Mr. Brist's mind.

It didn't work. I was cut loose into the world, a happy dropout.

Four years later, I was welding for a fabricating shop in Griffith, Indiana, a flat, grey industrial town ten miles southwest of Gary. I had been laid off from Inland Steel the summer before. It was 1982, and men waited in lines for a job at Burger King. It took me six months to find this job. I would have stopped looking earlier, perhaps moved to Philadelphia where my family had relocated in 1980, but I had it in my head that work was the only life for me — a place where I fit in — even though work was getting harder and harder to find.

I was twenty-two and lived alone in a small house outside of Miller. Every two weeks or so my mother sent me a letter. She missed me, wanted me to come home, but I rarely answered her, and then only to ask for money. The letters sat in a shoebox in my closet. I had a beard, long hair, and had taken to wearing sunglasses inside buildings. I wore a welding jacket I had stolen from Inland. On the back, stamped in bright red with a white circle around it, was the letter "I."

I was smoking a cigarette, the work stacked like a mountain in front of me, when someone clapped me on the back.

"Hey buddy!"

I turned and there was Mac, horrible as life. I didn't think anyone could recognize me through the beard. We exchanged names, but he didn't even blink at hearing mine.

"You worked at Inland?" he said, really happy. "Shit, I welded for Republic. What local were you?"

For the next three weeks, Mac and I worked together. He was only temporary labor. When the job was done, so was he. This wasn't high school anymore, and it didn't matter if you had an undefeated wrestling record in 1977. What mattered was how fast you could weld. How smooth you could grind a bead. There were two kinds of people on the lakefront: those who worked and those who didn't. If you didn't work, you didn't have a face; you became part of the great shuffling mass that never looked up from their shoes. If you worked, you had a body and two hands; that's how the bosses treated you. It wasn't much better than not working, but no one who had a job would admit it. This was survival: everyone trying to make their spare change a dollar.

While Mac was there, P. K. Engineering and Manufacturing Incorporated of Griffith, Indiana, paid him six dollars and seventy-five cents an hour, and, as an incentive, twenty-five cents for every screw-cover box he finished. He worked like a madman. Usually, late in the morning, the bosses came downstairs and walked through the shop. Mac, who never stopped working except to clean the splatter from the nozzle of the MIG, couldn't see them until they came up behind him and tapped his shoulder. Then he would lift the hood that all morning had covered his face, and you would see the white circles of his eyes, the rest of his face blackened with grinding dust.

"Nice job, fella. Keep up the good work. Maybe we can find a place for you."

Mac thought the guy would be true to his word, but I knew better. I didn't have the heart, or the heartlessness, to tell him the guy didn't mean it. It was just a way to make him work harder. But at the same time, it was a power I could hold over Mac. I knew from talking with the shop foreman there would be no new openings — then, or in the future. All I had to do to crush Greg Macowski would be to tell him the truth. But staring across the table at him, I felt, for once in my life, like a team player. I smiled, gave Mac the thumbs-up.

Tuesdays and Thursdays I bought lunch at the Lake View Restaurant, where we ate platefuls of all-you-can-eat perch for $2.55, drank beer, and watched the waves bash the shore of Lake Michigan. Afterward, we smoked a joint or two in his van, talking about our days at the mills.

"I had to get a job," he said. "I had a wife, and I'd blown everything I had on the security and first month's rent for an apartment. I didn't have a dime left for groceries."

"You're married, Greg?" It was news to me. After I was expelled, I went straight to work. Occasionally, I would go back to Crown Point, but never to talk. It was easy to believe, even then, that he didn't know who I was behind the beard, the sunglasses, the long hair. The seventeen-year-old loner ceased to exist for anyone, including me. Still, I couldn't be sure, so whenever we spoke, I purposely avoided the topics of school and wrestling. But it shocked me to know his life had changed in other ways. Married? When I thought of Mac, I always pictured his face straining behind that left hook, all his attention on me. Perhaps what I wanted was for him to remember me heroically taking his beating. It seemed ridiculous — adolescent — to imagine that this sturdy breadwinner would recall a thirty-second punchout.

"Shit, I've been married since I got out of high school — four years this October." He fished in his pocket and flashed his ring at me. "I've known Janet since I was thirteen. Never been with nobody else."

"Great . . . great," I said, not knowing what else to make of it. He took a long drag off the joint, held it, then blew the smoke into the windshield. "I had a wrestling scholarship when I graduated high school." He raised his eyebrows and dipped his chin as if the news still impressed him. "The University of Oklahoma was going to give me a free ride. They even sent a guy to my house to talk to me and my dad. 'Four years,' man, that's what the guy said. Four years and all I had to do was wrestle."

"So why are you still here?"

"I told you." He looked at me like I hadn't been listening. "I got married. Janet didn't want to go someplace she'd never been to before. She wanted to be near her family when the babies started coming. She thought Oklahoma was all pickup trucks and hillbillies with no teeth. And I wasn't so sure about another four years of school. My grades weren't so good — I bet you would have done all right, though. I mean, if it was you instead of me. You always read books — "

"How did you know that?"

"I know," he said without flinching. "C'mon, you think I could forget anything about high school?"

There was silence. I sat looking at his nostrils, the two rings of dirt around the edges. The dirt never came out of us. Some nights I could blow my nose for hours and still the black clots would form. Other than that, his face was smooth and clean, a boy's face. The scar still shiny and pink. The hair no longer the close buzz of the wrestler, but loosely tied in a bandana.

"Why'd you do it, Mac?"

"Man, you don't know how much Coach hated you."

"I can guess." Often I would come late to practice, sometimes stoned. I got bored with warm-ups, quitting somewhere between push-ups and squat-thrusts. As punishment, I had to spend the next two hours maneuvering under Tuna, our grunting heavyweight, and still I wouldn't stop arguing with Coach.

Mac laughed. "No, really. He thought you were trying to fuck with him."

"I was," I said. There was something in Coach's devotion to making us act on his command that appalled me. "Discipline!" he would scream at us. "If you have it, you can't lose!" I knew it burned him to watch me win.

"I know. But, man, it was *his* team. He liked gorillas, you know, real grapplers. He wanted you gone. One night after practice — you weren't there — he tells us to give you the treatment. Everything. So, when I saw you smiling at me in the locker room, I figured that was a good enough reason."

He was baiting me. I think he wanted me to find some anger, a little revenge. Perhaps he even wanted to find a little of that rage for himself. But it just wasn't there for either of us. We had both worked since high school. We couldn't wash the dirt from under our nails. I ate Cheetos and drank Old Style for dinner. He had a wife and bills on the kitchen table. I couldn't start my car on a cold day. The list went on and on. Life had changed — and yet, there we were, trying to work ourselves up over a locker-room brawl that happened years ago.

I laughed it off. "Jesus, Greg, my face hurt for a week."

"I'll bet. I wish I could hit like that again."

"Huh?"

"Nothing. You know, you were good. Kinda boring to watch, but you got the job done."

"Ah well," I said. "What's it matter?"

He started the engine, and we drove back to work.

The job was finished early. The company handed out a bonus for completing the contract ahead of schedule. Greg was gone the next day.

I saw Macowski again nine months later. It was night, and I had just bought a sixpack from the White Hen Pantry outside Merrillville. I popped the tab on the first beer, took a long drink and watched the men in the sheetmetal shop across the street. The bay doors were open and a soft blue light washed over the pavement. They were working a late shift. One man in a railroad jacket and baseball cap slowly hammered a long metal sheet like he was going to do it forever.

The lakefront had changed. The huge steelmills were dying and, with them, a way of life. The talk in bars no longer focused on where you worked, but on where you didn't. Warehouses stood vacant. The sky clung to its thin roots of factory smoke. Sunlight poured into the streets where we had never seen it before. Now I could see the faces of people, brilliant with defeat, stained with years of work, reddened by wind and fire. Men walked their shadows along brick walls, torpid, indistinguishable from one another except in height and girth, their bodies shouldering the same invisible load or longing.

As I walked back to my car, headlights lit on the windows. They blazed across the blackened glass. I thought of Bill Ezri, the man who taught me to weld. Years before, he had told me to leave this place because there was "a light in my eye." Of course, only he could see it, but he was persistent. "You only get it once in your life," he said. "Don't waste it — not here." He was a thin, wiry man with hard black eyes. He had two sons who followed him into the mills and a daughter who was his only hope.

I was unlocking my car door when a van pulled into the lot, its horn sounded and the headlights flashed. It stopped in the parking space next to mine, and out stepped Mac.

He was thinner. He seemed older. His shoulders sloped. His clothes looked too large. I recognized the red and black checkerboard shirt from the last time I saw him, when it fit like a skin.

"Hey, Paul! You got time for a joint?"

We sat in his van, finished the six pack and two or three joints, talking and laughing about nothing I can remember, except that he had finally found a steady job, working as a janitor for NIPSCO.

"Hey, it's a job. My wife is thrilled." There was a pause. "So, how's your love life?"

"Not bad. I had a date the other day. We went to a museum in Chicago."

"Woooo. Working hard since I last saw you."

"Yeah, well, I just met Stephanie. She's in college. In Gary. You know, that extension Indiana has on Broadway."

He nodded. "What's she do?"

"Nothing. Goes to school."

"No — what's she do in school?"

"English." I was embarrassed. It was strange talking about women with Greg. "She thinks I should go to college."

We stared at each other for a couple of seconds. Streetlight floated inside the van and it turned his eyes the color of grey stone. He took a roach-clip hanging from the rearview mirror, there with his wife's pink bridal garter and a silver chain on which he'd strung his driver's license. It was a different person in the picture.

"Greg, I just wanted to say I'm sorry about what happened at P. K.. I really thought they were going to give you a job."

"Aww, it's alright. Hey, you remember that first day I saw you? Man, were you shitted. I can still see that stupid look on your kisser — ." He stopped, made his face go dumb with a dopey smile and big eyes.

I winced. "Yeah, well, I was pretty surprised to see you."

"I knew who you were," he said, putting his old face back on, "but I didn't want you not to talk to me — I mean, after what happened in school."

The same old Greg — always bringing up the past. Our past — Mac and I — never changed. It grew older, as we did, gained or lost a few pounds, grew its hair out, shaved its beard, wore contact lenses instead of glasses, but it never surprised either of us. It wasn't like meeting a stranger.

"I would have talked to you. But, I think, after a while it would have been different."

"How so?"

I took my time, lit a cigarette, stared out the windshield. I looked for a way to tell him he was running in the wrong direction.

"Look at those guys, Greg." I pointed to the sheetmetal shop. Two men loaded a blank into a hand brake. "They've probably known each other for years. Don't even have to talk to know what the other's thinking. Just like an old married couple. By the looks of them, they're probably used to it by now. They spend every day together. I mean what could they talk about that's not old news?"

He shook his head. He lit a cigarette from a pack on the dashboard. "Didn't you ever want to go back — to school, I mean. Did you ever want to go back and do it all over?"

"I'm trying to."

"No, that's not what I mean."

I knew what he meant. I shook my head. "No."

"Well," he said. "I do. Man, those were great times. The best! What I couldn't do. It was so fucking good — wasn't it?"

"Yeah, you were," I said.

He flicked the cigarette into the back of the van. It fell in with others that littered the floor like white nails. It glowed for a bit then burned out in the blackness. I could make out boxes marked "Cleaning Solvent." Rags were thrown about like so many lost hands. Brooms. Brushes. A couple of spare tires strapped to the wall. A tool box covered with dust. Road maps. It smelled of gasoline and what I thought was Pine-Sol. Mostly it was dark, a dark you could see through.

"You were good." I smiled to prove it. "It seems unbelievable the shit we get ourselves into, but you got to believe there's something better coming out of all this."

He lit the end of another roach, inhaled deeply, and opened his mouth, but nothing came out, not even smoke. Something terrible was climbing up his throat and I didn't want to hear its name.

"Fuck you! Something better? Something better? This is all I've got. You're telling me it's a waste, to forget it. Fuck you, man. You want to hear something? Want to hear something really good? Listen up: I've been sterile since last year. Cancer. Man, my balls are gone!"

I reached out and took hold of his wrist, but he pulled it away.

"No, I'm not going to die. Dying would be too simple. It's worse than that." He choked on the next sentence. "I promised her kids."

I looked stupidly at my lap. He fumbled in his pockets for keys and slammed them into the ignition. "I got to go, man. I'll see you around."

I pulled off the road and sat on the hood of my car, waiting for the sun to rise — there wasn't much else to do. It must have been around four in the morning. I should have gone home, but that seemed like the wrong place to be. The air was brisk. I liked it. My whole body gave in to the cold: my fingers and toes numbing first, then the slow, steady crawl up my arms and legs until the shudders ran relays up my spine. Above, the stars were hidden behind a low cloud cover. I imagined them persisting through an infinite darkness, spelling out their impossible strategy toward dawn. It was good knowing my body occupied a definite space within the blackness. As small as it was, it had its beginning, and its end, where the cold started in my fingers and toes. Poor Mac. He was looking for some reason why it was all happening to him. He wanted to go back, to begin again, wonderful in his body.

In an hour the sun would shatter across the waters of the Delaware. My mother would begin another day at the kitchen table. My father, dressing quickly in the bathroom, would smell of Old Spice and toothpaste when he came downstairs and kissed her on the mouth. He would notice the bowl of fruit she always kept on top of the refrigerator. He would appreciate the oranges.

I knew the part of him that was happiest in his past. I could still remember late afternoons when he would come home from work and sit alone in his chair, his memory swimming with leaves, the sky slowly dressing in its dark suit. At the top of the stairs, I watched as his head tilted back, his hands turned palm up on the armrest. In his mind, he would meet the boy he once was. The small child with black hair and flashing teeth who always waited for his future to arrive under the blooming tulip tree. "Wasn't this my life?" he would ask. And what could the boy do but shrug his shoulders, and let the man he would become touch again his rough denims, the raised feathers of wheat on his shining, new penny?

Cruel that the body never forgets its past. Sitting on the hood of my car, bound by gravity and the senses, what did I see in the dark? What did I sniff out in the wind? Whose voice was clearest in that brisk silence? All I would ever know entered through the five kingdoms of one hand. And though I could hold nothing of the future, good sense let me assume the posture of the blind with my hands raised before me in an honest admission of fear, in a pure gesture of persistence.

LAURENCE GOLDSTEIN

THE SPORTS COMPLEX

They sweat and stretch in pain; they push weighted levers
and wrestle rubber knobs right or left, and always
on the perimeter, runners in shorts circle a track.
This is the Straining House. But will perpetual effort
do more than harden and swell muscles, including the heart?
Will charity increase with ease of breath, or poetry
be more cherished for the pull-lift rhythm of bars
or the kinetic frenzy of cycling and climbing of moving stairs?

Here for basketball, I think of Pindar who praised
the exertion of force on the wrestling mat, or the boxer's blow
that makes a name immortal for crushing a jaw. Nikeus,
I'll cite you at random to show how well the system works.
But these athletes will not live in verse; they toil
for other gain than first place in the Complex intramurals
or the now-reprehended wolf-whistle of the thoroughfares.

Better so. Who would be Ajax as the Greeks remembered him?
He earned Achilles' fancy armor by his brute strength,
a tiger who beat the Trojans down, but had no defense
when the sly generals Agamemnon and Menelaus
took the spoils for themselves, and gray-eyed Athena
spread her net for the hapless hunk: he murdered cattle
in his madness, thinking them Greeks, and when sanity returned
he sharpened his bloody sword, propped it in the ground
and ran it through a body no warrior could overwhelm.

I ask myself for a moral as I choose a ball, dribble
into the key and jump-shoot. No muscle comes of this;
more likely muscle damage as I leap and fall on tendons

weak enough to feel the shock. I have a backbone
so brittle in my forties I am warned away from bodysurfing,
my teenage skill. (Even Magic pulled hamstrings
for all the practice and craft of his everyday play.)
Shooting keeps me limber, like these fey bodybuilders,
we members of the chorus, never to be featured by name.
"It's a hard thing," we say in Sophocles' tragedy of Ajax,
"that I must range and plod, with never a fair course
to bring me near my goal." Unless ranging and plodding
is the goal, the incessant untrophied training till death.

Ball or no ball, we are goal-tending in our unremitting
half-measures of satisfaction, made a little tauter
and faster by exercise, annealed and better kneaded
into a shape and speed more acceptable to the gods.
Let's push that bar then, pump iron, as if Pindar
declared our vain and strenuous drill praiseworthy
and inscribed our American names in the temple of fame.
Imaginary victors, we wrap our tarnished selves
with the breastplate of the hero Achilles, and deadlift
the shield fashioned in the underworld for one Fate loved enough
to make of his funeral games the graceful culture of sport.

CHARLES JOHNSON

A PHENOMENOLOGY
OF THE BLACK BODY

A bawdy old black folktale celebrates the physical superiority of black men:

> Two white farmers sat before the stove in a general store in Alabama, arguing over who had the longest tool as an old Negro named Willis swept the front porch. They agreed to compare lengths. The man with the longest would get $25 for each additional inch. The first unzipped his fly. Six inches. The second did the same. Seven. The first turned to Willis, and said, "Let's see yours, Willis." The janitor trembled and shook his head. "Nassuh, Ah doan think Ah'd better do that, sar." The white man became angry. "I said for you to get in on this heah bet, Willis!" Afraid to say no, the janitor uncoiled his tool on the table—it took a while, friend: Willis just kept throwing it out like a fishing line. Twelve inches. Someone said, "God damn!" The two men gave Willis $125, and he raced home to show the money to his wife Maybelle. Staring skeptically at her husband, Maybelle asked. "You got alla that just for being big?" Willis whooped and went into hysterics. "Honey, that was the easiest money Ah ever made! Them white folks just better thank the Lord Ah wasn't on hard."

Laughing at the good fortune of Willis, we may lose sight of the fact that his triumph is based on cultural assumptions that lock him into the body and, to echo W. E. B. DuBois, create in his life a "double-consciousness" in need of resolution. This essay seeks to define the ambiguity of his situation and describe the harrowing constraints upon both Willis and his white competitors.

Our past experience as a people can often be understood through its expression in language, myths, stereotypes, symbols, and folktales like this one. As multi-layered complexes, they present collectively shared

121

and communicated meanings. But before we can talk intelligently about the "black experience" of the body, in this or any other narrative, we must first get clear on what is essential to all experience — the correlate of consciousness and its content, *noesis-noema*, or subject and object. A rule for phenomenology is that there is never an object without a corresponding subject, and that "Consciousness is always consciousness *of* something," to quote Edmund Husserl. Given the universality of these structures for consciousness, it is reasonable to say that there is neither an impenetrable "white" or "black" experience, which are mutually exclusive, but rather that there are diverse human variations upon experience, which can always be communicated imaginatively or vicariously across racial, political, and cultural lines through language in its two analytic forms: philosophy and literature. Perhaps this point is disagreeable to proponents of cultural pluralism, but it is a presupposition of the philosophy of experience — phenomenology — that is here assumed as a working methodology. The symbol of the black body, for example, if interrogated, should disclose a racial experience wrought mythically. Our folk literature simultaneously conceals and reveals our primordial racial situation, and must be carefully unpacked if we wish to wrench self-understanding from it.

Black writers, particularly novelists and poets in search of fresh ways of seeing things familiar, frequently feel the power of folk myths and stereotypes and, so moved, wrestle with uncovering their meaning. Weaving in and out of Frantz Fanon's works are thematizations of black consciousness from the vantage point of existential phenomenology, but without a turn to the body as the radix for interpreting racial experience. In his controversial essay "The Primevil Mitosis," Eldridge Cleaver brooks the stereotype of Black American physicality by now checking his own feelings (as an experiencing subject) against the myth, now rendering its terms rigidly abstract, now pursuing its more painful political implications. His conclusion: "The gulf between the Mind and Body will be seen to coincide with the gulf between the two races."[1] But is there such a gulf between the Mind and Body?

Cleaver assumes a basic division between the bodily and mental experiences of blacks and whites. Racism is the given, historically constituted and lying in wait for black consciousness, concealing the ethical dualism which has — over long centuries of Western cultural development — made white "good" and black "evil." Cleaver, focusing on one aspect of the phenomenon, the psycho-physical, finds that blacks are stripped of a mental life, which leaves them only a bodily existence (albeit a superior one like that of our janitor Willis), and he assigns them the name, "The Supermasculine Menial." He writes: "The body is tropical, warm, hot; Fire! It is soft, pleasing to the touch, luscious to the kiss. The blood is hot. Muscles are strength."[2] Alienated from this sensuous profile of the body, whites are characterized by Cleaver as "The Omnipotent Administrator." Weakness, frailty, cowardice, effeminacy, decay, and impotence are profiles associated with the white man's situation of abstraction from the body. Here, Cleaver's concerns in *Soul on Ice* are basically political, sexual, and polemical, not philosophical. But his attempt to explain our experience of embodiment may yield more philosophically than the author knows. His division recalls Paul Ricoeur's belief that, "It is possible for man to take two divergent and non-reconcilable perspectives upon himself because within man there is a non-coincidence which is that of the *finite* and the *infinite*,"[3] or of the physical and mental, consciousness and the body. It is even more illuminating when compared to Fanon's statement that, "There are times when the black man is locked into his body."[4]

Sexuality is not truly at issue in *Soul on Ice*. That is merely the manifestation of a larger problem of consciousness and the body in the black experience. The issue at stake is how blacks experience their own bodies within a world of racial restriction. By speaking descriptively, by casting the problem in absolute and often simple terms, Cleaver offers us the occasion for a broader consideration of experience, the body, and black consciousness.

Modern philosophy in the West since Descartes has entertained the idea that man is not identical with his physical being. In a crude formulation, man is presented mythologically and often philosophically as a mixture of mind and matter, spirit and flesh, consciousness and body, carnal shell and *Ka*, and remains to himself something of a mystery. The dialectic of matter and mind, subject and object, is a thread running the length of Western intellectual history, beginning with Plato's world of flux and world of forms. The later sundering of man and the world into mental and physical substances by Descartes in the *Meditations* throws light on the issue Cleaver is trying to bring to clarity—consciousness is experienced as being identical with, yet curiously distinct from, the body. One could almost categorize Western philosophy along the lines of whether a particular approach is primarily concerned with the subject of experience, consciousness, idealism, or the soul; if it emphasizes the object, matter, materialism, the body; or if it seeks a reconciliation between the two. Maurice Merleau-Ponty offers a simple but concise formulation to correct this false dualism that underlies the division between "The Omnipotent Administrator" and "The Supermasculine Menial": "I am my body."[5] It is that which reeves the subject to a world, anchors him in history, thus individualizing him, and makes possible perception and "meaning." It is my point of reference on the universe. I, as subject, am often at "one" with it, yet my relation as a human self to my body is also that of *radical otherness*. I *am* my body while I am also *not* my body (or I experience myself as not simply reducible to my body as the empirical object of physics, chemistry, neurology). Experience without "embodied consciousness" is as unthinkable as experience without the *noesis-noema* correlate: it is the irreducible way we are in the world. I am conscious of the world through the medium of my body.

To say that the body is our anchorage in the world is to bring this discussion to a consideration of "intentionality," the structure which gives meaning to experience. Intentions are at the heart of consciousness, or the *noesis*-pole, to the extent that they determine the manner in which we perceive the world. At this instant, let us say that I am a white administrator on campus. A strapping black student with a full natural, dashiki, coal-black complexion, and dark sunglasses comes into my office with a "dip-down," rolling gait. If my hobby is painting, perhaps I look toward the colorfulness of his clothing, and see him as a future subject for my canvas. Suppose I have just read Claude McKay's *Home to Harlem*, a novel which emphasizes the natural spontaneity of blacks; in this case I see the rhythms of his walk, the musicality of his movements in contrast to my own. Or, finally, suppose I am concerned that my daughter is being bused across town to a black school—Will she encounter people like this? In each instance the same student presents these multiple profiles of himself; they *are* his appearances, and each discloses a different "meaning." We have yet to speak of *his* experience upon entering the room and what my intentionality causes to arise in his consciousness. To "intend" an object or content of consciousness is to be "in-formed" by it as well as to *give form* to it. The mind is in no way passive; it is a participant in each act of knowing—self and object being inseparable poles of experience. It is also possible *not* to see other "meanings" or profiles presented by the object if the perceiver is locked within the "Natural Attitude," as Husserl calls it, and has been conditioned culturally or racially to fix himself upon certain "meanings." Rollo May, for example, reports on a patient who could not see an object placed before him on a table — it remained invisible on the basis of his inability to bring it forth intentionally as a content of consciousness.[6]

But consciousness is "embodied." Our desires, too, are "embodied," and it is clearly the case that every act of intending involves, to some extent, "interest." By this I mean that acting, willing, and intending are closely related. I see the student in a certain way because I fear for my daughter while she is across town. To *per*ceive a content is to *con*ceive that content. "The theory of the body image is, implicitly, a theory of perception."[7]

My body for me is not an assemblage of organs juxtaposed in space; my possession of it is undivided, and I know where my limbs are through a *body image*, know, when I sit at my desk, how my crossed feet appear, though I cannot see them. In all perception within a figure-ground relationship, where I either bring an object forth for attention or let it remain undifferentiated in the "ground," my body is the third term: it points me to the left or right, determines up and down, allows me to know space because as "embodied consciousness" I am in space, and know time because embodiment has temporality as one of its structures.

Right and left, established by the body, are sources of the lawful and forbidden; the body is emblematic; if I am "downcast," the body gestures accordingly with a drooping posture. "The body is our general medium for having a world."[8] The blind man's stick is no longer alien to him, not a mere object, but his bodily extension; the woman with a feather in her hat keeps a safe distance between it and things that might snap it off, but without looking: she *feels* these distances. All this is understood by the term *body image*, or in the work of Fanon, *body schema*. We see that motility is basic to intentionality.

Our first phenomenological act in a thematization of the black body involves a suspension or bracketing of all sociological and scientific theories concerning race. We wish to purify a field in which the body becomes the primary focus of racial consciousness. Whether black or white, the body is still experienced as having an ambiguity, a non-coincidence of mind and matter. I *am* my body, but clearly there is magic in the fact that when I say "Spread your fingers" the digits on my hand do so. I see my hand on my desk and sometimes it is alien; perhaps I do not even recognize it as *mine* when I see it in a photograph. Stranger still, I know that I cannot see myself as others see me, white and black, as if the secret of my body and the objectivity of its "outside" belongs, not to me, but to everyone else. Furthermore, I am black. I do not see what the white other sees in my skin, but I am aware of his intentionality, and—yes—aware that I often disclose something discomfiting to him. My body gives me the world, but, as that world is given, it is one in which I can be unseen. I walk down the hallway at the university and pass a professor I know well. He glances up quickly, yet does not acknowledge that he knows me. He has seen a black, a body, that remains for him always in the background, seldom figured forth save as maid, taxi driver, or janitor. Passing, he sees me as he sees the fire extinguisher to my left, that chair outside the door. I have been seen, yet not seen; acknowledged as present to him, but in a peculiar way. I call down the hallway, "Professor Peterson!" Recognizing me, he says, "Ah, Charles," and figures me forth. He offers me his hand and, shaking it, I see perhaps what he has seen: the darkness of the black body suggests "stain" primordially. For him, and at odd moments for me, this stain of my skin gives in a sudden stroke of intentionality "darkness," "guilt," "evil," an entire galaxy of meanings. Yet, it is *I* who perceive myself as "stained," as though I were an object for myself and no longer a subject. In fact, the stain of the black body seems figuratively to darken consciousness itself, to overshadow my existence as a subject. Is it this way for him? Cleaver writes:

> The chip on the Supermasculine Menial's shoulders is the fact that he has been robbed of his mind. In an uncannily effective manner, the society in which he lives assumed in its very structure that he, minus a mind, is the embodiment of Brute Power. The bias and reflexes of the society are against the cultivation of even the functioning of his mind, and it is borne in upon him from all sides that the society is deaf, dumb, and blind to his mind.[9]

That is, incapable of the intentionality that would allow the Supermasculine Menial to disclose an interiority. We shall call this situation the "black-as-body." Quoting Fanon: "In the white world the man of color encounters difficulties in the development of his bodily schema. Consciousness of the body is solely a negating activity . . . the body is surrounded by an atmosphere of uncertainty."[10] I am aware of each of my limbs through my *body image*; similarly, I am aware of my skin surface, my epidermal encasement through my *body image*, and particularly when I am "seen." "Saying that I have a body is thus a way of saying that I can be seen as an object and that I try to be seen as a subject, that another can be my master, so that shame and shamelessness express the dialectic of the plurality of consciousness, and have a metaphysical significance."[11] Fanon warns that "though Sartre's speculations on the existence of the Other may be correct . . . their application to a black consciousness proves fallacious. That is because the white man is not only the Other, but also the master, whether real or imaginary." And again: "Jean-Paul Sartre has forgotten that the Negro suffers in his body quite differently from the white man."[12]

The experience of the black-as-body becomes, not merely a Self-Other conflict, nor simply Hegel's torturous Master-Slave dialectic, but a variation on both these conditions, intensified by the particularity of the body's appearance as black, as "stained," lacking interiority and, as Fanon writes, as being "overdetermined from without." The body as opaque and consciousness as invisible is developed in Cleaver's brief essay. And if that consciousness is not experienced by the Other as invisible, it is the repository for the offscum of racial relations — to black subjectivity is attributed the contents that white consciousness itself fears to contain or confront: bestial sexuality, uncleanliness, criminality, all the purported "dark things." In R. W. Shufeldt's *The Negro, A Menace to Civilization* (1907) and Thomas Dixon, Jr.'s *The Leopard's Spots*, the idea is extended to include black blood, which carries the germ of the underworld and the traits of lower orders of animals; one drop of black blood, for example, will cause a white family to revert to Negroid characteristics even after a full century; the mulatto, though possessing white blood, is depicted as dangerous because his surface "outside," not being stained, betrays the criminality and animality of his interior.[13]

The stereotype with which we began discloses the black-as-body but, as a pure literary presentation, it conceals the original situation of "embodied consciousness" made a problem for itself by "stain." Consider the concern our grandparents had with body complexion, "brightening the race" through careful marriage, the terrible importance of fair skin, curly hair, and "yellah women." They were not fools, these old folks; they knew what they experienced. And understood skin-bleaching creams and straightening combs as important because these changed their stained "outsides" upon which, in this social system, the depth of their "insides" would be gauged by others. (Indeed, critic Robert Bone has called Christianity in James Baldwin's *Go Tell it on the Mountain* a "spiritual bleaching cream.") Stain recalls defilement, guilt, sin, corpses that contaminate, menstruating women; and with them come the theological meanings of punishment, ostracism, and the need to be "cleansed." It was never so much that, "If you're light, you're alright," meant that whiteness was rightness on the basis of the lack of pigmentation alone; rather, it meant that, "Washing a Moor white over three generations," degree by painful degree, led to his social recognition by the Other as human subject, as — in some cases — his possessing a soul, an "inside."

I am walking down Broadway in Manhattan, platform shoes clicking on the hot pavement, thinking as I stroll of, say, Boolean expansions. I turn, thirsty, into a bar. The dimly-lit room, obscured by shadows, is occupied by whites. Goodbye, Boolean expansions. I am *seen*. But, as a black, seen as stained body, as physicality, basically opaque to others — a possibility that, of course, whites themselves have in a room of blacks. Their look, an intending beam focusing my way, suddenly realizes something larval in me. My world is epidermalized, collapsed like a house of cards into the stained casement of my skin.[14] My subjectivity is turned inside out like a shirtcuff. "And so it is not I who make a meaning for myself, but it is the meaning that was already there, pre-existing, waiting for me,"[15] much like a mugger at a boardwalk's end. All I am, can be to them, is as nakedly presented as the genitals of a plant since they cannot see my other profiles. Epidermalization spreads throughout the body like an odor, like an echoing sound. This feeling differs little from that of sexuality: a sudden dizziness and disorientation, an acute awareness of my outside, of its being for others, a tight swell at my temples. But it is not the pathological feeling of "inferiority" alone that Fanon speaks of when my being is stolen — it is Cleaver's perception of the black-as-body. Yet, Fanon is correct. "For not only must the black man be black; he must be black in relation to the white man."[16] Because it is from whites that the intention, the "meaning" of the black body comes. I sit at the bar, ignoring the Others; but the body is acutely aware of them, knows immediately when someone outside my peripheral vision has stood up. It is intense, as though consciousness has shifted to the skin's seen surfaces.

Our body responds totally to this abrupt epidermalization; consciousness for the subject is violently emptied of content: one, in fact, draws a "blank," though clearly for the white Other my interiority is, if not invisible, a space filled with sensuality, crime, or childlike simplicity. There are physiological reactions: the pulse and adrenalin increase, the seen skin becomes moist, as if the body is in open conspiracy with the white Other to confirm the sudden eclipse of my consciousness entirely by corporeality. I feel its sleepy awkwardness, and know myself not as subject but as slumberous, torpid matter. The Other awaits my slurring my words; my mouth, dry as ash, seems ready to realize his expectation. He awaits a signal of my "Negroness" — perhaps my brutalizing the language when I order a beer: some signal that we in our bodies are not the same. If I am the sort of "Negro" brought up to be a "credit to the race," I must forever be on guard against my body betraying me in public; I must suppress the profile that their frozen intentionality brings forth — I police my actions, and take precautions against myself so the myth of stain, evil, and physicality, like a Platonic form, does not appear in me.

Or, let us say, I sit sipping espresso with a white friend in the Village, discussing Borges, Barthelme, Baraka, basketball, the incredible Pele. I've smoked myself into a sore throat; I sip the scum-surfaced coffee merely to wet my lips, to ease my throat. Our conversation turns circuitously and comes to Walt Frazier. The Other slaps my knee soundly. He says, "Man, that cat is the most beautiful animal I've ever seen on a basketball court. I mean, he moves like — like a cheetah, or a big jungle cat." Make no mistake: this comes from him as the highest compliment. He is "hip," you see, liberal, a Left Bank intellectual — it is merely a *faux pas*. He has not reduced us to a "nothingness." The reduction is to "muscles are strength." Paradoxically, we are reduced to the body as the subject of physics — Brute Power. Yet, as with the rush of sexuality, a torpor glazes over my consciousness, a languor arises like a sleepiness in my limbs. The thickness of the world's texture is thinned. The body commonly extends itself in vehicles, buildings, machines, clothing. "Consciousness is being toward the thing through the intermediary of the body — to move one's body is to aim at things through it; it is to allow oneself to respond to their call."[17] But the black-as-body must see such a call as dubious, even though the "White Only" signs have been torn down, because there remain strict territorial boundaries, real or imagined, when we experience the searing Sartrean "look" of the hate-stare, when the world is epidermalized. Our body in these cases comes awake, translates itself as total physicality — it, oddly enough, feels as if it is listening with its limbs to the Other as my interiority shrivels like something burned, falls into confusion, feels threatened and, if it does not make me constitute myself as hatred (unable to change the world, I emotionally change myself), it momentarily, like a misty field, hazes over.

But we have not completely answered the question raised by Cleaver. There are black modes of flight from the black-as-body situation to consider. So far we have said that in a situation structured by a color-caste system, a black's consciousness and his lived-world (*Lebenswelt*) are frequently epidermalized and thrown into confusion when others intend him as the black-as-body. Once I am so one-sidely seen, I have several options open to me on the level of consciousness. These are also stages in recent black history:

(A) I accept this being seen only from the outside, accept my human possibility of being matter *sans* mind for the Others. I craftily use this invisibility of my interior to deceive, and thus to win survival, as the folk-hero Trickster John frequently does in the "Old Marster and John" cycle. My stain is like the heavy make-up of a clown; it conceals me completely. The motto of this useful opacity is the rhyme: "Got one mind for whitefolks to see / Got another one that's really me." That is, not being acknowledged as a subject is my strength, my chance for cunning and masquerade, for guerrilla warfare: I am a spy in the Big House. I cynically play with their frozen intentions, presuppositions, and stereotypes; I shuffle and appear lazy to avoid work, or — if I am a modern — I manipulate their basic fear of me as Darkness and Brute Power to win concessions. It is what Ralph Ellison calls "Rinehartism" in his novel *Invisible Man*. In Richard Wright's "novel-of-ideas," *The Outsider*, the protagonist is Cross Damon, a black existential hero with an extensive background in Heidegger, Husserl, and French phenomenology, who is freed from his former life by a freak subway wreck in Chicago. He assumes a new identity, but needs a false birth certificate. He thinks: "He would have to present to the officials a Negro so scared and ignorant that no white man would ever dream that he was up to anything deceptive." By shuffling, head-scratching, eye-blinking, and butchering the language, Cross pulls off the grotesque deception, and the author explains:

> And as he stood there manipulating their responses, Cross knew exactly what kind of man he would pretend to be to kill suspicion if he ever got into trouble. In his role as an ignorant, frightened Negro, each white man — except those few who were free from the race bias of their group — would leap to supply him with a background and an identity; each white man would project out on him his own conception of the Negro and he could safely hide behind it. . . . He knew that deep in their hearts those two white clerks knew that no human being on earth was as dense as he made himself out to be, but they wanted, needed to believe it of Negroes and it helped them to feel racially superior. They were pretending, just as he had been pretending.[18]

(B) Perhaps I display my eloquence, culture, and my charm to demonstrate to the Other that I, despite my stained skin, do indeed have an inside. "Y'know, I was just thinking about Boolean expansions," I tell the barkeeper. I self-consciously sprinkle my speech with French (my interiority is Continental, you see). Perhaps I pretend that I am not Afro-American at all, but part Indian, Jamaican, or an African — a flight from the historical experience of American antebellum slavery in which epidermalization reaches its acme.

(C) Or I am radical, and seize the situation at its root by reversing the negative meaning of the body and, therefore, the black-as-body: "It is beautiful," I say, "I am a child of the Sun." The situation of the black-as-body possessing non-cognitive traits is not rejected in this most recent variation of cultural nationalism, but rather stood upon its head: the meaning still issues from the white Other. I applaud my athletic, amorous, and dancing ability, my street-wisdom and savoir-faire, my "soul," the food my body eats ("Yeah," I scream at my white friend in the Village, "we're naturally superior to you at sports. Uh huhn, and we satisfy our women better *too!*"); I speak of the communal ("single-body") social life of my African ancestors before the fifteenth-century slave trade, their bodily closeness to the earth. I am Antaeus in this persuasion of the alienated black self's phenomenological pilgrimage to itself, and the whites — flesh-starved invaders, freebooters, buccaneers, seamen who bring syphilis to ancient Africa — are alienated physically from the earth. They see their lost humanity in me. They steal me to take it home. If I am a member of the early Nation of Islam and believe in its mythology of Yacub, the black scientist who created a "white beast" from the black community, I intend the whites as quasi-men "grafted" from the original black-as-body until, by degrees, the Caucasian appears as a pale and pitiful abstraction from myself, ontologically removed several stages from the basic reality which I represent.

Curiously, this persuasion in which stain and the black-as-body are inverted is ahistorical; it must involve a complete reconstitution of cultural meanings with the black body as its foundation: two thousand years of color and symbolism must be recast. Hence, we see the black-as-body in this profile generating new cultural forms: African dress (body extensions), Swahili (what my body speaks), the Nation of Islam and Black Church of Christ (my interiority is black, you see), but behind such a cultural revolution, which I create, is the enigma of the black-as-body in a state of stain. I portray my body to myself as "luscious to the kiss," beautiful, "tropical," soulful, sensuous — as "Fire!" My knowledge is natural, from "Nature" (another vast body) and is called "mother-wit," a form of knowing antithetical to the lifeless thoughts in the upper recesses of the Omnipotent Administrator's brain. I intend the white body as pitifully unstained, stiff, decadent, rigid, unnatural, cerebral, and pasty like something left under my kitchen sink, away from the skin-darkening sun, for too long a time. No attempt to bridge the false dualism of the Supermasculine Menial and the Omnipotent Administrator, between the body and consciousness, is made in these variations.

It should be clear that what is described in Cleaver's "The Primevil Mitosis" is a general human possibility based upon the ability of "embodied consciousness" to be made a problem for itself within a racial caste system. As we have seen, the problem is not diminished by the customary strategies for escaping it. The black body remains an ambiguous object in our society, still susceptible to whatever meanings the white gaze assigns to it.

Postscript, 1993

This essay, which originally appeared in the Winter 1976 issue of *Ju-Ju: Research Papers in Afro-American Studies*, was written in 1975 as my "style paper" for the Ph.D. program in philosophy at

SUNY-Stony Brook. Back then all doctoral candidates were required to submit for the faculty's approval an essay using the methods of one of the three principal schools of twentieth-century philosophy — analytic or British, American philosophy (pragmatism), or phenomenology — and since aesthetics was my field of concentration, I chose the latter. If memory serves, this was easily one of the hardest years of my life. As a graduate student living on a teaching assistantship, I was broke, but that June saw the birth of our son Malik, and the feverish writing of the first draft for *Oxherding Tale*, a novel I would publish seven years later. I remember monkishly retreating into one of the foulest apartment buildings in Port Jefferson, New York (it was all we could afford that summer) and, when I wasn't working on the novel, reading Sartre's *Being and Nothingness*, Heidegger's *Being and Time*, and Merleau-Ponty's *The Phenomenology of Perception* back-to-back in about the space of a month. Out of that context of unemployment and impoverishment and general concerns for my son, and fresh from my immersion in these seminal works of the German and French phenomenological movements, this essay was conjured.

Looking back across eighteen years at this descriptive analysis, I realize that my hope was to examine the black male body as a cultural object and to inquire into how it has been interpreted, manipulated, and given to us, particularly in popular culture. In general, too little has changed in the social world since the essay was first published. Indeed, for a few years things got worse. In the Bush campaign's exploitation of Willie Horton to frighten voters in 1988, in the racial slur about "Gorillas in the Mist" from the policeman who beat Rodney King as he would a dangerous animal, in the television footage of black male destructiveness during the Los Angeles riot, in the rise of the white supremacy movement in the last decade, in Pat Buchanan's attack on NEA for funding a film about gay black men (and ex-Klansman David Duke's startling though brief political success), in the decimation of black communities by AIDS, in the sexual harassment charges against Clarence Thomas, who according to Anita Hill described himself as "Long Dong Silver," in the sexist "gangster" lyrics offered by Ice T and other rap artists, in the gang-banging legions of Crips and Bloods, in the relentless barrage of statistics about murder among young black men and their failure to support their families, and even in the popular novels of several black women authors during the decade of the

1980s, we find that the black male as "Negro beast" — violent, sex-obsessed, irresponsible, and stupid — still has great currency and acceptance in our culture.

However, it's important to point out that none of these cultural meanings cluster around the black *female* body. In an amazing and revolutionary feat of cultural reconstruction, contemporary black women have made dominant the profile of the female body as, first and foremost, *spiritual*: a communal-body of politically progressive, long-suffering women who are responsible, hard-working and compassionate, who support each other in all ways, protect and nurture their children and live meaningful lives without black male assistance. The black female body is, in fact, frequently offered to us as the *original* body of a humankind descended from a black Eve of Africa. Clearly, this profile owes much to both black cultural nationalism of the late 1960s (variation "C" in the essay) and to the embracing of feminism by many black women in the 1980s. Nevertheless, like the Negro Beast stereotype, the Ur-mother profile is a mythology that obscures and one-dimensionalizes our possibilities for experiencing each black person as individual, historical, and so unique that — as in the case of my son or daughter, for example — it must be said that no one like them has ever lived before or will ever live again.

Recently one of my colleagues in African-American Studies said to me that black women have succeeded in culturally "defining" themselves in their own terms and not those of the racial (or gender) Other. If he's right, then we have no choice but to conclude that black males have *not* done this quite as well as their female counterparts. As my friend, a gentle and scholarly man, put it: "People don't know who we are. Even *we* aren't sure who we are."

But isn't that precisely the perennial human dilemma? That we are, after all, beings who must fashion moment by moment what meaning our lives will have, beings in *process* who are subject in a single lifetime to change, transformation, self-contradiction, and constant evolution? In phenomenological terms, one can only achieve adequateness in describing the black male body by employing what some philosophers have called "genetic phenomenology," *i.e.*, by examining an individual as he (or she) exhibits over time a series of profiles or disclosures of being. For a life is process, not product (or pre-given meaning). It more resembles the verb, not the noun.

This, just maybe, explains the current interest of young people in the unusual life of Malcolm X. There is much for critics of culture and philosophers to discuss in Spike Lee's monumental film tribute to this slain leader. Begin with the opening scene when Malcolm Little — a drug-dealer, pimp, and thief — visits a barber shop and has lye combed into his hair, which straightens it so thin another customer says, "It looks white." Go next to Malcolm in solitary confinement at Charlestown State Prison, where he is made to live like a caged animal. Then contrast both of these scenes to Malcolm X on his knees in a temple in Mecca, his hands raised to Allah, an ancient, haunting Muslim prayer sliding from his black throat like song. Here, the black male body is the instrument of the Most High. It is a global body connected to America, Africa, and the Middle East. It is capable of surrender and strength. It is cleansed of drugs, tobacco, and alcohol. It is the temple, the repository, of two millennia of Islamic scholarship, the living vessel for a culture that achieved a remarkably high level of sophistication when Europe was struggling through its Dark Ages — indeed, the culture that preserved Aristotle and transmitted him back to the West. For the first time in motion-picture history, and perhaps in pop culture, the black male body is experienced as the embodiment of intellectual, political, and spiritual ideals.

And yet all these profiles are of *one* life. If Malcolm X had not been slain in 1965, we doubtlessly would have witnessed more, an unfolding of idea and image that, for the phenomenologist, can only suggest the open-ended character of being. If there has been some slim progress since I first published "A Phenomenology of the Black Body," it is of this sort. A gradual accumulation of profiles that expand and qualify our experience of black men: General Colin Powell coolly professional at the center of the Persian Gulf conflict, athlete Arthur Ashe, widely admired for his courage and humanitarianism, astronaut Ron McNair honored for his contributions to the nation and NASA, Seattle mayor Norm Rice laboring, day in day out, to serve an American city that still works. Any accounts we have of black males in the future must, I believe, take these men — and the meanings their lives embody — into consideration.

NOTES

[1]Eldridge Cleaver, *Soul on Ice* (New York: Dell, 1968), 174.

[2]*Ibid.*, 169.

[3]Cited in Don Ihde, *Hermeneutic Phenomenology: The Philosophy of Paul Ricoeur* (Northwestern University Press, 1971), 56.

[4]Franz Fanon, *Black Skin, White Masks* (New York: Grove Press, 1967), 225.

[5]Maurice Merleau-Ponty, T*he Phenomenology of Perception*, trans. Colin Smith (New York: The Humanities Press, 1970). The discussion of the body is developed in Part One.

[6]Rollo May, *Love and Will* (New York: Dell, 1969), 229.

[7]Merleau-Ponty, *op. cit.*, 206.

[8]*Ibid.*, 146.

[9]Cleaver, *op. cit.*, 171.

[10]Fanon, *op. cit.*, 110.

[11]Merleau-Ponty, *op. cit.*, 167.

[12]Fanon, *op. cit.*, 138.

[13]George Kent, *Blackness and the Adventure of Western Civilization* (Chicago: Third World Press, 1972), 173.

[14]The term "epidermalization" was first used in a phenomenological sense by Professor Thomas Slaughter, of the Afro-American Studies Department at Rutgers, in his unpublished paper, "Epidermalizing the World."

[15]Fanon, *op. cit.*, 134.

[16]*Ibid.*, 110.

[17]Merleau-Ponty, *op. cit.*, 138.

[18]Richard Wright, *The Outsider* (New York: Harper & Row, 1953), 159.

CHRISTIANNE BALK

DRESS-ME-UP DAVID

Comes shrink-wrapped in plastic at the local
health food store, propped up between bamboo
tea strainers and bags of dried kumquats, his fabulously
full body now a complete set of flat
kitchen magnets, though if you look carefully

you might see the man Michelangelo saw
desiring something in the distance
with his entire body, unashamed
and poised, as if through his eyes we might see
the cost of carving two tons of pure white

marble into flesh, beloved
foreground wild for the one standing just out
of sight. What price, those willing thighs, unsettled
and unsettling cock, tangled hair, undistracted
gaze, patient hands, oh, perfectly balanced

stance withholding the almost imperceptible
lean of the body's longing to go as
far as the eyes can see and farther. One
shot in broad daylight in the Piazza
della Signoria! Who can imagine being divided

like that? Carried away, soaked in potassium
bromide, silver nitrate, gallic acid,
rolled out and pressed down
on huge sheets of flexible, vinyl-topped,
magnetic metal fabric. You can do

what you want with the tiny, low-cut briefs
he comes with, the denim jacket, jeans, flannel
shirt, boots, hat, peel them off or layer them
one by one on top of him on the front of your
refrigerator to hold up

grocery lists? phone bills? snapshots of the ones you love?

INJURY

This is the child of lifting luggage wrongly.
The resistance of weight that reintroduces
us to gravity. The unthinking pull upward
that spasms us out of ourselves.

The suitcase said, No,
and my body echoed
that heavy word,
a deep shudder within slumbered muscles
that crumpled me from easy flight.

There is suddenly nothing outside
this small world of pain,
where everything becomes empiric
and the world ruptures down to one focus.
I see nothing beyond this body on fire.

Porter hands lower me
into the passenger seat of someone's car,
put the seat back prone. I stare
up, surprised at the blueness of the sky.
The plane tickets in my breast-pocket
ricochet my heartbeat.

Wheeled into the hospital,
I am parked to wait
with colorful others and we are all
the same identity.
Patient. Dole-eyed.
Waiting to be probed, molded, reset.

Walk out singular.
In injury, we are only collectively singular.
Patients. Dole-eyed.
Most of us samely cradling
a part of ourselves.

We think of *whole* when we are incomplete.
Except for the dull ache, I do not exist
from the waist down.
And how heavy the testes,
how insistent on their presence they become.
Is this the one injury every man fears?
Is this an ache anything like labor?
Is this the rending we inflict on women?

While the physician explains
the strained, inguinal ligament
that snakes down from hip to center,
I concentrate on how it never existed before this,
how it aches now like an abortion of self.

Heavy with the comfort of medication,
apart from the waiting others,
I am wheeled out to singularity again.

Home in bed, learning the word, dependent,
I am no longer myself, no more
my easy name. I am
this new throb that tempos my sleep.
I dare not move,
but lie still as obedience, swaddled
in white elastic that holds me in.

In darkness and injury, we are anonymous.
What I cannot perform, I become defined by.
In darkness, the shape that shares my bed
lies on its back and I do not move myself over to it.
Bereft of ability, we reduce
to forms without function.

There will be tedious nights of rocking
from this new invalid to the old person.
The journey to our old definitions
may be impatient
but the necessary voice says,
lie still to heal.
Relearn slowly how to bend,
how to step gingerly,
how to lift,
how to be
in the ligaments that lend us,
momentarily,
to each other and to ourselves.

DAVID LEHMAN

ON THE NATURE OF DESIRE

1.

There are, said my old philosophy professor, two kinds
Of people in the world: those who divide everything in two
And those who don't. At the dinner party, Janice was talking

About computers. IBMs are masculine, she said. Macintoshes
Are feminine. That's exactly what some people say
About art and nature, said her husband, Don. Do you really

Believe that, asked Mark. I mean, should hurricanes be named
After women, as in the old days, and is the construction of a city
The quintessential male act, Nature subdued by Apollo's merry
    men?

2.

Nature, then, is the great eruption — flood, earthquake,
Tidal wave, volcano — that interrupts the World Series
And sends men running to their cars and their private visions

Of sublime waterfalls in the early nineteenth century when
Man could feel alone in a benevolent universe whose god
Was not an almighty moralist but the outburst of an imagination

Capable of anything. Nature is the calamity that overwhelms
    man
With terror yet draws him into it, and he creeps to the edge
Of the canyon, holding the hand of the woman he loves.

3.

The laws governing isosceles triangles do not apply
To man, wife and child. The professor of mathematics is one
Of two men in love with the same woman. The other is his son

By a previous mistress. Both are fearless.
They know that nature is a woman, a forest on fire
That can't stop burning. The goal is not to quench the fire

But to let it burn. The dancing around the fire goes on
All night, and the victorious couple is the last
To drop down exhausted and consummate their love.

4.

I saw her again this evening. She had the face of the woman
With the braided hair at the desk in the public library,
Where she used to work before she grew up and I moved away.

When I got up close I could tell how young she was — maybe 17,
The age we were when we met. I was reading *The Sun Also
    Rises*
And she walked over, brought me a pile of books about
    Hemingway,

And let her hand linger on mine, accidentally brushed.
Neither of us understood the nature of our desire,
Just that it was mutual. Our ignorance fed the fire.

5.

In those days you could have a girl in your dormitory room
Twice a month, on Saturday night, from seven in the evening
Until one a.m. The lights were out, but the dust of my window

Caught the glare of a streetlamp and the reflection of a neon
"Chop Suey" sign. An imaginary wind lifted her skirt,

And she smiled, letting me look. "You know, you could be
    expelled

For this." She had theories: she was Catholic, I was Jewish.
She was ashamed of her breasts, I was proud of my poems.
The antitheses were alluring in the early morning light.

6.

There are those who insist that all differences except
The biological are trivial and that the oppositions
Between Apollo and Dionysus, nature and culture and so on,

Are all of them sentimental and false, because they concern
Only the man and the woman, neglecting the third who walks
    always
Beside them. The great mystery is time and how we lost it

And cannot get it back, cannot convert memory into action,
The slim-breasted girl in the public library; can barely recall
The face in the photograph, the body beneath my own.

7.

Man in the state of nature was unalienated from his labor
Or in a state of constant warfare with his fellow primates.
They fought over an ordinary woman in an ordinary bar,

As if the fear of death didn't matter. The survivor wins her.
She is convinced he has put her on a pedestal in order
To look up her skirt: once a philosopher, twice a pervert.

Watching the couple's antics in bed are his mother and father,
Her mother and father, and the Marquis de Sade.
The son, asleep in the next room, is guarded by angels.

8.

In summer camp, the girl knows that any partner,
However unappealing, is better than no partner at all,
So she agrees to dance with him, a slow dance, an awkward
      waltz,

And when the torture is over, and their bodies separate,
He is shocked at what he sees: "Your dress is bleeding."
The boy becomes a man when his desire distracts him

From his fear, and he cannot resist the return to her womb
Though it rhymes with death at every orifice. The dress
Is put on to be taken off, the bed made to be undone.

9.

Why, then, is this city full of randy men, anxious
To cheat on their wives, and lonely women, who learned to
      say no
To importunate suitors long ago? If the scholars of sex

Are right, every Eve defends herself against her own desire
While trying to allay Adam's fear. If the poets of sex
Are right, the exchange of body fluids is a function

Of natural thirst, and love is the speechless joy
That lasts until it dies, and the couple close their eyes,
Tired, unashamed, nude and asleep for their hour together.

PRESSURE

if I rest my fingers here,
if I lay my cheek like one petal
of a rubbery orchid against your cheek,
will you rise from your knees,
will you pull your wrists free of these leather cuffs,
teach me the history of the stitches in your spine,
that mole and the cold rims of your ears?
you are brown along your legs,
Indian red across the hills of your shoulders,
only your buttocks stayed pale
under boxers you wore on a beach somewhere
on a handful of islands on a map,
curling your toes in the sand,
flexing the soles of your feet at the sun.
your lips to my shoulder seal a red death
in this room, where two stalks of orchids reach high like hands
and drop, and the sound of the air is soft
as the mushroom carpet,
white as the lace you fling around your hips.
here is the perfect stocking,
here, clasp it
between the two buttons of the garter, rise on legs
cased in the shimmer of a butterfly's crushed wings,
I can smell the desiccated powder in the air,
I can feel you reach with the arms of dying orchids,
your lips pursed like a cherub's,
your face red with pressure as if at a deadline,
nipples clipped between miniature planks of wood.
take it off, take it all off,
wipe the tears that slide glass over your eyes.

if I strike a match will you pour flames from your eyes,
birds of paradise red and orange at the sharpest points,
will your mouth leak a kiss onto my tongue
to run down your neck and across your burnt shoulder?
at least touch my tongue
with your tongue, with some salt of remorse
at the corners of your eyes, cross your arms
behind my shoulder blades and press me close
so my stomach caves
at your stomach solid against me.
hold my face in your hands, you burn
with the pent heat of vacations taken in winter,
beaches advertised in travel agencies,
grass skirts never the color of grass but of autumn leaves,
blue cocktails and a white sun to watch over you
year round, burning away symptoms of sadness.
don't kneel, don't submit
with your kisses on these stockings I wear for you,
lighter than breath,
your hands shaping calves and the hurt of an arched foot,
your eyes driving through mine, driving blue thunder
and I don't dare blink, I can't blink,
I swallow the white shroud of this room,
tug at the shroud of hair brushed back from your forehead,
know that you will leave with your nipples
matching the heat of your shoulders
the stripes of the crop cardinal across your buttocks,
now simmering, then fading.
don't say you came to learn about pain
when you will leave with all the colors inside me,
wear them for days on your back and breast
like the branding of an island sun.

TO BE HORST

The man stood in the cafe's doorway staring openly and with no expectation of recompense at a girl who sat three paces away from him. His monochrome, leonine face, bracketed between curly hair and beard of that shade called red only because it is not what is usually called brown, was covered so contiguously with freckles that the places where flesh tones broke through were the real freckles. It was a face puzzled, stymied, suddenly decisive, wrongly decisive: a face full of error, of error simple and compound, error seen and missed, error mourned and error dreaded, error unerased. A single heavy Cyclopean eyebrow bore down on his eyes like a frown. He wore a collection of baggy, bulbous, but untorn plaids; he had a regular table in the window of the cafe where he would sit for hours, never reading. Nobody who worked there had ever seen him with anybody.

The girl, about twenty, raised to him a well-arranged and blank white face. The man pointed to his sternum and lofted that bar over his eyes as high as it would go. Pushing against the thick brunt of shock, he began toward her in small slow steps, anxious not to disturb whatever delicate balance in the atmosphere made pretty girls look back at him today.

"Are you Horst?" she asked him.

"*Horst?*" He squeezed out the word on a long exhalation, an exhaustion: his chest caved, his shoulders folded in around it, and his clothes seemed to loosen as he shrank inside them. "No, I'm not Horst," he said, almost inaudibly. "But I'd like to be."

His hand fell away from his chest, as if it could no longer resist the pull of gravity; he broke at the waist and sagged into a chair. From there, ten feet away, he watched the girl steadily, his fingers spreading and contracting on the marble tabletop. Presently a man came in, introduced himself to the girl, and sat down with her.

148

Horst was a striking young man with dark brown hair, tanned olive skin and blue eyes. In or around the eyes was a weary ease that did not change when he saw the girl: he knew — approached her with the knowledge — that he could have her if he cared to. The eyes said *Hello, I am tired, Try to wake me up, I may be awakening, No, I am sorry, You tried, It is me, I cannot feel, I am a wanderer, Hello, I am tired, Try to wake me up.*

The red-haired man's eyes moved from the girl to Horst, and did not move from Horst. He was imagining what it might be like to be Horst. He could taste the drink that Horst drank, could see what Horst saw, breathe the air Horst breathed. He had forgotten entirely about the girl: she was merely a Horst-induced mirage; a manifestation, a byproduct, a proof of Horstness in a universe of Horststlessness; she was just one of many things that would happen to him in a life, the life ahead of him, of being Horst. Horst was the answer; the girl had been only the question. He stared inquisitively, to penetrate the mystery of being Horst; acquisitively, to wrench from Horst all of the Horstian secrets; he stared as if receiving an encrypted radio signal, as if this stare, so close by, could not possibly intrude upon the privacy of Horst, as if Horst, returning the stare, would look only into a mirror.

Horst into Horst equals Horst: something seemed to take hold of his nose, jerk it Horstward; something gently pinched the skin around his eyes into small weary crinkles. He held himself absolutely still as a sort of carbonation foamed up along the surface of the table and etched new whorls and eddies into his fingerprints. As his eyes changed, a smile stole into them. Soon now, very soon, the admirers would begin to come.

Poseidon. Greek bronze, ca. 450 B.C.
National Museum, Athens.

RUDOLF ARNHEIM

A GOD'S PERFECTION

Perfection of the body and mind comes with being a god. When Poseidon, the god of the seas, is shown imperfectly as a mortal entangled in much violence, as he often is on Baroque fountains, he foregoes this distinction. But presented as a trident-hurling ruler by the Greek bronze sculpture of the 5th century B.C., he is revealed as divinely perfect. Poseidon is still an attacker, but the throwing of the weapon is no longer the frantic effort of a capricious will. Rather, the weapon detaches itself from the man by a transfusion of energy from man to weapon, provided by the pervasive rippling of muscles that animates the god's body. The gentle swell shows the body as a wavy rhythm of consonant forces; and this empowerment of the whole, this action by nonaction, makes the weapon fly off under its own impulse. It is an exemplary demonstration of what the Japanese master of archery taught the Western philosopher Eugen Herrigel, who wanted to understand the wisdom of Zen Buddhism.

Action by nonaction, the formula for all sculpture that respects the timelessness of its medium, is also displayed by the symmetry prevailing in the figure. Poseidon's body has just emerged from the basic stance, so well known to us as the spread-eagle figure of the Vitruvian man, in which Leonardo gave us once and for all the prototype of male appearance. But this stance is also, and more relevantly, the root position for the Yoga exercises, the basic *asana* from which one proceeds to the sideways profile position of directed action.

Without letting us forget the timeless symmetry from which it sprang, the body's turn to action differentiates the functions of the limbs. The left leg commits the weight of the body to displacement and advance, while the swiveling right leg lifts the whole figure beyond the human enslavement of gravity. Liberated from the load of matter, the god appears as the embodiment of pure energy, spiritualized action.

151

The body is here under the command of the head, facing the goal. The right arm activates the hurl, the left arm keeps the body steady and steers its direction. Total concentration defines the goal, but the goal remains in the infinite as a target never reached. It is an endless quest, which — as we think of the human species — transcends even the completion of masculinity by femininity. Beyond such human finality of union, the divine figure's sexual organ remains confined to the symmetry of nonaction, while the spirit of Poseidon's glance knows of no such finality.

Only when the body is nude can it reveal the interaction of all its parts, the universal dynamics which alone displays the spirituality of the image. Slightly superhuman in size, Poseidon's statue was presented as a votive offering to a temple devoted to him. Only recently, less than seventy years ago, the bronze statue was recovered from the Aegean Sea, appropriately near Cape Artemision, where according to the Greeks' belief, Poseidon had come to their help by shipwrecking the Persian attackers. I thought of him when I sat among the marble columns of his temple remaining on the Sunion promontory south of Athens. High above the waters, I was impressed with the endlessness of the god's realm and the quiet ubiquity of his power.

ANDREW CAMPBELL and NATHAN GRIFFITH

THE MALE BODY AND
CONTEMPORARY ART

When asked to write an essay about contemporary visual representations of the male body, we welcomed the opportunity to examine how issues of maleness and masculinity have embedded themselves within the high culture of recent art. However, we are of the opinion that the "male body" does not exist. It is nothing more than a physical support for a "masculine" identity that is constructed by the ways in which it is clothed, is arranged or arranges itself, and the social/sexual context in which it interacts with similarly or dissimilarly sexed bodies. Therefore our commission presented certain problems. These problems inevitably centered around the prerogative of choice. Given the possibilities, how should we proceed? Should we concentrate on a particular medium, a particular conceptual underpinning, or simply on works that appealed to our individual tastes in art? How were we to frame this subject?

In a sense, these questions have determined the direction of our argument and the nature of our selection. Nevertheless, within these expansive parameters two approaches seemed to predominate. The first and by far most abundant locates meaning within the sexuality of the image. Characterized more specifically as a focus upon the homoerotic, this approach has been exemplified in the last three years by an explosion of material on the photographic representation of the male nude.[1] This approach is counterpointed by another, as indicated by the groundbreaking 1991 group exhibition, *No More Heroes: Unveiling Masculinity*, held at San Francisco Camerawork.[2] This second model incorporates the erotic potential of the image as only one aspect among many, the whole of which constructs a more expansive notion of the male body and its relationship to masculinity.

With this distinction in mind, the question then became, whether to maintain a clear focus and highlight the various means by which the male body has been requisitioned as homoerotic subject, or attempt on a broader level to suggest the variety of masculinities that a male body can bear. Our approach works within the parameters of each analytical framework simultaneously, to seek within images the sexual as well as the extra-sexual. It is an approach that has led to particular choices for this portfolio.

Among other things, it has led us to amplify the definition of "contemporary." While wishing to concentrate on visual images produced within the last five years to coincide with the growth of critical interest in the male body, we also recognized that the adjective "contemporary" indicates art that has been produced within the last generation. As a result we have decided to include some earlier works, works which are less famous, perhaps on account of their submersion within a larger conceptual series (as in the case of Jonathan Borofsky), or due to their overshadowing within the later success of the artist (as for Joel-Peter Witkin). But, as has already been implied, "contemporary" also indicates a conceptual awareness of the male body, an awareness defined relatively either as a result of the feminist movement, or the growth of a more general institutionalized "gender studies." In keeping with these concerns, the earlier works have been included for their thematic poignancy and their ability to illustrate certain significant modes of presentation that the male body has undergone.

With such concerns in mind, we have also privileged certain modes of production. Most strikingly, we have emphasized photography in its paradoxical role as a tool for both naturalizing and fracturing the relationship between the image and its subject. (For example, Joel-Peter Witkin's photographs testify both to the visual facticity of his subjects and to the artifice of their imagery.) And within the medium, we have chosen a number of what may be called homoerotic photographs, some of which may be disturbing in their frankness, but all of which illustrate the part the gay community has played in the tactical deconstruction of the male body as a purely heterosexual site. In addition, we have selected a significant number of works that disrupt the male body as a site of patriarchal power (evidenced in the work of Anne Rowland), or as a sexually dangerous other (that of Andres Serrano). The end result is that we have favored those types of images that problematize the very notion of a male identity defined and characterized by an archaic, euro-american, heterosexual, phallogocentric system of signification that feminism, and more recently gender studies, have schematically implicated. To this end, we will demonstrate that even those artists that might find themselves existing within this system adopt it as a point of contention through which to (re)present "masculinity."

Jim Cogswell's paintings are images of people caught alone or together in a variety of settings and circumstances. Persons rendered are young and old, male and female. Cogswell's own body serves as the originary point through which they come to life. He eschews the use of models, fashioning images of others largely through his own form.[3] The others that he renders are fictions. The bodies that he represents do not exist except as manifestations of the painter himself.

The painting *Thirst* (Fig. 2) is a self-portrait. The artist's identity is not disguised through the bulk of extra flesh or an altered visage but is an accurate transcription of what he sees in the mirror. This male body is the central element. It affects a pose denoting activity. The act of drinking intimates that there may be a narrative belonging to the image, supported by the specific locale within which the pose is enacted. In and of itself, this act might constitute a story. However, such an ordinary act is incongruous with the exalted treatment rendered through paint and brush. It is incongruous with the experience of such unheroic naked male flesh.

The seams of the painting unravel when the body is viewed as object, one among many objects within the frame of the work. The accoutrements of the room are assembled: the body, a painting on the wall, the carafe and funnel, the urn and the plant, the wagon wheel on a ledge, the glass held in hand. Together they form a conglomerate of potential meanings; together they might construct a narrative.

There are common bonds established. Biomorphic and cylindrical objects are juxtaposed against the planar outline of the painting on the far wall. They are juxtaposed against the geometry of the interior of the room. They share a common form and purpose. Each is a container, the carafe and glass for liquid, the urn for life, the body for substance ingested in physical and sensory form. Like the markings of paint on the rectangular canvas, they are all things through which narrative might ensue. But they resist the telling of stories.

They speak only for their identity as vessels and of their utilitarian status.

Among them the body is privileged, through centrality, size, and shared corporeal similarity with the viewer of the image. The body becomes the primary vessel, the container for meaning. Yet, the meaning of this body does not lie in its ability to convey the fundamental nature of Cogswell the man or a narrative of his life. The meaning of this body lies with the questions it evokes about the nature of representation, its power of persuasion, and its ties to "reality." While the body in this painting and others speaks for bodies in the world, Cogswell's body gives them form. They are essentially a simulation of his own. Removed from actual existence in the world and subjected to the world of the framed canvas, they become a simulation of that simulation.

A painting of 1990, *Circular Mirror* (Fig. 1), underscores several of the themes within *Thirst*. Like its predecessor, *Circular Mirror* implies something beyond the stasis of its title. While the painting appears to be a reworking of the classic Narcissus myth, the presence of the extra male figure intervenes in the closed circuit of the original narrative. The additional character, perhaps as metaphor for another viewing audience, is curiously disinterested, but his act illuminates the preoccupation of the principal actor as all the more selfish. While there may be certain parallel concerns in *Thirst* and *Circular Mirror* connected to satiation and satisfaction, *Mirror's* central figure appears to be traversing the tenuous line between practical need and perpetual, unfullfillable desire. Bearing in mind the metonymic relationship between painter and subject, the dual role that Cogswell maintains, we also need to consider the "narcissistic" relationship between this painter and himself-as-image. And yet the disinterest of the painting's secondary figure implies that the vanity of his neighbor is not as dangerous as it was for his mythic relation; the mirror, too, is portable, implying its flexibility of use, even a potential communal value. While the vainglorious position that Narcissus originally occupied is clearly being redirected, the merits of self-imaging are also being repositioned. When Cogswell pictures others, he pictures himself. But as he pictures himself he asks what it means to picture at all. For all the selfishness of the central figure, we as viewers are also drawn to the mirror, visually and verbally. Jim Cogswell's (self-)imaging clearly invites us all to look at ourselves in the mirror, and question our own image-making.

Peter Howson's graphic works present themselves as physical counterparts to the muscled, predominantly male figures that adorn his canvases. These constructions of grotesque men are at once tangible, tactile, and even brutal at times. While his robust brushwork clearly connects him to the New Scottish Painting, another feature that places Howson's art within this group moniker is the masculinism of his subject matter.[4] As with Cogswell, the act of painting becomes for Howson a (modernist) metaphor for male (pro)creative desire. This sketch of 1991, *The Masked Wrestler* (Fig. 3), conveys an assertiveness, perhaps even more so because of its "unfinished" state. The strength, and sense of volume, of this sketch are also symptomatic of New Scottish Painting, which owes more to draughtsmanship as an underpinning than the painterly bravado of, say, Abstract Expressionism.

As in Howson's latest series of paintings, *The Blind Leading the Blind* (1991), overdeveloped caricatures stand frozen in dramatic postures, gesturing, flexing, screaming silently. Yet, these representations of Scots bums and heavies, of Glasgow's "dossers" and "wee hard men," retain a certain human dignity if only in the passion of their stance and the theatrical chiaroscuro Howson employs throughout his work. This sense of pathos echoes older masters such as Francisco Goya, and as such its retrospective gaze seems to establish itself as traditional. This is not to imply that Howson's work (with its references to Goya and Breughel) is regressively nostalgic, or that its subjects and handling are somewhat less original (for all the problematics involved with that term), but rather that Howson's work is aware of itself as stemming from, and being a constituent part of, a history of painting. That self-reflexivity, in and of itself, should also problematize the modernist myth of (male) originality.

In the dramatic images from *The Blind Leading the Blind* series, and in this pastel sketch, machismo finds itself sporadically manifest in rather more menacing terms. But Howson's works mimic the hyperbolic gestures that "masculinity" marks as its own. *The Masked Wrestler*, almost larger than life, demonstrates the conflicting stylization — sometimes terrifying, sometimes gloriously camp — that accompanies the production and interpretation of its "masculine" image. As with Jim Cogswell, this accute self-awareness of image and imaging renders the ambiguous relationship between the "male body" and its "masculine" image all the more evident.

Nancy Van Goethem's 1990 series, *American Men* (Fig. 4) offers a view inside the body, beyond the exterior shell, to their humanity. The inspiration for this series of sixty ink drawings came from a reaction against "the gaze." For Van Goethem the gaze, a particular dynamic of looking, was determined by centuries of male artists, a gaze which idealizes, sexualizes, and patronizes, a gaze which ultimately objectifies the perceived and derives pleasure only for itself. Her intention, to quote her personal statement, was, "not to make an 'object' of the male, but rather to display a certain mapping of their faces, moods, expressions." Unfortunately this single image from the series cannot do justice to the project as a whole. The complete series numbers some sixty drawings displaying different facets of character; equally, an *American Women* series has been completed, and intended to be displayed simultaneously.

The portraits are largely taken from memory of the myriad faces swarming New York City; a smaller portion, approximately one-third, were abstracted from photographic sources, either her own or images taken from the media. As a result none of these drawings really constitutes a subject, but instead retains certain (perhaps idealized) character attributes.

There is an overall melancholy to the series that is certainly related to Van Goethem's choice of medium. Both the monochrome of whitened paper and Sumi inks, and the "tears" of ink that stream down each visage contribute to this introspective sadness, one not evident in her brightly colored painted works. But these portraits present more than mere emblems for the intrinsic sorrows of urbanism. Their construction suggests something profoundly more interior. One advantage to using ink washes is the creation of layers of color, even a sense of the translucent. The heads of her "sitters" betray this translucency to a far greater extent than their clothing, which is either evenly patterned or blocked out.

Each of the heads displays an almost architectonic construction beneath its surface, delineating the topography of their faces. However, topography is not an adequate word to describe such a geographics of the male face. The sense of melancholy also arises from a quality of vulnerability, of psychological penetration, of being able to see through disguises. Topography implies a superficiality, a shallowness, while Van Goethem's drawings offer multiple depths of perspective. Rather than exposing the impossibility of a concrete meaning, she distills, reduces, even simplifies, these male visages before our eyes. Each of these images with its respective subframes proffers at least some kind of reclamative project, some kind of deeper worth. The male body is still objectified by Van Goethem, but in such a way as to suggest her subjects' potential. Her frameworks are points of origin rather than points of enclosure.

Representations of the gendered body are on occasion asked to speak for the universal. To this end, the *Backs* (Fig. 5) of Magdalena Abakanowicz provide the point of departure for a discourse upon the nature of human experience in the world. Life-size and larger, their origins are an actual human man and the cast of his body.

These *Backs* take form in resin-dipped burlap applied to a mold of plaster and left to harden as independent units. Multiple casts of this form have been produced. They appear as fragments of a body, only its back, from the shoulders to the knees. Often these backs are assembled and shown in installation. They have been placed in a variety of settings, in galleries and museums, on roads and beaches. They have been arranged in a multitude of configurations, lines, and rows, through regimentation and through dispersal. They are set on the floor or on the ground.

Each shares a basic form that derives from their mutual mold. Yet each is unique. This basic form is marked by variation. The laying of burlap, the creases made, the thickness of the folds, exact individuality out of mundane sameness. Headless, expressionless, emphatic in their obstinance, they speak as individuals through random variations in their production and through the distinction of their position in a given configuration.

Through their sameness, they parody the homogeneity of the human race. Through their individuality, they speak for its differentiation. These abstract forms are a skin that emulates the body, a shell that signifies "man's" physical presence in the universe. These backs literally take the form of the male body, yet they do not speak for that body. They "express the spiritual condition of human beings in Modern society, characterized by anxiety, alienation, and loss of values."[5]

The backs take form as husks, brown burned-out corpses, charred remains. Their entrails have been extracted, their muscles and bones removed. These skin-like shells evince a sense of spiritual and physical pain. They speak the anguish of bodies brutalized. These backs are analogs of the actual body that gave them form, and metaphors for bodies having suffered in days gone by.

The ensemble is stiff and lifeless. They are the trace of an abstract notion of the body that we define as essential to the human condition. They are the remnants of separation, a split from the mind, the hollow remains of Cartesian dualism determining the body's relevance in the world. Intellect is voided through the dispersal of their heads, spirituality by the removal of their hearts. What remains are empirical remnants, a being determined by the physical presence of its body in the world.

Nancy Grossman perceives herself as an outsider, an other, an identity constructed through the anti-Semitic taunts of her mother's family, developed out of the trauma of incest, determined by her position as a woman. Her art takes form largely through the repetition of symbolic motifs that isolate the roots of her otherness in the oppression of society and culture.

The bound male figure is common to her oeuvre. It is constructed as sculpted heads, encased in leather, secured by cords and zippers. This body is represented in drawings and prints, full-length or in pieces, chained and tied, writhing and contorted. It has been rendered as a form, a single sculpted body, in *Male Figure Sculpture* (Fig. 6).

This male body is a metaphor for the sculptural process that created it.[6] Big legs and arms and the well-defined torso are evidence of the obsessive lengths to which men will go to create the perfect image, to pursue an ideal, to construct a specimen characteristic of that ideal. Through sculpting, the male body is rendered beautiful. In this case, the legs are poised. One pushes forward, the other pulls back. Their position throws the buttocks upward. A bountiful curve is effected. Ideal form comes alive. It recalls the Grecian youth as a sign of perfection and grace. The body is rendered sexual. Thighs frame the genital region, articulating it, concentrating it, privileging the penis through centrality. The body is rendered powerful. Its lungs are expansive and its chest pushes outward. The rib cage is marked. Muscles ripple and connect the torso to large arms which are cast up, over the head, covering the head.

The body is idealized as beautiful in its powerful sexuality and through a yielding pose, not unlike the *Dying Slave* of Michelangelo (Fig. 7). Both of these male bodies are characterized by a pathetic sense of beauty. Both are given over to slavery and submission uncharacteristic of modern conceptions of "man." Here, there is a conjunction between Grossman and Howson. In their works the myth of the strong (heterosexual) man as an identity behind which to hide is overtly presented as artificial, a disguise which cannot conceal its seams.

Like Michelangelo's slave who battles his prison of stone and loses, Grossman's figure combats a brutality enacted through leather that binds, covers, and contains its sculpted body. For Grossman this occurrence is rendered through the guise of sadomasochism, a relationship to the world defined by physical pain and mental anguish. This figure is marked in its maleness. The body is large and muscular, its organ is prominent. Yet, body and organ alike are bound and constricted. In spite of its manliness, in spite of its apparent strength, the body is rendered ineffectual. It has no means by which to exercise control. Bindings signify its estrangement and alienation. Leather seals its skin from contact. Zippers prevent its senses from operating. This body is closed off to others, removed from contact with the world. It is rendered impotent through a sexuality of fear and trepidation.

This body is symbolic. It is symptomatic of the physical manifestations of terror implicit in an experience of the institutions of society. Violence, war, rape, and murder oppress Grossman's figure. It in turn stands for our own oppression, an oppression that may be registered through our unwillingness to disbelieve in the potent symbolic union of male body, masculinity, and power. It may also be testament to the force with which patriarchy sutures each of these elements together as a means of procreative self-justification. Through restraint this figure is isolated and its appearance is rendered monstrous. It stands separate and apart, characterized by an otherness endemic to its lot in life, endemic to us all, indicative of the force of the institution, which can turn even the masculine and its privileged status into a quaking, fearful marker of lost power.

Joel-Peter Witkin's photography immediately unsettles our perception of the normal. His otherwise perfectly printed images appear scarred and wraith-like, conveying a sense of entrapment not unlike the caged figures of Francis Bacon. And witnessing these images, of Bacon and Witkin alike, a viewer finds himself or herself contained, caged within the closed circuit of the viewing experience, heightened in this case by the overwhelming facticity of the photograph.

There are certain elements that disrupt a perception of Witkin's work, and specifically *Canova's Venus* (Fig. 8). The titles of his pieces encode the pictorial elements, very often vectoring them in dangerous directions. Along with his works, *Las Meninas* and *The Kiss*, *Canova's Venus* is forcibly inserted into the discourse of art-historical tradition. Yet these references are not merely facile and mimetic. *The Kiss* recollects Géricault's paintings of dismembered body parts, as decapitated heads enact a postmortem, gay kiss, evoking, curtailing, even terrorizing our memories of Brancusi, Klimt, and Rodin. *Canova's Venus* performs a similar knee-jerk act, maneuvering past Canova, and simultaneously challenging Henry Fox Talbot's similarly posed photographic portrait of his wife from the 1840s. In true postmodern fashion (which then ironizes itself), Witkin places himself in the position of a cultural bandit, mimicking, parodying, possibly violating the tradition which he cannot, in a metairony, fail to acknowledge and locate himself within.

While the "male" body of art history and historiography is subtly challenged, the male Venus within the frame creates a different series of tensions. This goddess of love seems more like a Caravaggesque Cupid, vulnerable yet aloof, titillating yet not altogether attainable. In a further historical twist, this young man recalls another series of adolescent boys — those photographed in the last decades of the nineteenth century by the Baron Wilhelm von Gloeden, whose work Witkin owns. However, unlike the sunlit, kitsch classicism of von Gloeden, there is in Witkin's pastiches a sense of intrusion into an underworld that perhaps one might not wish to see. The covered face, like those of so many of Witkin's subjects, allows our scotopic gaze to go unnoticed or unacknowledged. And the voyeurism is further withheld by the obviously *staged* "realities" within the photographic frame. A second ingredient reflects and refracts our titillated scopic desire. The opacity of large areas of the prints, selectively and simultaneously obscuring and revealing, and in places fostering absolute denial by the manual action of needle into negative, creates a certain erotics of vision. The viewer's eye surveys the bodily evidence in fascinated discomfort, never fully deflected back at itself, but never allowed full visual access.

In the more "extreme" of his work, as in *Hermaphrodite with Christ* (1985), Witkin plays havoc with physiological and thereby

sexual norms, celebrating his viewers' visual and psychological dis-
ruption. In the afterword of his latest book, *Gods of Earth and
Heaven*,[7] which reads more like a want ad, Witkin requests the
following: "I need physical wonders — a person, thing or act so
extraordinary as to inspire wonder. . . . All manner of visual perver-
sions. Beings from other planets. Anyone bearing the wounds of
Christ. Anyone claiming to be God. God." After all, as the story
goes, God made man in his own image, and as the title of his latest
monograph suggests, Witkin has created images of men as, or who
may in fact be, gods. His use of photography as an evidenciary
medium — Roland Barthes' "that-*has*-been" — underpins the factual
fictions that he inscribes as both gloriously real and really made up.
And such is the paradox in which this modern Venus operates, vacil-
lating between horror and absurdity.

Elements of *Canova's Venus* — the obvious revealing of the genita-
lia, the veiling of the face, the scratching of the negative combined
with the chemical staining — act out a sadism upon the original body
of the man photographed. Yet as other photographers are keen to
point out, Witkin still produces a perfect print from his "abused"
negatives — perfect in their lack of material violence acted out on the
physical body of the paper — unlike Arnulf Rainer or Doug and Mike
Starn. Joel-Peter Witkin's image of "Venus" ultimately seems to
revere this male body, sealing it temporally beneath the classically
smooth sheen of the print's surface, intact despite its oddities, aberrations, and disruptions of the traditions of art history, heterosexual
desire, and photographic practice.

Mark I. Chester pictures the people he knows: friends, lovers,
acquaintances. His images are photographs, and as such are documents of those who engage in sadomasochistic practice. They are
mostly images of gay men who engage in radical gay sex. These men
stand apart from both normative homosexuality and heterosexuality. These images and the men they record move deep within the
realm of transgression and excess. They are mysterious and painful,
beautiful and repugnant.

Many people find Chester's images troubling. For most of us,
their subject is elusive, incomprehensible. Sex positioned on the side
of pleasure is not supposed to hurt. But those who practice radical
sex know that sex can and does hurt. In radical gay sex, each man is
given over to the will of another. Desire is instilled at the site of

dominance and submission. But radical sex is not necessarily a gay practice. It is a ritual played out by many people in one form or another, consciously or not. However, in its all-male form, it is potent and disturbing. The straight man cannot help but respond viscerally to these images, when fantasies of domination turn toward him. He might find them seductive or he might be repulsed as the consequences of his relationship to these images are played out in his imagination.

In this they share a relationship with Grossman's *Male Figure Sculpture*. There is an assertion, active and passive, of male, phallic power in the taking and giving of pleasure. It is on this tenuous ridgeline at which trusts are enacted and tested, where ferocity is pitted against the threshold of endurance, that conflicting heterosexual concepts of masculinity are challenged. And it is images such as these that have lit the fires of censorship, fires which would erase any challenge to normative heterosexuality.

Most emphatically, these images are about men who love men and the sexual nature of that love. Chester's *Hanged Man* (Fig. 9) is a photograph.[8] Despite the stasis of the image and the pose, the subject is not dead. But he is an image, the record of an occurrence in a room, with a body, one leg shackled, hoisted into the air, hung from a ceiling out of view. This image records a way of life characterized by the shackle, the mask, and the gloves, framed in leather, facilitated by screws in the wall. Defined by the hard penis.

The character pictured submits to chain and leather, to Chester the photographer who binds him in chains. He submits to the camera that binds him to an image and sights him with its scopophilic lens. We are witness to the games that Chester plays with his friends, with his camera, and through his camera. Sexual dominance goes hand in hand with mastery over his image. His subject submits to us as we stand behind the camera and before the image with our own scopic eye and look.

This is a record of the nature of that arousal. The leather mask, boots, and riding pants, the apparatus, the chains, locks, and hoist all play a part. They are accoutrements, objects that typify this mode of sexual practice. They are fetishistic: the texture of leather and its scent, the sound of chains all enact desire. Leather binds and constrains. It presses against the flesh while it blinds and deafens. It denies tactile access to any other surface. There is nothing to see, nothing to smell but leather. There is nothing to feel but the pressure of a body at odds with its posture.

We see this body struggling for composure, for balance. We imagine the body, its systems gone awry, blood rushing to its head. The veins in its neck and arms bulge. The muscles are taut. We see this man fighting to breathe, breathing only through his mouth, a mouth that gasps for air as the box cuts into his back. This mouth gasps as we imagine the body turned upside down and the weight of its liver and entrails pressing hard, down onto the lungs. The man nears unconsciousness. He seems dead. He straddles his own coffin. He makes the sign of the cross. He marks the moment when sex and death come together in Freud's "little death." For him, they come together in pain. He is aroused. His penis stands hard, erect, encased in a leather sheath, enlarged by that sheath. Its effect is doubled by bulges in his pants, tripled by the penile extension of arms, legs, and head. We see the penile shapes, but the penis itself is only a contour, a bulge. We read it through the body exposed: the stiff arms and neck, the pulsating veins, the head, and open mouth. Our subject is ecstatic.

But we do not see that ecstasy. We only see its trace, in the body marked, contained, adjusted. Chester's camera metaphorically captures that moment. It defines that moment through composition, light, and manipulation by the artist's hand binding the body. He records the male body in pain and submission, the male body exposing desire. We are witness to that desire and its iconic nature as it strikes us for a moment. That desire is determined for us by the look of the photograph.

Frank Rich recently wrote: "The new blood culture is the bizarre pop byproduct of a national obsession with all bodily fluids. It's a high pitched, often hysterical acting out of the subliminal fantasies, both directly and erotic, of a country that has awakened to the fact that the most insidious post-cold-war enemy is a virus."[9]

While Andres Serrano's 1988 *Untitled VII* (*Ejaculate in Trajectory*) (Fig. 10) presents us with the absent but necessarily male body, it would be imprudent to consider Serrano's image outside the highly politicized zone of bodily fluids. What is curious about AIDS, the new disease that overshadows our lives, is the foregrounding and policing of the body as a sexual organ and the instigation of new sexual mores.

In his article, Rich goes on to write: "Its [AIDS'] undiminished threat has made the connection between sex and death, an eternal nexus of high culture, into a pop fixation, finally filtering down to the vocabulary of commercial images." Serrano stated in a personal interview, "I didn't set out to do a body of work about AIDS, but I realize that in the age of AIDS those pictures could work, even could refer to AIDS, and they should." While both Anne Rice and Madonna have contributed to the fetishization of the condom, and to the perilous but defendable defile running between pleasure and death, Serrano's untethered ejaculate seems liberated in its contagial self-pleasure. Despite the ambiguity of its scenarios, the real and the mythic narratives frozen in the stasis of the print, the masturbatory fantasy acted out remains symbolically dangerous.

In practical terms it has meant that the series has undergone various "un-namings." While it was originally shown untitled, the series was parenthetically identified after an unforgiving review. Images from this series have subsequently been subject to a certain curatorial censorship in the choice to omit "Ejaculate in Trajectory" in favor of the more "sophisticated," cool untitle. One wonders what would(n't) have happened if *Piss Christ* (1987) had undergone the same process?

Serrano's interest in bodily fluids goes technically in hand with his decision to use the Cibachrome process in which prints are produced from a color slide, generating much stronger tonal values. Body fluids, when back-lit, provide flat planes of consistent translucent color, allowing him to emphasize the flatness of the picture plane. A successful case could be made in a formal comparison between Serrano and, say, Mondrian, Rothko, or Newman. But for all Serrano's interest in technique, and his unwillingness to stake a single meaning to his photographs, he remains very cognizant of the upheaval that his images can provoke. For instance, he referred to his intensely close-up photographs of sanitary napkins as being a necessary balance for these "male" images, while he also referred to the semen shots' *apparent* lack of ethnicity.

But bearing in mind the autobiographical element of the fluids famously involved in the *Piss* series, combined with a deduction wrested from the artist's nameplate, it becomes obvious that this is not a white man's sperm flying across the frame of the photograph. The photograph captures the act of an "other," it frames a sexuality. The Clarence Thomas-Anita Hill incident reminded this country that it was still hung-up over the discussion of sex and sexuality, especially as it pertained to the sexual mythos of the (black) other. In addition, the artwork also engages in an unsettling discourse shared by Robert Mapplethorpe and his *Perfect Moment* exhibition as it was defined by Jesse Helms's homophobic trauma and his complaints about *Embrace* (1983), the miscegenational embrace of white and black (men) desiring each other.

For all the generous egalitarianism of Serrano's acknowledgement of the multiple and often antagonistic views surrounding his pieces, what appears so much more important is the means by which his media, "his" body fluids — urine, menstrual blood, milk, semen — have become politically substantive and manipulated to suit various ends. "In my later works," he stated in our interview, "like the 'fluid' pictures, there is very little trace of ethnicity on the surface of it. But I think I've been Europeanized as much as every one else in the society, and the work is a reflection of that too." For all the necessary "male-ness" of this series, Serrano's images consistently remind us how masculinity, too, is traversed by the qualifiers of sexuality, class, age, and especially race.

In 1969 Jonathan Borofsky began counting. He counts on paper, one number after the other, as a mental activity, as a means by which to focus his mind.   Numbers are his signature. The art that he makes is marked by these numbers, specifically the number he has reached when a piece is produced. Each number marks time: a time of creation, a time in Borofsky's life, a moment in time. Counting verifies Borofsky's existence on earth.

At 2668379 and 2670098 Jonathan Borofsky conceived separate images. Here, they come together as one, informed by two criteria, one substantive, the other ethereal, the act of drawing and his own state of mind. When he draws, he draws on paper, walls, and canvas. What he draws are self-portraits, but what he renders are not representations of his physical self. These drawings are pictorial manifestations of the chaos in his head.

This chaos is a compendium of forms and recurring events: dreams, symbolic objects, manifestations of Borofsky's identity. They exist for the public in installations, as drawings on a wall, objects in a room, paintings hung from a ceiling. Aspects of the compendium are repeated in single installations. Over the course of time they have been transcribed again and again; coupled with unique images such as geometric forms, the names of famous black men, Chinese women weaving, and flying blimps. The drawing/painting illustrated is detached from the compendium, an ensemble on paper without benefit of reference to the rest of the chaos in Borofsky's head. *Selfportrait at 2,668,379 and 2,670,098* (Fig. 11) is ostensibly a profile, a bust portrait of Borofsky sketchily rendered in acrylic paint and charcoal. It is also a male body, a man with the ears of an animal. The two are bound together. One speaks through the other. The full figure might stand for the activities of the mind, the thoughts that go on in this profile head.

This figure has horns and holds a staff. He is a devil engulfed in the flame-like gesticulations that form the head. Aggression and evil are played out by the demon, in the look of the body and the look in the eyes that penetrate our own. The horns are long and hard. These penile projections bind the theme of penetration to conventional markers of maleness. The devil-man is rendered as a dominating force. These horns are ears, they denote a man guided not by intellect but through sense and intuition, a man not bound by culture but conditioned through perception and interaction with the natural world. This animal-man is "being" in the world. His ears point upward, receiving sound in the physical world, receiving the energy of the spiritual world that lies above and beyond them. Spirituality is marked on his body. It bears the sign of the Jewish star, a personal symbol for Borofsky, a tie to religion. This star is marked on his forehead, the site of the third eye, the point where yogic power is taken into the body. This spiritual-man is a transcendent being.

Borofsky is a philosopher whose bodies are marked by symbolic contradiction. This particular body is a complex of meanings bound by the predilections of society, determined to escape them, and subsumed by an intrinsic animal nature. It operates within a series of dialectical frameworks that endeavor to question the most basic assumptions developed through introspection. Borofsky's self-portrait, all his self-portraits, stand for him, his perception of himself, and his existence defined through the social, animal, and spiritual. By rendering the complex that is himself, perceived by himself, he exposes fundamental aspects of the enigma through which we define our subjecthood.

We have examined the male body in its capacity as a purveyor of a meaning exterior to itself, as a metaphor for experience (Grossman), for private identities (Chester), or indeed for art's history (Witkin). But it is also necessary to examine the ways in which meaning can be attached to the male body, as it is clothed, and as it undresses itself. In Lorna Simpson's piece, *She* (Fig. 12), this issue is clearly rendered, highlighting the problematics of dress as an adequate metonym for sex.

She, like many of Simpson's images, is a multi-paneled work offering several almost identical views of someone's mid-section. Each frame contains a suited figure, seated, adopting various poses and gestures. Within these compact cropped images, images lacking faces, heads, even a potentially telling hairstyle, there is little possibility for gauging the stature and the build of the sitter, let alone the sex. Within the photographs themselves, we are only left with the suit and hand positions as indices of identity. Like *The Crying Game*, the movie that has awakened us, both forcibly and controversially to the transgressions of dress and sexuality, the text panel of "She," at the top of the piece, announces itself like "the big secret." Assuming that we would have identified the sitter within the images as male according to the ambiguous clues that we are given, we are now left to resolve the difference between text and image. Perhaps by some ingenious detective work and close inspection, the neckline or the slim wrists and fingers would announce their origins as female parts, perhaps not. Either way, and unlike *The Crying Game*, the conundrum with which we are left seems deliberately irresolvable.

Simply resolving the puzzle by reminding ourselves that women nowadays are more freely able to wear men's clothes seems ridiculously naive, especially bearing in mind Simpson's other works. In much of her art, the relationship between word and text surrenders a series of puns, slippage, and elisions. Within *She*, due to the paucity of the verbal aspect, there is no comic relief to be gained from the interactive elements. There is a parallel to be made between this piece and René Magritte's painting *The Treachery of Images* (1926): a pipe with its famous subtext, "*Ceci n'est pas une pipe.*" In *She* the declaration of denial is acted out in the dysfunctional relationship of photograph and word. But that relationship does highlight certain things about the photographs, the suit, the gestures, and the word itself. While Magritte's title speaks of treachery, and the suit appears to be a disguise within the confrontational relationship of sign systems, there is not necessarily an essential truth being upheld here. "She" as an approriate pronoun to describe the sitter is rendered as problematic and as abstract a signifier as that of the suit. Rather than proposing or enforcing a male/female dualism, Simpson's piece rigorously questions the solidity of dualisms such as this, and instead appears to celebrate difference in its most liberatory forms.

Andrew Uchin's work also examines, through various tactics, the politics of gender construction, and thereby male identity, in the formative homosocial milieu of the (middle-class) family. Where our previous artists have dealt with the male body as an icon of power, and masculinity as the tentative emanation of that power, Uchin's work explores the site at which this semblance of power is generated but necessarily problematized. It is the site at which male bodies communicate, interact, and possibly touch, but only within specific, elusive codes of behavior.

His earlier series, *Family Letters* (1986–90), is comparatively intimate in its exploration of the communication between father and son. Each image partially discloses the text of a rather banal letter, so banal as to allow multiple complex readings. "Andy! This is an example of what we talked about. Love, Dad." The underlaid images that accompany, and to an extent are programmed by, the letter's text present, among other themes, a boy dressed up as a cowboy with pistols at the ready, two naked men wrestling, and an interracial marriage photograph. While the images appear as solitary examples of "what we talked about," exactly which question they illustrate remains enigmatic. From the implied transmission of information from father to son, a power channel is nevertheless highlighted, and by extrapolation even the simplest possibilities for male intimacy remain riddled with diverse power relations that define familial modes of communication.

His latest group of works, the *Trophy Series* (Fig. 13), deals with the icons of masculinity erected in the American home. Each of these images is mounted, like a sports trophy or memorial plaque, on wood veneer, presumably to match the "den" environment in which they will ultimately be placed. While these plaques raise issues of gendered, private spaces and of privileged (male) audiences, they remain absolutely self-consciously insipid. Like Uchin's "family letter," they are generic to the point of blandness—we all know what they look like.

Where the *Family Letters* series questions the levels of communication and textual/verbal intimacy between son and father, between student and male mentor, the *Trophy Series* attends to more corpo-real signifiers of homosociality. In the *Untitled* piece illustrated here, the extension of the anonymous male hands into the frame and toward the neck and cheek of the smoker, frozen at an apparently incongruous moment, generates an erotic tension between the two men, heightened by the grainy murk within which they are set. Is that a nervous smile? Is that a caress or the removal of the visible cigarette to light another taken from the barely visible packet in the other anonymous hand? The circular frame encloses this ceremo-nial, just as the den segregates areas of activity within the home; this is a private moment, shared between two men. Within this homoso-cial enclave certain tactile taboos appear permitted, or are at least a hair's breadth away from consummation.

Uchin's photographic work revels in the capture of the apparently insignificant moment, the subconscious action, the missed encoun-ter. The ambiguous legibility of *Untitled* (its title also implies its symbolic dislocation) arises from its lack of context, from its lack of socialization. But the region that the *Trophy Series*, and the *Family Letters* series, occupies, or rather threatens to expose, is the appar-ently innocuous region of physical, male sociality. What Uchin is potentially exposing is the extent to which the boundaries of (hetero-sexual) homosociality are maintained by a series of ideological con-ventions that seek to segregate areas of normal and abnormal male behavior, and regulate the activity of the male body within those segregated zones. Such conventions operate within similar segre-gated social spaces (and to an extent these are mutually dependent conditions) — such as the bar, the factory, the gym, and the den — and while modified by factors including class, religion, and ethnic background, these conventions ensure the heterosexual legitimacy of intimate male contact.

In Carol Novak's work, the male body is the site of sexual desire in a turnabout from the business-as-usual world of image production. *Sex God* (Fig. 14) ostensibly refers to the myth of Elvis Presley, his sexual powers, and the personal entrapment these powers enacted upon him. Though *Sex God* is not a literal image of Presley, it defines the unique character of his situation as one who became, in Novak's words, the "reversal of our cultural model of female as spectacle/sex object." The sexual component of Presley's music and performance left him at the mercy of his many female fans. It left him at the mercy of the boyfriends and fathers who felt obliged to protect "their" women. He became a prisoner of his conflicted desires as he attempted to perform his sexuality while maintaining his personal freedom and safety.

In *Sex God* the male body is trapped, contained, isolated by the apparatus of the cage. It is reduced to only a torso, left to stand for man as the mark of his sexuality. The body is rendered in the fashion of a Greek Adonis, a bulk of muscles and flesh; configured in large pectorals, a flat stomach, lean hips, and wide shoulders. The body is faceless. It contains no distinguishing marks. There are no means by which to discern its identity. The body is headless. It cannot reason. Nor can it take pleasure in observing the gaze upon it, or feel the hands that claw at the cage, the hands that crave to touch the flesh inside. The body is without appendages. It cannot fight or run. The body is without a phallus, the symbol of power and dominance, and as such it is rendered impotent. It has been emasculated.

This body is subjected to the whims of those who might act upon it. Its performance becomes only display and that display is only a ruse. The body is confined to the perpetual state of its own performative act. Entrapment is the only way to save it from the annihilation of those bodies that pursue it. Entrapment is the only way to save this body from itself. Like Nancy Grossman's bound head, Novak's cage literalizes the sense of masculine power turned against itself.

Anne Rowland's 1992 series, *Dictu Sanctificare*, was a direct response to the influence of organized religion on everyday artistic life. As Rowland states: " . . . if Christianity is going to be invoked to directly affect visual art, as well as prevent exhibitions in this country, then it would be logical to do work concerning the way Christianity represents itself, and has been represented." In this work Rowland references then-Governor Clinton's invocation to prayer after the L.A. riots, Sandra Day O'Connor's proclamation of the U.S.A. as a "Christian nation," and ex-President Bush's continuous affiliatory references to the Divine Being. Within this context, patriotism, nationalism, and religious faith are shown to be intertwined and mutually interdependent.

The show *Dictu Sanctificare* incorporated various evidenciary photographs of biblical anatomies including *Angel's Wing, God's Penis*, and here *Some of Adam's Ribs* (Fig. 15). Her photographs of holy anatomy deconstruct some of the power-laden, mythic icons that religion, and specifically Christianity, propound. The show's title translated—"it is said to be sanctified" or "to sanctify by saying"—proposes a series of ironies, and at its most sinister implicates organized religion in a matrix of biased gender power relationships. The tautology of self-justification that Rowland sees in organized religion, of course, extends further into the public sphere as her comments above make explicit.

While textual references, the preached word, and the plethora of Christian paintings and sculpture testify to the authenticity of Adam's existence as the first man, Rowland's images question that body of evidence while they question their own status as photographic documents. Despite our awareness of the photograph's susceptibility to manipulation, the use of photography obviously implies certain truth statements, the least of which being that the anatomy represented must have been situated in front of the camera. But the indistinct vignettes that frame these specimens obviously impede our recognition of these bodily artifacts as copies of copies. However, the prizing of these bodily images from their "original" frameworks, either anatomical or art historical texts, calls into question the very genesis of (Christian) iconography. Nevertheless, her practice of isolating body parts, and presenting them in series as if pinned and mounted in a velveteen butterfly case, generates the solemn atmosphere of a votive reliquary.

There is a wonderfully kitsch aura to Rowland's work, its slightly saccharine taste certainly due to the act of displacement. But kitsch also maintains an implicit politic, a campness that interrogates certain male myths of genius and creativity. While Rowland's work claims an authenticity, it challenges itself, and spirally implicates its points of origin and the origins of those origins *ad infinitum*. As kitsch, her work cannot take itself seriously as merely a visual artifact, but rather looks in on itself as statement. Despite our temptation to dismiss some of her work as churlish, the effect of the series and her use of photography invites us to look further into these images, and our investment in their iconography. On this ambiguous textual level, at which images float more freely before they are anchored into an ideological discourse, Rowland's images are akin to Andres Serrano's infamous *Piss Christ*. Both forcefully challenge the claims of symbolic property made "in the name of" an image, reissuing those images (be they plastic crucifixes, or reproductions of "high" Christian art) in modified formats to torque an apparently naturalized, invisible ideological discourse that otherwise makes a claim to symbolic autonomy.

Rather than inventing the holy anatomy, Rowland illustrates — according to the multifaceted symbolic evidence — the Bible and an entire history of Christian art. However, the deconstructive tendency that underlies the medium and presentation of her work is extended explicitly toward the subject matter of her series as well. The male bodies within this series, those of the Holy Triumvirate, and that implied by the progenital spare rib, are all similarly tested, stressed, and put under tension. We as viewers are left to complete the cycle of gender(s) and gendering. Within the boundaries of the *Dictu Sanctificare* series, and by implication far beyond those boundaries, where the male body is resolutely present, the woman's body is either absent or muted by its inclusion within familiar patriarchal structures such as the *Holy Family*. The male body, within the Christian myth of origin, is presented by Rowland as a powerful fiction upon which socialized conventions are generated.

Ken Giles has consistently dealt with the issue of masculinities throughout his photographic work while simultaneously exploring the sensual qualities of that medium. In a recent series, of which *Portrait of a Young Man* (Fig. 16) is a constituent, Giles employed the relatively primitive cyanotype process. One aspect of this process is that each image is made from a contact print, i.e., the image is exposed to light with the negative lying directly on top of the paper, ensuring a direct correlation in size between negative and print. In order to achieve the "legal size" print, Giles enlarged the original negative through a photocopier until that correct size was achieved. On top of the cyan blue base image, he worked purple pastel into the hand-made rice paper. As a result, the images from this series are rather precious, both physically and visually.

In distinction to his larger pieces, these smaller works share a similar compositional feature. His male figures shy away from the gaze of the viewer, almost shriveling before our eyes in his unfamiliar landscapes. However, the coloration of these figures animates rather than petrifies their otherwise frozen frames. They seem caught actively hiding from, but never absolutely denying, the gaze of their viewers. Unlike Joel-Peter Witkin's specimens, who emanate a grotesque air, Giles's young men remain rather more liminal. Instead of offering themselves to the camera, they defend their anonymity. Despite the vague textual encoding of his title, and the possibility of making literary connections to it, "The Young Man's" only concrete signifier of his selfhood is his sex. The "Young Man" is only that. As a result of this lack of nominative identity, he appears rather fragile.

One consistent theme that has framed this discussion about the male body has been that of vision, and its somewhat cryogenic power. For Freud, and more metaphorically for Lacan, the construction of (sexual) difference, and thereby some normalized level of identity, was based on the principal action of vision. And it is the significant and signifying action of vision that, particularly within the discourse of psychoanalysis, abets the conjunction of penis and power: the penis's exteriority and, thereby, visibility as a concrete marker of (sexual) identity. Following a conceptual theme similar to that of Witkin and Uchin, and utilizing the same principal medium of photography, Giles's photographs freeze the vision that constructs sexual difference. However, it is during this point of stasis that the action of the eye itself becomes visible. Where Witkin's work offers itself as unsettling fact, Giles's photographs question the absolutism of the judgmental gaze. Exaggerated in the perpetual present of the print, the instantaneous, statuesque, and exterior view of this young man is presented as somewhat inadequate, incapable of intuiting the nuances of sexuality, of personality.

But it is at this conjunction of vision and image, or of *je* and *moi* to use Lacan's terms, that another important conjunction can be made between Giles's *Young Man* and Jim Cogswell's *Circular Mirror*. Throughout this essay slippages have appeared between normalized "masculinity" and its aberrations; however, the element of self-doubt that lurks beneath both these works also appears to underscore the scrutiny that "masculinity" puts itself under. It is surely doubt that Cogswell's central figure finds himself caught within, and a perception of inadequacy that riddles Giles's young man. And it is the constant diacritical fear of seeming "feminine" — soft, emotional, intuitive — that lurks at the heart of this doubt. While Giles's young man cowers tragically in his perceived inadequacy, it is also important to remember that for all the traits of power that masculinity lays claim to, it finds itself anxiously attempting to live up to its claims.

The term masculinity has no meaning in and of itself. It only has meanings brought to it through social construction and history. The male body is only one aspect of what masculinity might be. This body has component parts and in some way these parts differ from those that occupy the body that we would define as female. But to say precisely what is male or masculine or manly is a difficult thing. Such things can only be prescribed. However, traditional notions of masculinity no longer hold in our culture. Masculinity, and femininity for that matter, are now more than ever tenuous notions. The artists about whom we write perceive the precariousness of this situation. That is why, perhaps, they choose to confront masculinity and the male body for themselves. That is why we choose to include them in this essay.

NOTES

[1]These studies are a testament to the powerful historical trend of gay photography in the United States, a trend only recently recognized by the community at large in the cause célèbre of Robert Mapplethorpe. See Allen Ellenzweig, *The Homoerotic Photograph: from Durieu/Delacroix to Mapplethorpe* (New York: Columbia University Press, 1992); Melody Davis, *The Male Nude in Contemporary Photography* (Philadelphia: Temple University Press, 1991); Emmanuel Cooper, *Fully Exposed: The Male Nude* (London: Unwin Hyman, 1990). The one possible exception to this homoeroticized male body is *The Male Nude: A Modern View: an exhibition* (New York: Rizzoli, 1985).

[2]The power of the show's theme and its images garnered it a place among *Art in America's Top Ten* exhibitions for 1991. Two of the artists illustrated in this essay, Andrew Uchin and Anne Rowland, had their works shown in this exhibition.

[3]Interview with the artist, March 1993.

[4]The advent of this strategic label was heralded by *The Vigorous Imagination* exhibition at the Scottish National Gallery of Modern Art in 1984.

[5]Masao Kobayashi, *Magdelena Abakanowicz* (Sezon, Japan: Sezon Museum of Art, 1991), 4.

[6]Arlene Raven, *Nancy Grossman* (Brookville, New York: Hillwood Art Museum, 1991), 46.

[7]Joel-Peter Witkin, *Gods of Earth and Heaven* (Altadena: Twelvetrees Press, 1989).

[8]*Hanged Man*, from a series of fine arts photographs, "Sexual Portraits and Private Acts from the Warzone," 1986–1989.

[9]With reference to the movie *Bram Stoker's Dracula*. See Frank Rich, "Style" section, *New York Times* (December 6, 1992), 7.

[10]This piece, begun in 1969, consists of a series on notepad paper that has been numbered consecutively. The continuing project is used as a reference point for establishing the numbers that he will title other works with. As these other works are finished, he will adopt the number he had written into the earlier project as an identifying mark.

THE MALE BODY

AND CONTEMPORARY ART

A PORTFOLIO

Fig. 1. Jim Cogswell, *Circular Mirror*, 1990. Oil on museumboard, 22″ x 23.″ Photograph courtesy of the artist.

Fig. 2. Jim Cogswell, *Thirst*, 1988. Oil on canvas, 56″ x 44.″ Collection of
James Goode, Washington, D. C. Photograph courtesy of the artist.

Fig. 3. Peter Howson, *Masked Wrestler*, 1989. Pastel on paper, 25 3/4″ x 20 1/2.″ Photograph courtesy of the Joy Emery Gallery, San Francisco.

Fig. 4. Nancy Van Goethem, from the *American Men* series, 1990–1991. Sumi ink on painted ph balanced paper, each 40″ x 26.″ Photograph courtesy of the artist.

Fig. 5. Magdalena Abakanowicz, *Backs*, 1976–80. Burlap and resin, various sizes. Private collection, Korea. Photograph courtesy of the Marlborough Gallery, New York.

Fig. 6. Nancy Grossman, *Male Figure Sculpture*, 1971. Leather-covered wood and zippers, 68″ high. Photograph courtesy of the artist.

Fig. 7. Michelangelo Buonarroti, *The Dying Slave*, before 1513. Marble, 90″ high. Collection of The Louvre, Paris.

Fig. 8. Joel-Peter Witkin, *Canova's Venus*, 1982. Copyright Joel-Peter Witkin. Photograph courtesy of the Pace/MacGill Gallery, New York, and the Fraenkel Gallery, San Francisco.

Fig. 9. Mark I. Chester, *Hanged Man*, from a series of fine art photographs, "Sexual Portraits and Private Acts from the Warzone," 1986–1989. Copyright Mark I. Chester. Photograph courtesy of the artist.

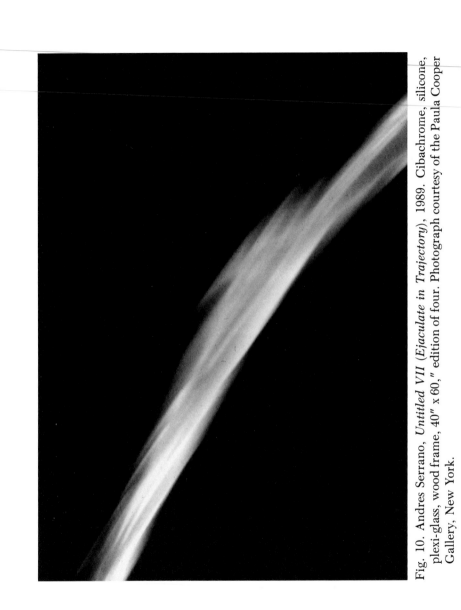

Fig. 10. Andres Serrano, *Untitled VII (Ejaculate in Trajectory)*, 1989. Cibachrome, silicone, plexi-glass, wood frame, 40" x 60," edition of four. Photograph courtesy of the Paula Cooper Gallery, New York.

Fig. 11. Jonathan Borofsky, *Selfportrait at 2,668,379 and 2,670,098*, 1979–1980. Acrylic and charcoal on paper, 83 3/4″ x 48.″ Collection of the Whitney Museum of American Art. Photograph courtesy of the Paula Cooper Gallery, New York.

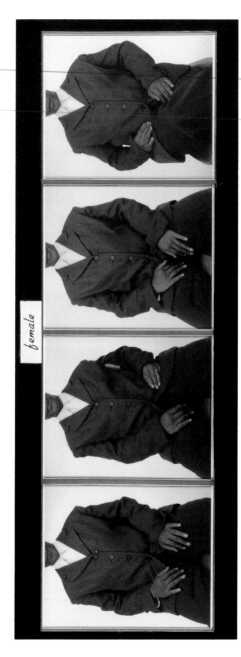

Fig. 12. Lorna Simpson, *She*, 1992. Color Polaroid, 29" x 85 1/4." Photograph courtesy of Museum of Fine Arts, Boston.

Fig. 13. Andrew Uchin, *Untitled*, from the *Trophy Series*, 1991. Cibachrome print with wood burl veneer frame, 23″ x 19″ x 2.″ Copyright
Andrew Uchin. Photograph courtesy of the artist.

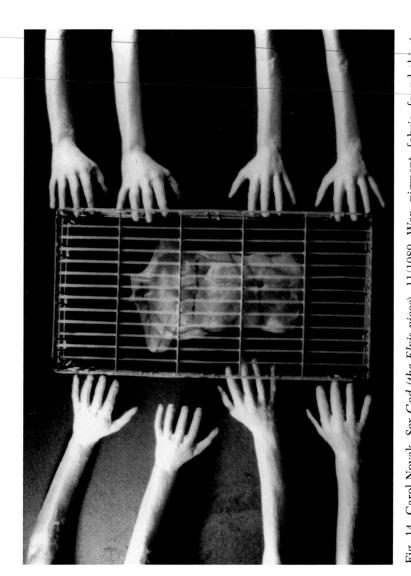

Fig. 14. Carol Novak, *Sex God (the Elvis piece)*, 11/1989. Wax, pigment, fabric, found object, 60″ x 102″ x 14.″ Photograph courtesy of the artist.

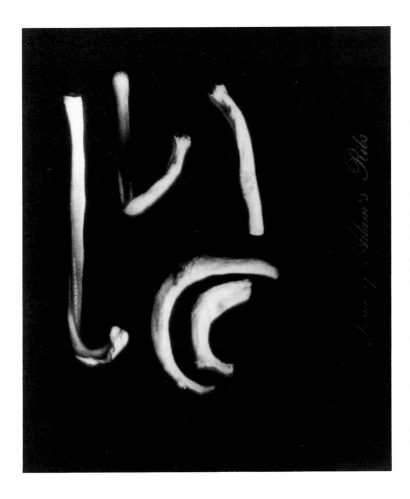

Fig. 15. Anne Rowland, *Some of Adam's Ribs*, from the body of work *Dictu Sanctificare*, 1990. Type C print, 14" x 11." Photograph courtesy of the artist.

Fig. 16. Ken Giles, *Portrait of a Young Man*, 1992. Altered cyanotype print. Photograph courtesy of the artist.

DAVID R. SLAVITT

TIRESIAS AND NARCISSUS

from Ovid's *Metamorphoses*, Book III

In heaven, peace had returned, or at least a truce, and Jove
relaxing one evening and drinking a bit more wine than he should
    have,
got into one of those odd discussions — this one with Juno,
a flight of fancy, really, that turned into earnest debate.
Resolved: That the pleasure women take from the sexual act
is greater than that of men. Not so, his wife insisted.
And how would one know? To whom could one look for such
    expertise?
There was, of course, Tiresias — impartial, or one who had taken
both parts, as it were. Once, with a blow of his walking staff,
he had interfered with a pair of copulating serpents
he'd found on the road — in an act of such impious rashness
that he had been changed at once from man into woman, and
    lived
for seven years in that form. In the eighth, she encountered again
that same pair of serpents, to whom she addressed herself
with awe: "Since you have this magical power, to change the
    gender
of one who strikes you, I do so again." With a ritualistic
tap she struck them again, and was changed at once to a male,
as he had been before. To him, who had been a her,
the gods put their dispute. When their judge answered: "Women
have more pleasure, by far," Juno was much displeased,
and blinded him on the spot. Jupiter could not undo
her cruel deed but gave in recompense the rare
gift of second-sight, by which one can know the future.

179

Quickly, the seer's fame spread through Boeotian towns
and beyond, as people came to consult him. One of the first
was Liriope, the nymph, who once had bathed in the river
where Cesiphus, its god, had seized her in his embrace,
held her in his current, and ravished her. In time,
the nymph brought forth a son, an amazingly pretty boy,
whom she named Narcissus. For this, her baby, she came to
     inquire
of the blind seer how he would live, and what fullness of years
he might expect. The prophet replied: "He will live long,
if he does not know himself." Absurd? Or a mystery? No one
could understand or explain what his answer meant. But the
     truth
came out in its own good time, in his life and peculiar death
in the sixteenth year of his age. No longer a boy, not yet
a man, he was truly gorgeous. He had a perfection that stopped
the hearts of tender maidens and handsome young men, but none
who yearned for him was favored, or even noticed. His pride
was icy; his heart, cold. His obliviousness was complete
until, one day, when he was out in the woods hunting deer,
calling out to scare them and drive them into his nets,
and Echo heard him. A nymph, she was singular in her habits,
could not initiate speech, but could not refrain from an answer
when somebody else addressed her. Up to that time, she lived
not as a disembodied voice, but her conversation
was limited to repeating the last words she had heard.
This was a punishment Juno had visited on her because
of what the sly nymph had done on several occasions when Juno
had come in search of her errant husband, and Echo waylaid
     her,
detained her in clever banter, and given the other nymphs
the time to get away clean. Jupiter, always alone,
would express his delight in this visit from Juno — who soon
     caught on
and said to the garrulous vixen, "Your tongue has tricked me
     enough.
Your powers of speech will diminish to the repetition of short
phrases." And from that moment, Echo could merely echo
the tail end of what she had heard. Now having seen Narcissus,

she was struck by his beauty, enamored, followed along behind
     him,
going from bush to bush, eager for yet a closer
look at this marvelous creature. The closer she came, the more
ardently she burned, as a torch with its quick-burning sulfur
will burst into flame from another torch that is held nearby.
She longs to come closer, to speak, to accost him with winning
     words,
but what can she say? Her curse prevents her from speaking first.
Her tongue is meat in her mouth, until the charm of his own
voice can break the spell. And now that he's separated
from his friends and companions, he calls into the underbrush,
"Is anyone here?" and she answers in joy and with passion,
     "Here."
He looks around but sees no one. "Come!" he calls, and she
     answers,
in the height of rapture, "Come!" Once more he looks and calls
     out,
"Why do you hide?" and she chides him, or teases, and answers,
     "You hide."
He thinks it's a game and invites, "Now let us meet," and she
     answers
with the word she has yearned to pronounce: "Meet," and then
     she appears,
approaches, and tries to embrace him, throwing her arms round
     his
neck, but he flees as he always has. "Keep away! I'd sooner
die than have you touch me." Stricken, what can she say
but the woeful phrase, "You touch me!" before she retreats to the
     woods
she has lived in all her life, to hide her shame in the shadows
of leafy dells and dark caves? She pines, dwindles away,
grows gaunt in her grief, and her body wastes away into
     nothing.
Only her bare bones are left and her voice, until, after a time,
those delicate bones become stone and there's nothing but pure
     plaint
that hangs ashamed in the air of the woods and mountainsides.
     All unaware, Narcissus went his blithe way, behaving
in just this manner to all, nymphs of the woods and water,

and of mountains too, not to mention the human females and
     males
who longed for his impossible beauty. One such rejected
gallant protested and prayed to the heavens to grant Narcissus
the pains of his unrequited ardor. Let him know how it feels
to yearn without hope. And one of the serious goddesses heard
     him,
Nemesis, the righteous, who granted this just supplication.
There was a pond, a small but perfect body of water
way off in a distant part of the wood, where no shepherds came
nor goatherds with their flocks. Its surface was burnished silver,
and grass and waving reeds framed it and kept the winds
from touching its pristine surface. To this unearthly spot
Narcissus came one day, hot from the chase and tired,
and with an enormous thirst which he knelt down to slake . . .
     but another
thirst is born, an impossible longing for what he sees
reflected in the water's surface. That face, that body,
he adores, loves, yearns for with all his heart. He is smitten
utterly, and he feels what the goddess has in her justice
visited on him to feel. He knows it is hopeless, knows
it is only his reflection, his own face looking down,
but there it is, looking up, handsome beyond belief,
with a negligent saucy look that invites as it also repels
and fascinates. He is lost, as motionless now as a marble
statue. But is there a statue as perfect in form and proportion,
as precise in its execution, as subtle in how it is colored,
the way that blush of the cheek gives way to the whiter flesh
     tone
of jaw and neck? He is sunk in the pond, in the rapture, adores
himself, is adored to be so adored. He lowers his head
and tries to kiss the face, reaches his hands to embrace
the elusive other, the self, the object to which he is subject
forever. It shimmers away, coy, elusive, mocking . . .
as he has mocked so many, so often. He cannot desist,
cannot resist. He is crazed, knows it, and tells himself:
"Get up, turn away, forget it. What you seek, you have. It's
     merely
an image, nothing. The face you see in the pond will be gone

the moment you leave . . . " But that thought is unendurable,
     awful,
as if he had contemplated a murder. He tries again,
reasoning with himself, that he can come back any time,
look in the pond, and find that face looking up from the water.
It will be waiting for him — but the thought of its faithful
     patience
melts his heart. He is ruined and cannot order his muscles
to lug his body away. He lies there, stretched out on the grass
and gazes down with eyes that are hungry for what they feed on,
thirsty for what they drink. They cannot get their fill,
hating even to yield to the need to blink. He looks up
at the trees that surround the pond and calls out to them to
     witness.
"Of all the lovers who come here, and there must have been
     many, has ever
a passion appeared before you as desperate as this, as forlorn?
I am deluded and know it, but what love is not delusion?
And ought not love to be judged by its distance from dreary
     reason,
the height of its flight, the depth of its madness? Beside myself,
I love what I see and yearn for this face so defiantly close,
so tantalizing. The plane of the pond's surface is hardly
as thick as a wall or a city gate, but it keeps me away
from the face I love, that upturned and yearning face that adores
     me
as much as I long for him. Our hearts are one, but our bodies
reach out across a chasm as wide and as deep as the world
can offer anywhere. Oh, my darling, my love, come!
I see you smile when I smile, and weep when I weep, and I see
your invitation, your humor, your grief, your innate
     understanding
of every idle thought that crosses my mind, your immediate
sympathy and affection. . . . And in my own heart I can feel
that same quick apperception of your slightest mercurial mood.
I am ashamed of my folly but also proud, defiant,
having found my love in despite of the laws of man and nature.
My life is worthless to me, for only in death may I hope
to be rid of this unendurable agony of desire.
I hate the idea that he should perish but know he is willing

as I am to undergo that wonderful *Liebestod*
by which we may be at last united forever. There's no
other or easier way. We'll die with the same last breath."
He turned again to the face, the adored, that beloved face
that beckoned and tantalized from beneath the water's surface.
They wept, his tears falling downward and the other's falling
     upward
to meet and ruffle that cruel plane, and the mirror image
rippled and blurred. Narcissus cried out in torment: "Come
     back!
Do not desert me. Stay! If I cannot touch, I can look,
as you can gaze up at me in exquisite consolation.
Oh, my adorable one!" And he crooned and groaned as lovers
have done, and do, and he beat his breast, and tugged at the
     hem
of his tunic in his distraction. . . . And looked, alas, even better,
that flush of emotion providing a special glow to his cheek,
just as an apple has at its moment of perfect ripeness
that ideal tinge of red, or a cluster of grapes in the morning
beaded with dew seems to pose for a painter's representation.
But he glances down to see how the face has subtly changed,
implausibly but exquisitely improved, and his heart is shattered
anew. He melts, collapses as wax in a candle melts,
or frost on a window pane as the rays of the sun assuage
the night's chill. He languishes, pines. . . . He is like a
log in the fireplace that burns and consumes itself. His flush
fades to a woeful pallor, and he wastes away to a gaunt
caricature of himself that Echo might have delighted
to see — except for the pity she felt and the love. "Alas!"
the stricken boy calls out, and Echo gives back his word,
"Alas!" with her own grief descanting on his. He beats
his grieving breast and the sound repeats in the empty air.
And then, as he weakens further, he calls out a last "Farewell,"
to which she replies with her own heartbreaking, heartbroken
     "Farewell."
His head drooped like a flower, and death at least sealed those
     eyes
that had undone him or been undone by their owner's beauty.
Down in the underworld, where all of us have to go,
he gazed once more at his image in the still pool of the Styx,

and felt the same sweet pangs, while on earth his naiad sisters
wailed and beat their breasts and tore their hair in mourning,
and the dryads joined in the keening and lamentation, and Echo,
faithful and loving, resounded each of their moans and cries.
They prepared his funeral pyre and came to the shore of the
      pond
to fetch the body . . . but it was gone, replaced by a flower,
with a handsome yellow center surrounded by petals of white.

LEO BRAUDY

IN MY FIFTIES

Several years ago, I was awarded a grant to live for a few weeks on the grounds owned by a lavish but scholarly foundation in the foothills of the Italian Alps. My application had a full bibliography, along with an intricately plotted proposal and impeccable references, all designed to support my desire to take advantage of the Foundation's hospitality and good wishes while I organized my thoughts about issues of politics and gender in Restoration England.

I arrived toward the end of a rainy spring. The Alps were covered with mist, and a fine drizzle fell almost every day as I trudged my way along the garden paths to the small out-building that was assigned to me as a study. The building was originally either a church for wanderers in the vast estate who needed a timely place to pray or perhaps a blockhouse and guard tower to defend the now vanished battlements. Inside, no indication of its former function existed. There was a typewriter, a stack of paper, some pencils, and a large quantity of a peculiar style of Italian scotch tape, which I never succeeded in loosening from its roll.

I was there to work, and work I did for the first few days, while I was still prey to the dutiful guilt of having requested time and money to do something that I was now being asked to deliver. My bladder, however, was less dutiful or at least less guilty. The little studio was only a short walk from the main house, but the drizzling rain made the prospect of walking back every time I had to relieve myself unpleasant, even while the constant trickle down the studio windows encouraged my urge.

Luckily, there was a large French window that opened on a cliff that sloped steeply down to the village many hundreds of yards below. Trees were everywhere and there was no one in sight, unless I became paranoid about binoculars in the villas on the other side of the lake. Accordingly, long about mid-morning, I would just open the window and let go.

One day, unexpectedly, while I was pissing out the window and hoping no one was watching, I remembered Adam, a friend of mine when I was a teenager, who was always doing that kind of thing. Adam was the first purposefully contrary person I ever got to know well. I've met many contrary persons since then. Some of them were eccentric and likeable, others just hostile to anything they hadn't thought of themselves. Occasionally, I've even tried to cultivate a contrary streak in myself. But Adam was the first, and so he retains the status of model.

I had heard his name long before I met him. In the crowd that hung out in front of Barson's Soda Shop at 60th and Cedar in the early to mid-50s he was "famous" — "a boy of well renown," as a very affected celebrity-attuned girl used to call him. It didn't take much to get noticed on that corner, although every newcomer was feverishly trying to find just the right angle. An otherwise nondescript guy had a special syncopated way of snapping his fingers and slapping his hands that he would diffidently demonstrate on request. That was enough to give him a minor niche.

But most of the truly famous teenagers had some particular story that made their names. Everyone had heard about the time Otzy Gross, whom I never saw let alone met, broke the leg of an usher who was trying to tell him to keep quiet at the Esquire movies one Friday night. The usher resembled the rest of the teenagers there. The only difference was that he needed to make rather than spend money on a Friday night, and that he had to wear a smelly maroon jacket with a fake velvet collar as part of the bargain. He was certainly in no mood to mess with the notorious Otzy. But too many adults who had no business being at the movies on the weekend had been on his case about the noise Otzy and his friends were making and the hapless usher had to do something about it or be fired. Whereupon, according to the story, Otzy picked the usher up and tossed him a few rows, almost hitting a group of girls from Cardinal Dougherty and breaking the poor guy's leg in the process. As you can tell, my sympathies are more with the anonymous usher than with the famous Otzy. But it was a good story, if you managed to concentrate on the opposition to authority and feat of grandiose strength side of it.

No such stories were told of Adam, no stories at all that I knew of, and I hung around him for a fair amount of time. He was quite strong and certainly contemptuous of most authority, but his allure was due more to his aura than to anything he actually did. He looked tough, but he was also considered to be a good dancer, which in the early '50s was an important accomplishment in my crowd. When Chuck Berry sang about "Philadelphia, Pee-Ay" in "Sweet Little Sixteen," we knew he meant us, even though he was talking about the tv show *Bandstand*, where few Jews (or blacks, except for stars like Chuck Berry) ever went.

Dancing was the great release. Nothing beat it. A few kids drank, but not much, or at least the drinking was subordinate to the dancing. We didn't have drugs and when drugs came in, they weren't so much about movement as about staying still, watching, peering into the heart of things and coming up with some revelation of the way things really were, or what synapses were exploding in some corner of your head.

But dancing, that was it. Dancing was really the crucial break with the past. Parents might get irritated at rock & roll, but the dancing drove them crazy. It's hard to get this from any of the magazine images of the '50s, or even the films. In the rare Hollywood films that tried to show rock & roll, like *The Girl Can't Help It*, the music was domesticated into some nightclub environment it never inhabited, and the dancing looked as if some classical corps de ballet decided to try on bobby socks and pegged pants for size. All was awkward and jerky. Neither the flow of true rock & roll dancing, nor the spastic energy was captured.

Somehow dance was supposed to be the socializing force that would tap all this potentially anarchic power and turn it to positive social uses. *Bandstand*, which began locally in Philadelphia, was devoted to dancing, but when it went national (and was called *American Bandstand*), the style became homogenized as well. The dancers wore coats and ties, or blouses and dresses — for all the world as if they were setting up for a tea dance, circa 1957, a little different from their parents, but not very much.

The style was basically Italian South Philadelphia, and even though it was different from the foxtrot, it still seemed tight, although no doubt the smallness of the dance floor helped give that impression. The slow dances were a lot better, although they were censored. No two-handed, closeup slow dance was allowed. If you were a little more radically inclined, you could watch the Mitch

Thomas show from Wilmington on Channel 12. But even that simultaneously looser and more stylized dancing done by the black kids, because it was on television, had a tamed-down look. Neither was like what went on at real dances.

In ordinary dancing, Adam was competent but nothing special. But we hardly ever did anything we would consider ordinary. The basic style of slow dancing was called the Fish, which meant a couple glued up against each other and moved sinuously around the floor in their best approximation of a two-person sidle. That's how you did the Fish if you were ambitious. If not, you just stood there and rubbed and hoped someone would turn the lights down.

The Fish came along about every tenth dance, as a break from all the fast dances. Occasionally there was also a group dance, like the Stroll, in which boys faced girls in parallel lines, clapping on the downbeat. The heads of both lines paired off in turn, and eased down the middle to separate at the other end. The boy did it with one shoulder dropped and a hand raising his pants pocket as high as possible, trying to look like some cool black guy. The girl was imitating some other model. It wasn't a black girl style, and I was never sure of its origins, although their tight skirts, thick white socks, and loafers marked the look as vaguely Italian, in the usual South Philadelphia paraphrase.

Adam could fish with the best, although his slow dancing in general was too theatrical — a lot of fast dips, spins, and turnouts — to convey much sensuality. His dancing reputation was built primarily on jitterbug and especially on the flashy but solid way he could do what we called the Jersey Bounce. He would begin by rapidly twirling his partner around. This worked best if they were wearing crinolines. Then he would almost forcibly swing them away from himself and across the floor. There was a three- or four-beat pause for snapping his fingers in a cool way and making sure the other dancers had cleared enough space between them. Then the girl ran directly toward him at top speed. At the last second before they crashed together, he grabbed her and lifted her first to his left side and then to his right, up in the air and down between his legs, and then up in the air again for the grand finale. Of course these maneuvers required an equally athletic partner and Adam had those as well. No matter where we went in the city, from one synagogue dance to another, there was always an energetic, attractive young woman in the crowd whose eyes would light up when Adam appeared. She would immediately seize his hand for the next dance, where they would do their spectacular number, usually to the rhythmic applause of a surrounding crowd, who had stopped their own dancing to appreciate the master.

Adam did take out some of these girls, but most of them were for dancing only. I had a few dance-only girlfriends myself. Some dull Freudian might call it sexual displacement, although at the time it seemed a lot better than getting dressed up and going on a date — a complicated process that had yet in my experience to have anything to do with what I was told was sex. Even in more casual circumstances, when money and premeditation didn't enter in so much, I still considered sex to be primarily a matter of the penis. But dancing, especially these hours of endless athletic jitterbugging, brought the whole body into play. After an hour or so of dancing, eyes would start to glitter, muscles would relax, and people would be so drenched in sweat the dance floor resembled the crucible of some primordial soup out of which a new race would be born.

The relative anonymity of the dance was also appealing. The one or two times I actually tried to date a dance-only girlfriend ended up badly. Once the music was over, it turned out that we didn't have much to say to each other. We were all nominally Jewish or at least hung out with Jews. But often we came from opposite geographic and even social ends of Philadelphia, let alone different varieties of Jewishness. It was a lot better when all we knew of each other were our first names, what we looked like, and the fact that we could both fling our bodies around in some unison with the music and each other.

Yet even Adam's jitterbugging skill couldn't account for the looming presence of his personality over the people who knew or only had heard of him. He was also known as "the great makeout man," perhaps because of his many dancing partners, since he didn't really officially date that many girls. "Makeout man" was a term that could refer either to the number of attractive girls you seemed to have on a string (the male version) or to whether you were actually a good date and even a good kisser (the female version). Few of us did much formal dating, and a good part of the reputation of a great makeout man for both sexes was to be able to appear alone at a party or on a hangout corner and manage to end the evening necking with someone you just happened to meet. Like dancing or most of our other forms of teenage charisma, this was done in front of a crowd.

Our parents had been hyped by the media into worrying about teenagers who wanted to go steady. But making out was worth a lot more in male reputation than any premeditated date. No matter how much they bragged later about what they "got," it was mainly the wimps who couldn't stand the heat who went steady.

Part of Adam's reputation might also have been due to his money. Most of the kids we knew were the children of schoolteachers, small businessmen, or an occasional doctor or dentist (in an age before that meant automatic wealth). But his parents owned a huge metal-fabricating plant somewhere along the Delaware and, in the middle of a relatively modest neighborhood, they lived in a big house with a very visible tennis court. Even though Adam was my best friend, I was therefore wary of double-dating with him, because it was sure to wind up being more expensive than I could afford. Usually, he doubled with his older brother Bobby, who was sixteen and old enough to have a car. It was a green and white '57 Oldsmobile that Bobby spoke of with awe, as if its speed had nothing to do with his own foot on the accelerator. "Over 50," he would intone in a traffic-safety voice intended for our youthful benefit, "you're not driving a car, you're aiming it."

On the night Adam and I met, he was wearing pink Bermuda shorts and black knee socks. I don't remember what I was wearing, probably light brown chinos with a belt in the back and a nondescript short-sleeved shirt from Penney's. His rough face, heavy nose and strong features, along with a set of muscular arms and legs, made an odd combination with what until that moment I had considered to be a foppish, even somewhat faggy outfit. Fops and fags were usually closely associated in that world of insult, and it was a daring person indeed who in any way consciously signaled even the slightest aspect of either. Jerks and bullies of all sorts were constantly asking some unwary target to do something—usually it was look at his fingernails—that would "prove" that he was really a fag. The tipoff was if you held your hand palm away from you instead of bending your fingers with your palm facing you—or maybe it was the other way around.

Adam's character, I soon discovered, was always to run against the grain. The whole point was to be provocative. Typically, someone new to the scene would see him in those Bermuda shorts or some other seemingly outlandish outfit and then make a big show of bending his hand backward at the wrist and lisping "Hello, dear"—in the usual 'you're a fag' manner. Whereupon Adam was licensed to kick the shit out of him. This was accomplished by a series of heavy pushes that threatened to knock the attacker off his feet but never quite did, until he backed down. Since it was part of the mythology that all of 'them,' in addition to wearing Bermuda shorts, were cowards, the would-be mocker was so startled by being shoved with such strength that he backed down almost immediately, especially when he realized he was getting no support from the watching crowd — all friends, acquaintances, and admirers of Adam, who were waiting to see if this particular version of a familiar confrontation developed any intriguing nuances.

Excavating this chunk of the unwritten history of masculinity reminds me that perhaps Adam's reputation as a makeout man had less to do with the number of his girlfriends or how far he got with them than with the storied size of his prick. It is amazing to recall how much the usual banter and conversation among boys had to do with "the human penis," as the sex books called it then. Discussion of sizes, jokes about length and width, never stopped. Fag-baiting may have been one of the normal ways to attack a potential enemy and solicit audience approval at the same time. But invitations to 'suck my dick' were also the invariable response to any actual or fancied slight. To which the invariable retort was 'whip it out.' Sometimes this was done, but only by the literal-minded, who didn't quite understand the delicate system of vulnerabilities of which it was a part.

Barry Corlin, a very fat kid whose father ran a pharmacy near my Hebrew school, did this one memorable day. Barry was a member of another group of friends of mine who often played afternoon knuckleball between the end of junior high school and the beginning of Hebrew school. None of them knew Adam except through me.

Another member of the group (I can't really call it a gang) was Rob Sieckel, who had the heaviest beard and aspired to look like "a tough *schkut*" — which tended to mean any non-Jewish white male with a leather jacket and motorcycle boots. Sieckel was also the most foul-mouthed person I have ever met. Out poured a constant stream of obscenities and invective that no adult I knew could manage, at least not in my hearing. In his honor we had named any transcendently gross insult a "sieckelian" or, sometimes, a "robscenity." Normal insults were "ranks" or "sounds." But the pure sieckelian had to be totally and maddeningly irrelevant to whatever the hapless victim was trying to say. Here are a few examples.

Anyone: "Let's go to the movies." Sieckel: "Why, to see your mother blowing your father in the balcony?"

Anyone: "Where are you going for Passover?" Sieckel: "Anywhere they have matzoh that doesn't look like your mother's cunt scabs."

At its best, there was a certain virtuoso improvisation about this sort of grossness, and Rob pushed himself to make sure he maintained his reputation. Corlin was a good target because he had an earnest air that went along with his weight and the fact that he was somewhat older, although not enough to have a beard heavier than Sieckel's. This particular day Sieckel had driven Corlin to distraction by an endless obscene nattering about his fatness, his inability to play knuckleball properly, the saggy way he ran around the bases, and the way his droopy breasts made him look like a girl. Rob was especially inspired by the patterns of sweat that were staining Barry's shirt and pants. Barry wore more dressy clothes than any of us, probably because he had to work in his father's pharmacy as a stock clerk, but for Sieckel it was another evidence of his fagginess.

"Why don't you just shut the fuck up?" said Barry after a particularly galling set of sieckelians. "Make me," said Rob, jutting out his jaw in his best tough *schkut* style. "I'd rather make your mother," said Barry. He smirked at having scored one finally. But Rob was only waiting. "Make my mother?" he said triumphantly. "You wouldn't know what to do with that pathetic little dick of yours. You're so fat you can't even see it when you piss. No wonder your crotch is always soaked. You don't even know when it's working and when it isn't. Pee-you." He held his nose and chortled. "That's why no one wants to sit next to you in school."

It wasn't a brilliant set of "sounds," but it was having the desired effect. Barry was getting red from anger and embarrassment.

Sieckel and Corlin lived across the street from each other, and perhaps this proximity turned up the heat even more. Barry was older than the rest of us and already went to high school. Later he would sometimes drive us to school in his father's car. Rob's father would rarely let him have the car in the daytime. But he often used it on dates, especially after he joined a chapter of AZA, a Jewish fraternity, situated in the newer neighborhood of Overbrook Park, a step up from the row houses and apartments where we lived. Rob was always trying to get me to join as well. But I thought it was too expensive, even though I admired the black and red silk jackets they all wore, with their names in script on the front. If I could have gotten away with just getting the jacket, I might have been tempted; otherwise, all they seemed to do in their meetings was sit around and talk about girls and read dirty comic books starring Blondie and Dagwood or W. C. Fields and Jean Harlow, stolen from someone's father's nighttable drawer. That didn't seem to be enough reward to go around identified so obviously as a Jew, and a particular kind of West Philadelphia frathead Jew at that, pretending that he really lived in the suburbs.

Nevertheless, when Rob took me along to parties organized by his girlfriend in Oxford Circle, a few social steps up even from Overbrook Park, he introduced me as a pledge, as an evidence of what he considered to be my potential high status, along with his own more senior role. He also liked to call me "kid" and a lot of time was spent at lunch with him and his friends at Central discussing my precocious ability to enter into their view of the world even though I was all of two years younger.

My role at these parties and double dates was to take care of the girlfriend of his girlfriend. These girlfriends of the girlfriend were invariably a lot uglier than the center of attention. It was like some Jekyll and Hyde symbiosis. At every dance and on every street corner two girls would be standing together, best friends, one looking like a perfect Hollywood teen-age girl, with all the right accessories from hair to shoes, while next to her would be her best friend, covered with pimples, dressed in some grotesque parody of what constituted good grooming and style.

Did beautiful and popular girls with personality have some deadly guilt that forced them to run out and find some poor soul to gather into their sphere and thus purge the shame of being so perfect? Or was it some simpler matter of contrast: the beautiful girl seemed even more beautiful with her ugly stepsister foil, while the ugly girl, the imperfect girl, was assured of a lot more dates in this double situation than she would get if she were on her own. After all, she had attracted the attention of the queen of the hop, and like some duenna was often the only route to the queen's attention. In the code of high school courting, the gambit of the ugly girlfriend also added a nuance of moral superiority. "Ditch your friend and let's go somewhere" was a line that met with disaster. "Only a truly deep and sensitive person," replied the lovely Rachel or Sandra, drawing herself up, "could appreciate the virtues of my friend Doreen or Hilda, and I don't go anywhere without her." Sorry, schmuck, you flunked the test.

The really cool guys, therefore, always had a double of their own in tow to take care of the problem. I played this role in relation to several of my older boyfriends. And it wasn't a chore. At fourteen, I was too young to drive, but tall for my age. I could be presented as an up-and-coming protegé who could bear witness to the magnanimity of Rob or some other grand sixteen-year-old. Like most junior partners, I also was reassuring to parents who were somewhat nervous about their daughters dating individually, but felt perfectly at ease when two comparatively well-dressed and well-mannered young men appeared at their door. I got around to a lot of interesting parts of the city this way and saw the insides of a lot of homes very unlike my own. I also had the chance to make out with many ugly girls, since one of the not-so-hidden truths of the pretty girl/ ugly girl game was that the pretty girl flirted while the ugly girl "put out."

Not that they were so ugly. Many of them were quite attractive in their own ways, if you discounted the pimples, the gap teeth, the few extra pounds of weight, the lack of cashmere sweaters or whatever it was that assigned them to the lower realms of teenage female attractiveness. Another nuance of the situation was that the pretty girls had very strict parents who didn't have the grace to go out for the evening and leave their house empty, while the parents of the ugly girls were virtually non-existent. Maybe that's what gave their daughters the idea that they were ugly: no one was interested in protecting them.

As a result, ugly-girl houses were always the scenes of what passed for sex in my crowd. Couples would retire to different rooms, usually not bedrooms, since even ugly-girl parents could notice a rumpled bed. Then the wrestling would begin. Ah, the tremendous effort and contortion it took to grasp even the merest corner of a breast or crotch. I know I said that ugly girls put out. But of course you couldn't say that you knew they did or had and therefore should for you. That would be the end of the evening. Coy resistance was part of the game, on both sides. There was little or no chance of actual intercourse in these situations, just an interminable succession of power struggles worked out in miniature. In fact, even if the girl wasn't putting up a struggle, you had to pretend she was as a sop to her self-esteem. Thus, I began to school myself in something like the male version of faking an orgasm.

My global claim that there was little or no chance of actual intercourse in these situations really means there was no chance for me. If anything like that threatened to happen, terror and inexperience would have put me in a terminal panic. I was neither a great heel who could love them and leave them, nor did I have enough money to actually take the girl out. It was only when I was much older, after I had met many attractive women who confessed they had been considered the ugly girl in those couples, that I began to realize I had seriously misspent my early teenage years.

I can't vouch for my friends who were off in other rooms. But if they did get more than a little bare this or that, they were remarkably restrained about it. Most of the time, they just complained about how their pretty-girl date had forced them to "talk," the worst possible date activity, or how prolonged making out had given them blue balls.

I wonder if teenaged boys still get blue balls. Maybe only if they're Mormons or born-again Christians, although they probably wouldn't admit it. Blue balls were the result of having a constant erection for about five or six hours with no release in sight. They were amazingly painful, something between being kicked in the groin and having your testicles squeezed slowly in a vise. Or at least that's what we compared them to. Since you were supposed to be having fun and daring the realms of the forbidden, blue balls also carried a nice aura of punishment. No one blamed them on the girl. Underneath it all, we were basically polite little Jewish boys. Blue balls were a weird badge of honor: only those who had really been making out heavily could complain about it.

A few years later, when I was going out with a girl who was willing and even somewhat interested in jerking me off under the covers in her parent's tv room, I *still* got blue balls in an almost anachronistic fashion, as if I didn't quite believe I had graduated into the rarefied realms of release. I also got some astonishingly painful abrasions. Her makeout technique was no better than mine, and when it came to mutual masturbation, it was a lot worse. Like me, she tried to supply in energy what she lacked in finesse. Once, when our passion collided with the scabs from a set of still-healing sores, we searched the house in vain for hand lotion and wound up using bacon fat from the juice can that still sat on the back of her parents' stove in solemn tribute to their World War Two civilian preparedness. It did soothe things a bit, but when her parents came back from the movies, they sniffed around the room and finally accused us of sneaking food upstairs, which, unlike jerking off with bacon fat, we had been expressly told not to do.

*   *   *

I didn't mean to stray from Barry Corlin's mistake in thinking he could outdo Rob Sieckel in insults. Rob had sounded on Barry. Barry, instead of getting red and flustered as usual, had then uncharacteristically tried a sieckelian of his own by bringing Rob's mother into it. Rob then went on to detail the small size of Barry's dick, his body odor, his fatness, and was homing in on several more areas of insult. Barry was bigger than Rob and weighed a lot more and if he had been at all coordinated could easily have knocked Rob down. But we rarely got physical. Unlike the gentile kids or the black kids who would slap you around as well as yell at you, we did it all in words. But the surprising thing this day was that foolhardy Barry kept right on going.

"You think you're so tough, so cool, sounding on me all the time," said Barry. "I'm sick and fucking tired of you, Sieckel. Fuck you. Why don't you just suck my dick."

"Whip it out," said Rob, the formulaic response. Whenever anyone said "suck my dick," "whip it out" followed close behind. No more earth-shattering than "How are you?" "Fine. How are you?"

Only this time something happened. Barry whipped it out. I was halfway down the block playing the outfield, and they were standing around home plate, and so I couldn't see very well what was going on. There was a flurry of movement, Barry started yelling and Rob laughed his raucous laugh.

"What happened?" I asked Paul Goldstein, as I ran up to where everyone was standing. Paul was a twin and, like his brother Martin, wore a plaid shirt and corduroy pants. The street where we played was right next to his house. Paul grinned from ear to ear, which in his case wasn't really a cliché but true. He had a wide, pumpkiny face that was always filled with fun, while Martin was a thin dour type who hardly ever smiled and delivered the truth as he saw it in a harsh peremptory voice, to which there could be no response.

"It's finally happened," chortled Paul. "Corlin said 'suck my dick' and Sieckel said 'whip it out,' and Corlin *did*."

"He did?" I was amazed.

Paul could hardly contain his laughter. "He unzipped his fly and dug around, and Sieckel was bending down real close, just like he really meant to do it. Then, when he pulled it out, Sieckel hit it with his car keys."

At the corner, near the cement steps that led up to Paul and Martin's house, Sieckel was yelling more obscenities at the top of his lungs, while Corlin, holding his crotch, stumbled down the pavement toward his house above the pharmacy on the other side of Walnut.

"I wouldn't suck that pathetic excuse for a dick," roared Sieckel. "Take it home to mommy, she'll put some calamine lotion on it. It looks like a mosquito bite anyhow."

Rob's face was puffy with triumph. "What a dipshit that Corlin is," he said, turning to the rest of us. "Well, at least he's got a proper circumcision now."

We were about to get back to the knuckleball game, but Martin Goldstein said it all reminded him of a book on medieval torture he had been reading. "Barry wouldn't have been able to walk at all if those guys got their hands on him," he said with a bitter smile. Even when he was pleased, which often happened when he talked about new historical tortures he had discovered, Martin's face remained closed on itself, smooth and impassive.

"They would put you on this chair with a hole in the center and your balls would hang down and then they'd just cut them off, real slowly, just nicking them at first, unless you told them what they wanted to know, and then they still might cut them off, just for fun."

"Who's they?" asked Rob. Aside from his obscenity, Rob was always preoccupied with the facts, as befitted someone in a higher grade. "Who did it? The Inquisition?"

"No," said Martin. "It was the Huguenots or maybe the Catholics did it to the Huguenots."

"That's nothing," said Peter Rentler, who had just moved into the neighborhood a few months before. "I read in *Reader's Digest* about the Communists in Russia *right now*. There was this guy who they thought was an American spy and so they got this woman to really sex him up and then, when he was hard and all, quick as a wink they slipped a glass rod up his dick."

He looked around to see if we got what was happening with the appropriate gravity and horror. We were transfixed. The knuckleball game was forgotten. It was the first time Peter had said very much and it was a great debut.

"And then they *broke* the glass, right in his dick."

"Come on," said Rob the fact-hunter, "how does anybody know that?"

"Because," said Peter, lowering his voice, "the guy who wrote the article had to hold him *while he took a piss.*"

He finished triumphantly. Nobody said much. I was feeling a little queasy trying to imagine a broken glass rod in my urethra and the faces of the rest of the strayed knuckleballers were turning various shades of green.

Martin Goldstein took the opportunity of this sickly pause to switch the conversation to more ancient and heroic brands of torture.

"That's pretty good," he allowed. "But during the Middle Ages they did some really neat things. I read that in Poland the counts would take a spy and they'd tie him to a table in a room in the dungeon. Then over his stomach they'd put a metal bowl upside-down with three rats in it."

"Ugh," said Rob.

I played the straight man. "What's so bad about that?"

"Because when it got colder, the rats would instinctively seek warmth, and so they just eat their way out through the guy's stomach!"

That was so bizarre that everyone looked pleased and disgusted rather than just sick. It was time to get back to the game, but Rob still had a few sounds left over from the fight with Barry that he didn't want to waste.

"You know what Barry is, don't you?" Rob was talking to David, one of the younger kids who would watch us, hoping to be invited to play. They were all wary of Rob, but now that Barry had gone home in disgrace, there was a chance to be let in and David was taking it.

"No, what?" said David. David had a cluster of freckles down the middle of his forehead that gave him an intense, somewhat cross-eyed look. He wore his safety patrol belt everywhere, with its shiny silver badge pinned precisely in place. Everyone else's was frayed around the edges, but David's was spotless. His mother bleached it, he told me.

"Barry's a blivvy," said Rob.

"What's a blivvy?" asked David, as we all waited for the punchline that we knew so well.

"Five pounds of shit in a one-pound bag," hooted Rob. "Don't you know anything?"

He turned back to the game, and David wasn't invited in.

*   *   *

The "whip it out" incident was submerged if not forgotten by the next week. Rob continued to insult Barry, and Barry would struggle to land a few back, even scoring slightly every once in a while. But the true contest was over.

Barry became a pharmacist later. I saw him several times behind the counter in his father's store, mixing chemicals and powders, measuring and weighing. I don't know what Rob finally became, probably a lawyer. But it was all foretold that day. Barry had tried to take charge by insisting that Rob's casual obscene banter refer to reality. That would somehow prove that Rob was really unmanly, that it was all words, all bullshit. But reality, or Barry's unfortunately literal version of it, was what got him into trouble, made him vulnerable to someone who just improvised.

Still I felt sorry for him, as he limped along that pebbly narrow sidewalk, even as I thought what a good story it would make. I felt sorry for him because he had just gotten caught in a way that I knew I would never get caught because I was too careful. Caught with his pants down, as my father would say. He was a schlemiel who thought he was in control without realizing that schlemiels always forget that there's someone around just waiting to pull the rug out. That's why they're schlemiels. They're not really dumb. They just don't think ahead.

I remember this day that everyone else who was there has probably long forgotten because it crystallized something for me that I didn't really understand until much later. In his plodding, weighing and measuring way, Barry's misadventure had just made the truth a little more literal. The Cold War was after our dicks, pure and simple. During World War II, it was food. If I didn't eat, my mother told me I was Hitler's helper or insulting the starving kids in

China who only had praying mantises to eat. I saved fat in milk cartons that would be used to pack the anti-aircraft guns and cut out the tops and bottoms of juice cans so that they could be flattened and turned into tank turrets. But if World War II was about food, the Cold War was about sex. Just weaken for a moment, try to be logical and make language mean something, and right away somebody would wham you in the crotch — right here in America. And if you thought the Commies were any better, just lower your guard for an instant and they would slip a little glass rod up your urethra when you weren't looking and that would be the end of that.

If that sounds too grandiose and self-important, it was the way I thought then, and the years have only confirmed the feeling of living in the '50s it embodied for me. Why apologize for a habit of mind I shared with everyone else I could talk to? Don't ask for any more details. I can't be precise. It was some vague uneasiness engendered by going to all those science fiction movies, where you knew it wasn't really Mars vs. the Earth, but us vs. them. Or the ones where the person who looked just like your father really had a third eye just under his hairline.

Gloria Grahame, my favorite actress, served as the erotic focus of this general disbelief that what was on the surface was all there was to see. I never understood what the appeal of Marilyn Monroe was and I was long past being a teenager before I could get with James Dean. Too many phony girls I knew gushed over him, while she had that insufferable goo-goo voice that smart girls imitated to show they weren't really a threat. Big deal about the tits too. I was as preoccupied by tits as any other boy my age was or thought he was supposed to be. But in the movies at least they were just that, tits, and never conferred any special allure on the person who wore them. In real life, the point was to catch a glimpse, or cop a feel. Actually the ugly girls had them more often than the pretty girls. Another divine compensation? Or maybe the ugly girls just showed them off more. Who could tell unless you got close, which meant you had to take them out or be a makeout man — for which I had neither the loot nor the line.

There's a great insight in that episode from *Everything You Wanted to Know About Sex* when Woody Allen appears in a small-town police station to tell the incredulous cop at the desk that there's a giant tit ravaging the countryside. We can argue about the vengefulness part, but the detachability, the feeling that tits in the '50s had a life of their own, was right on target. Like the human penis, the human tits and the human crotch just floated there in the sexual soup, prey for anyone who fished. "He's like an octopus," giggled some of the less verbal girls, "all hands."

It was another double message, like "look, but don't touch." No wonder Gloria Grahame appealed to me, with her cool sarcasm and her lipstick where she had no lips. Promising other lips and other meanings beyond what I could see and couldn't imagine. But I tried.

You don't have to tell me that my friendships with Adam and Rob were similar. I know I played a similar role in both. Rob was older and Adam younger, but they set the terms of my sexual induction. While I stood ready to tell jokes and dredge up weird facts to amuse the ugly girlfriend, they spirited the object of their desires off to another room. At more public occasions, I helped provide conversation by my dancing style, which I was beginning to model on my nervous system's interpretation of Little Richard's "Long Tall Sally." Like the ugly girlfriend, I was a test too. Did the pretty girl know enough to like me or to pretend to?

I did finally gather up the nerve to ask Adam how big his prick actually was. We were in his parents' house, passing through one of its many dark rooms stuffed with elaborate furniture covered in plastic shrouds. It was early evening and I was accompanying Adam back to his room where he was going to get ready for a double date with his brother. Adam's usual motivation for these dates was that his brother let him drive while Bobby made out in the backseat.

"I don't know where Bobby finds these girls," he said distractedly, taking off his usual T-shirt and unwrapping a starched pink dress shirt fresh from the cleaners. "All they ever talk about is sex and who's going out with who."

It seemed like the right time to finally satisfy my curiosity.

"Pray tell me, my dear Mr. Vernon," I said, imitating a radio announcer with a Philadelphia accent trying to be refined. "Exactly how large is your famous organ?"

Adam looked at me uncertainly.

"Let's see the fucking thing," I said harshly, in the tones of Humphrey Bogart.

Adam reached up to a dusty library shelf and pulled down a book. I don't remember what the title was. He pulled his penis out of his shorts and stretched it along the spine of the book like a farmer stretching a turkey's neck or the Mad Hatter straightening out a flamingo in preparation for croquet.

"There you go," he said jauntily. Then embarrassment got the better of him. He tossed the book back on the shelf, stuffed his prick back inside his pants and continued dressing.

The moment was over. Adam began to complain again about the low quality of girls Bobby managed to round up.

"Big deal," I said, embarrassed myself and glad to change the subject. "At least it's a date. Let's do something this weekend."

"Sure," said Adam. And, as usual, we did.

Whatever I was — bridge, buffer, confidant, audience, distraction — I always went along for the ride. So they drove, and I sat alongside, searching the night for adventure, looking for the key that would unlock its mysteries. Even years later, standing at a window overlooking the gray roofs of northern Italy, adding my small stream to the drizzle and the drench, I found myself still comparing my body and its language to theirs, still wondering how it ever became my own.

PHILLIP LOPATE

PORTRAIT OF MY BODY

I am a man who tilts. When sitting, my head slants to the right; when walking, the upper part of my body reaches forward to catch a sneak preview of the street. One way or another, I seem to be off-center — or "uncentered," to use the jargon of holism. My lousy posture, a tendency to slump or put myself into lazy contorted misalignments, undoubtedly contributes to lower back pain. For awhile I correct my bad habits, do morning exercises, sit straight, breathe deeply, but always an inner demon that insists on approaching the world askew resists perpendicularity.

I think if I had broader shoulders I would be more squarely anchored. But my shoulders are narrow, barely wider than my hips. This has always made shopping for suits an embarrassing business. (Francoise Gilot's *Life with Picasso* tells how Picasso was so touchy about his disproportionate body — in his case all shoulders, no legs — that he insisted the tailor fit him at home.) When I was growing up in Brooklyn, my hero was Sandy Koufax, the Dodger's Jewish pitcher. In the doldrums of Hebrew choir practice at Feigenbaum's Mansion & Catering Hall, I would fantasize striking out the side, even whiffing twenty-seven batters in a row. Lack of shoulder development put an end to this identification; I became a writer instead of a Koufax.

It occurs to me that the restless angling of my head is an attempt to distract viewers' attention from its paltry base. I want people to look at my head, partly because I live in my head most of the time. My sister, a trained masseuse, often warns me of the penalties, like neck tension, which may arise from failing to integrate body and mind. Once, about ten years ago, she and I were at the beach, and she was scrutinizing my body with a sister's critical eye. "You're getting flabby," she said. "You should exercise every day. I do — look at me, not an ounce of fat." She pulled at her midriff, celebrating (as is her wont) her physical attributes with the third-person enthusiasm of a carnival barker.

"But," she threw me a bone, "you do have a powerful head. There's an intensity. . . ." A graduate student of mine (who was slightly loony) told someone that she regularly saw an aura around my head in class. One reason I like to teach is that it focuses fifteen or so dependent gazes on me with such paranoiac intensity as cannot help but generate an aura in my behalf.

I also have a commanding stare, large sad brown eyes which can be read as either gentle or severe. Once I watched several hours of myself on videotape. I discovered to my horror that my face moved at different rates: sometimes my mouth would be laughing, eyebrows circumflexed in mirth, while my eyes coolly gauged the interviewer to see what effect I was making. I am something of an actor. And, like many performers, the mood I sense in myself is that of energy-conserving watchfulness; but this expression is often mistaken (perhaps because of the way brown eyes are read in our culture) for sympathy. I see myself as determined to the point of stubbornness, selfish, even a bit cruel — in any case, I am all too aware of the limits of my compassion, so that it puzzles me when people report a first impression of me as gentle, kind, solicitous. In my youth I felt obliged to come across as dynamic, intimidating, the life of the party; now, surer of myself, I hold back some energy, thereby winning time to gather information and make better judgments. This results sometimes in a misimpression of my being mildly depressed. Of course, the simple truth is that I have less energy than I once did, and that accumulated experiences have made me, almost against my will, kinder and sadder.

Sometimes I can feel my mouth arching downward in an ironic smile, which at its best, reassures others that we need not take everything so seriously because we are all in the same comedy together, and, at its worst, expresses a superior skepticism. This smile, which can be charming when not supercilious, has elements of the bashful that mesh with the worldly — the shyness, let us say, of a cultivated man who is often embarrassed for others by their willful shallowness or self-deception. Many times, however, my ironic smile is nothing more than a neutral stall among people who do not seem to appreciate my "contribution." I hate that pain-in the-ass half-smile of mine; I want to jump in, participate, be loud, thoughtless, vulgar.

Often I give off a sort of psychic stench to myself, I do not like myself at all, but out of stubborn pride I act like a man who does. I appear for all the world poised, contented, sanguine when inside I may be feeling self-revulsion bordering on the suicidal. What a wonder to be so misread! Of course, if in the beginning I had thought I was coming across accurately, I never would have bothered to become a writer. And the truth is I am not misread, because another part of me is never less than fully contented with myself.

I am vain about these parts of my body: my eyes, my fingers, my legs. It is true that my legs are long and not unshapely, but my vanity about them has less to do with their comeliness than their contribution to my height. Montaigne, a man who was himself on the short side, wrote that "the beauty of stature is the only beauty of men." But even if Montaigne had never said it, I would continue to attribute a good deal of my self-worth and benevolent liberalism to being tall. When I go out into the street, I feel well-disposed toward the (mostly shorter) swarms of humanity; crowds not only do not dismay, but enliven me; and I am tempted to think that my passion for urbanism is linked to my height. By no means am I suggesting that only tall people love cities; merely that, in my case, part of the pleasure I derive from walking in crowded cities issues from confidence that I can see above the heads of others, and cut a fairly impressive, elevated figure as I saunter along the sidewalk.

Some of my best friends have been — short. Brilliant men, brimming with poetic and worldly ideas, they deserved all of my and the world's respect. Yet at times I have had to master an impulse to rumple their heads; and I suspect they have developed manners of a more formal, *noli me tangere* nature, larger in response to this petting impulse of taller others.

The accident of my tallness has inclined me to both a seemingly egalitarian informality and a desire to lead. Had I not been a writer I would surely have become a politician; I was even headed in that direction in my teens. Ever since I shot up to a little over six feet, I have had at my command what feels like a natural, Gregory Peck authority when addressing an audience. Far from expressing stage fright, I have actually sought out situations in which I could make speeches, give readings, sit on panel discussions, and generally tower over everyone else on stage. To be tall is to look down on the world, and meet its eyes on your terms. But this topic, the noblesse oblige of tall men, is a dangerously provoking one and so let us say no more about it.

The mental image of one's body changes slower than one's body. Mine was for a long while arrested in my early twenties, when I was tall and thin (165 pounds), and gobbled down whatever I felt like. I ate food that was cheap and filling, cheeseburgers, pizza, without any thought to putting on weight. But a young person's metabolism is more dietically forgiving. To compound the problem, the older you get, the more your palate grows cultivated — and the more life's setbacks make you inclined to fill the hollowness of disappointment with the pleasures of the table.

Between the age of thirty and forty I put on ten pounds, mostly around the midsection. Since then my gut has suffered another expansion, and I tip the scales at over 180. That I took awhile to notice the change may be shown by my continuing to purchase clothes at my primordial adult size (33 waist, 15$\frac{1}{2}$ collar), until a girlfriend starting pointing out that all my clothes were too tight. I rationalized this circumstance as the result of changing fashions (thinking myself still subconsciously loyal to the Sixties' penchant for skintight fits) and laundry shrinkage, rather than anything to do with my own body. She began buying me larger replacements at birthdays or holidays, and I found I enjoyed this "baggier" style that allowed me to button my trousers comfortably, or to wear a tie and, for the first time in years, close my top shirt button. But it took even longer before I was able to enter a clothing store myself and give the salesman realistically enlarged size numbers.

Clothes can disguise the defects of one's body, up to a point. I get dressed with great optimism, adding one color to another, mixing my favorite Japanese and Italian designers, matching the patterns and textures, selecting ties, then proceed to the bathroom mirror to judge the result. There is an ideal in my mind of the effect I am essaying by wearing a particular choice of garments, based, no doubt, on male models in fashion ads — and I fall so far short of this insouciant gigolo handsomeness that I cannot help but be a little disappointed when I turn up so depressingly myself, narrow-shouldered, talmudic, that firm, set mouth, that long narrow face, those appraising eyes, the Semitic hooked nose, all of which express both the strain of intellectual over-achieving and the *tabula rasa* of immaturity . . . for it is still, underneath, a boy in the mirror. A boy with rapidly receding hairline.

How is it that I've remained a boy all this time, into my late forties? I remember, at seventeen, drawing a self-portrait of myself as I looked in the mirror. I was so appalled at the weak chin and pleading eyes that I ended up focusing on the neckline of the cotton t-shirt. Ever since then I have tried to toughen myself up, but I still encounter in the glass that haunted uncertainty—shielded by a bluffing shell of cynicism, perhaps, but untouched by wisdom. So I approach the mirror warily, without lighting up as much as I would for the least of my acquaintances; I go one-on-one with that frowning schmuck.

And yet, it would be insulting to those who labor under the burden of true ugliness to palm myself off as an unattractive man. I'm at times almost handsome, if you squinted your eyes and rounded me off to the nearest beau ideal. I lack even a shred of cowboy virility, true, but I believe I fall into a category of adorable nerd or absent-minded professor that awakens the amorous curiosity of some women. "Cute" is a word often applied to me by those I've been fortunate enough to attract. Then again, I only attract women of a certain lopsided prettiness: the head-turning, professional beauties never fall for me. They seem to look right through me, in fact. Their utter lack of interest in my appeal has always fascinated me. Can it be so simple an explanation as that beauty calls to beauty, as wealth to wealth?

I think of poor (though not in his writing gifts) Cesare Pavese, who kept chasing after starlets, models and ballerinas—exquisite lovelies who couldn't appreciate his morose coffeehouse charm. Before he killed himself he wrote a poem addressed to one of them, "Death Will Come Bearing Your Eyes"—thereby unfairly promoting her from rejecting lover to unwitting executioner. Perhaps he believed that only beautiful women (not literary critics who kept awarding him prestigious prizes) saw him clearly, with 20/20 vision, and had the right to judge him. Had I been more headstrong, if masochistic, I might have followed his path and chased some beauty until she was forced to tell me, like an oracle, what it was about me, physically, that so failed to excite her. Then I might know something crucial about my body, before I passed into my next reincarnation.

Jung says somewhere that we pay dearly over many years to learn about ourselves what a stranger can see at a glance. This is the way I feel about my back. We none of us know what we look like from the back. It is the area of ourselves whose presentation we can least control, and which therefore may be the most honest part of us.

I divide backs into two kinds: my own and everyone else's. The others' backs are often mysterious, exquisite, and uncannily sympathetic. I have always loved backs. To walk behind a pretty woman in a backless dress, and savor how a good pair of shoulder blades, heightened by shadow, has the same power to pierce the heart as chiseled cheekbones! . . . I wonder what it says about me that I worship a part of the body that signals a turning away. Does it mean I'm a glutton for being abandoned, or a timid voyeur who prefers a surreptitious gaze that will not be met and challenged? I only know I have often felt the deepest love at just that moment when the beloved turns her back to me to get some sleep.

I have no auto-erotic feelings about my own back. I cannot even picture it; visually it is a stranger to me. I know it only as an annoyance, which came into my consciousness twenty years ago, when I started getting lower back pain. Yes, we all know that homo sapiens is constructed incorrectly; our erect posture puts too much pressure on the base of the spine; more work-days are lost because of lower back pain than any other cause. Being a writer, I sit all day, compounding the problem. My back is the enemy of my writing life: if I don't do exercises daily I immediately ache, and if I do, I am still not spared. I could say more, but there is nothing duller than lower back pain. So common, mundane an ailment brings no credit to the sufferer. One has to dramatize it somehow, as in the phrase "I threw my back out."

Here is a gossip column about my body: My eyebrows grow quite bushy across my forehead, and whenever I get my hair cut, the barber asks me diplomatically if I want them trimmed or not. (I generally say no, associating bushy eyebrows with Balzacian virility, *élan vital*; but sometimes I acquiesce, to soothe his fastidiousness). . . . My belly button is a modest, embedded slit, not a jaunty swirl like my father's. Still, I like to sniff the odor that comes from jabbing my finger in it: a very ripe, underground smell, impossible to describe, but let us say a combination of old gym socks and stuffed derma (the Yiddish word for this oniony dish of ground intestines is, fittingly, *kishkas*). . . . I have a scar on my tongue from childhood, which I can only surmise I received by landing it on a sharp object, somehow. Or perhaps I bit it hard. I have the habit of sticking my tongue out like a dog when exerting myself physically, as though to urge my muscles on; and maybe I accidentally chomped into it at such a moment. . . . I gnash my teeth, sleeping or waking. Awake, the sensation makes me feel alert and in contact with the world when I start to drift off in a daydream. Another way of grounding myself is to pinch my cheek — drawing a pocket of flesh downward and squeezing it — as I once saw JFK do in a filmed motorcade. I do this cheek-pinching especially when I am trying to keep mentally focused during teaching or other public situations. I also scratch the nape of my neck under public stress, so much so that I raise welts or sores which then eventually grow scabs; and I take great delight in secretly picking the scabs off. . . . My nose itches whenever I think about it, and I scratch it often, especially lying in bed trying to fall asleep (maybe because I am conscious of my breathing then). I also pick my nose with formidable thoroughness when no one, I hope, is looking. . . . There is a white scar about the size of a quarter on the juicy part of my knee; I got it as a boy running into a car fender, and I can still remember staring with detached calm at the blood that gushed from it like a pretty, half-eaten peach. Otherwise, the sight of my own blood makes me awfully nervous. I used to faint dead away when a blood sample was taken, and now I can only control the impulse to do so by biting the insides of my cheeks, while steadfastly looking away from the needle's action. . . . I like to clean out my ear wax as often as possible (the smell is curiously sulfurous; I associate it with the bodies of dead insects). I refuse to listen to warnings that it is dangerous to stick cleaning objects into your ears. I love Q-tips immoderately, I buy them in huge quantities and store them the way a former refugee will stock canned foodstuffs. . . . My toes are long and apelike; I have very little fellow feeling for them; they are so far away, they may as well belong to someone else. . . . My flattish buttocks are not offensively large but neither do they have the "dream" configuration one sees in jeans ads. Perhaps for this reason, it disturbed me puritanically when asses started to be treated by Madison Avenue, around the Seventies, as crucial sexual equipment, and I began receiving compositions from teenage girl students which declared that they liked some boy because he had "a cute butt." It confused me; I had thought the action was elsewhere.

About my penis there is nothing, I think, unusual. It has a brown stem, and a pink mushroom head where the foreskin is pulled back. Like most heterosexual males, I have little comparative knowledge to go by, so that I always feel like an outsider when I am around women or gay men who talk zestfully about differences in penises. I am afraid that they might judge me harshly, ridicule me like the boys who stripped me of my bathing suit in summer camp when I was ten. But perhaps they would simply declare it an ordinary penis, which changes size with the stimulus or weather or time of day. Actually, my penis does have a peculiarity: it has two peeing holes. They are very close to each other, so that usually only one stream of urine issues, but sometimes a hair gets caught across them, or some such contretemps, and they squirt out in two directions at once.

This part of me, which is so synecdochically identified with the male body (as the term "male member" indicates) has given me both too little, and too much, information about what it means to be a man. It has a personality like a cat. I have prayed to it to behave better, to be less frisky, or more; I have followed its nose in matters of love, ignoring good sense, and paid the price; but I have also come to appreciate that it has its own specialized form of intelligence which must be listened to, or another price will be extracted.

Even to say the word "impotence" aloud makes me nervous. I used to tremble when I saw it in print, and its close relation, "importance," if hastily scanned, had the same effect, as if they were publishing a secret about me. But why should it be *my* secret, when my penis has regularly given me erections lo these many years — except for about a dozen times, mostly when I was younger? Because, even if it has not been that big a problem for me, it has dominated my thinking as an adult male. I've no sooner to go to bed with a woman than I'm in suspense. The power of the flaccid penis's statement, "I don't want you," is so stark, so cruelly direct, that it continues to exert a fascination out of all proportion to its actual incidence. Those few times when I was unable to function were like a wall forcing me to take another path — just as, after I tried to kill myself at seventeen, I was obliged to give up pessimism for a time. Each had instructed me by its too painful manner that I could not handle the world as I had previously construed it, that my confusion and rage were being found out. I would have to get more wily or else grow up.

Yet for the very reason that I was compelled to leave them behind, these two options of my youth, suicide and impotence, continue to command an underground loyalty, as though they were more "honest" than the devious strategies of potency and survival which I adopted. Put it this way: sometimes we encounter a person who has had a nervous breakdown years before, and who seems cemented over sloppily, his vulnerability ruthlessly guarded against as dangerous; we sense he left a crucial part of himself back in the chaos of breakdown, and has since grown rigidly jovial. So suicide and impotence became for me "the roads not taken," the paths I had repressed.

Whenever I hear someone tell an anecdote about impotence — a woman who coaxed an ex-priest who had been celibate and unable to make love, first by lying next to him for six months without any touching, then by cuddling for six more months, then by easing him slowly into a sexual embrace — I think they are talking about me. I identify completely; this, in spite of the fact, which I promise not to repeat again, that I have generally been able to do it whenever called upon. Believe it or not, I am not boasting when I say that; a part of me is contemptuous of this virility, as though it were merely a mechanical trick, which violated my true nature, that of an impotent man absolutely frightened of women, absolutely secluded, cut off.

I now see the way I have idealized impotence; I've connected it with pushing the world away, as a kind of integrity, Molière's *The Misanthrope* — connected it with that part of me which, gregarious socializer that I am, continues to insist that I am a recluse, too good for this life. Of course it is not true that I am terrified of women. I exaggerate my terror of them for dramatic effect, or for the purposes of a good scare.

My final word about impotence: Once, in a period when I was going out with many women, as though purposely trying to ignore my hyper-sensitive side and force it to grow callous, by thrusting myself into foreign situations (not only sexual) and seeing if I was able to "rise to the occasion," I dated a woman who was attractive, tall and blonde, named Susan. She had something to do with the pop music business, was a follower of the visionary religious futurist, Teilhard de Chardin, and considered herself a religious pacifist. In fact, she told me her telephone number in the form of the anagram, N-O-T-O-W-A-R. I thought she was joking and laughed aloud, but she gave me a solemn look. In passing, I should say that all the women with whom I was impotent or close to it had solemn natures. The sex act has always seemed to me in many ways ridiculous, and I am most comfortable when a woman who enters the sheets with me shares that sense of the comic pomposity behind such a grandiloquently rhetorical use of the flesh. It is as though the prose of the body were being drastically squeezed into metrical verse. I would not have known how to stop guffawing had I been D. H. Lawrence's lover, and I am sure he would have been pretty annoyed at me. But a smile, saying, "All this will pass," has an erotic effect on me like nothing else.

They claim that men who have long, long fingers also have lengthy penises. I can tell you with a surety that my fingers are long and sensitive, the most perfect, elegant, handsome part of my anatomy. They are not entirely perfect—the last knuckle of my right middle finger is twisted permanently, broken in a softball game when I was trying to block the plate—but even this slight disfigurement, harbinger of mortality, adds to the pleasure I take in my hands' rugged beauty. My penis does not nearly excite in me the same contemplative delight when I look at it as do my fingers. Pianists' hands, I have been told often; and, though I do not play the piano, I derive an aesthetic satisfaction from them that is as pure and Apollonian as any I am capable of. I can stare at my fingers for hours. No wonder I have them so often in my mouth, biting my fingernails to bring them closer. When I write, I almost feel that they, and not my intellect, are the clever progenitors of the text. Whatever narcissism, fetishism, and proud sense of masculinity I possess about my body must begin and end with my fingers.

BRENDA HILLMAN

MALE NIPPLES

— not utter, not
useless, the uselessness of desire, the slight
depression around the center

.

— When the motorcycle boy would light
    his cigarette, I longed
for the flat nipples, the scars, the contralto 'when'

.

and after I saw that the flower
of hell is not hell,
    but a flower —

.

— How the flesh goes in on some.
On the handsome ones who have worked out,
the slightly debased flesh —

.

    which will not
    let my dangerous
    mouth rest there

.

How the beautiful boys' nipples in the pool
in Arizona looked
"underwatery" — pennies which have been thrown in

.

— and after I saw
that the flower of hell
was not one bit hell, but a flower —

.

convinced him to take only
his shirt off. They were, well, one
was brown and one was like the inside of a story —

.
— the ones of divers,
how they point down under the wetsuits:
glad scavengers!

.
    when I first put
my tongue on his (having decided
    he is not my mother) —

.
Oh, the bodies I loved were very tired.
I liked their skin. And
I was no sad animal no graveyard —

.
— and after I saw that desire
is hell, that the flower of hell
is not hell but a flower, well,

.
— So I told the little hairs
around his nipple: lie flat! and they did,
like a campfire later, without the stories —

.
those of soldiers in the desert war and often
his left one tastes "metallic" as in
childhood, when I licked my brother's b.b. gun

.
Kept not finishing
    people I loved.
I tried, — but.

.
The top lip of a Corona beer
is about the size
of one of his —

.
    And after I saw that the flower
    of hell is desire, the almost, well
I still had desire —

.
— So the moon came up
    pink tonight
like one of what had been missed

VASECTOMY

It is clear
the first time they make love again
—the wife's wound stitched
tight into a young girl's
drawstring purse, gold
coins intact, the last baby's
difficult passage erased,
the stitches melting into butter,
the husband's broken sex
tender, a damaged eggplant
after the delicate operation,
the procedure as delicate as eye surgery—
it is clear
they needn't be careful.
Money worries, birth control devices
are flushed down the toilet
like the thwarted sperm
diverted to another stream.
Now the husband and wife
can feast through the darkest days.
They send the children to bed early,
most nights the husband hums, whistles
and splashes on aftershave,
resurrecting memories of his wild youth.
His first love in the back of a pickup truck.
The wife lies in the dark—a wound
her husband can't see in the dark—
the basket of her belly
filled with rotting eggs,
the ones that didn't get picked.

She thinks of the lost possibilities,
the one that remains hidden in the grass
unnamed but yearned for —
the idea of a bright one,
stranded,
star-gazer, poet, mathematician.

ROBERT BLY

BLESSINGS ON THE STOMACH,
THE BODY'S INNER FURNACE

I think the stomach must have gone to the dark goblins given grace far out in the groping tundras, and learned from them how to magically father the children of heat. How delicately the body carries in the loaves of carrot, onion and brown rice, and throws these heat-seeds into the furnace, near where the furnace-keeper lies sleeping, all awash in awakening murders.

And the liver, the ileum, the duodenum, the jejunum, the caecum, the fore-gut and the hind-gut gather, secrete, comfort and hatch the new food, and the thyroid and pancreas call up the heat preserved for eras under the ice, bits of sunlight that got caught in a stone, tiny sexual flames in the sparrow's foot, the fire from the dry shavings in our tongue. . . . So that our brains go about warmed and fiery, and after that can explode into the cello concertos, and imagine the giant blinking at the top of the beanstalk . . . the barbarous fingers scratching its head. . . .

Then we know ourselves companions to the bark-eating porcupines out for their morning walk, friends even to the mineral stars, whose inner furnaces heated them so well they produce their coppery light. So someone in us says, Blessing then on our inner stove, on which the furnace-keeper sleeps even in the day; and blessing on all these calefactors, cookstoves, kilns, boilers, caldrons, urns, tinderboxes, Franklins, retorts, stewpans and corncob-ranges; because of them we can exchange sparks of light through the souls in our eyes when we meet our lover on the dance floor at someone else's wedding.

EDWARD FIELD

OLD ACQUAINTANCE

Old friend, we've come through
in pretty good shape, so far,
better, in fact,
than during those angst-filled years
when you wrecked my life
and I wrecked yours. Remember?
But, back then, we didn't appreciate each other,
did we—like an ill-matched couple,
a bad job by an incompetent marriage broker,
or who just got married out of general horniness
rather than any real compatibility.

I never liked your looks or size
and you had ideas of your own
I couldn't figure out,
though I responded to your goading
and roamed the nights away.
My God, what you led me into,
and I got you into some pretty tight fixes myself.

Life is less strenuous now.
In our golden years, you make few demands.
We've both come to like a bit of a wank,
with none of the old recriminations after.
And I've even learned to admire,
as I pose in the mirror,
the angle of your dangle,
your silky length,
respect your sulky independence.
I wonder that I ever thought you

insufficient, myself underendowed —
or else you've grown.
Best of all, I'm impressed
by how good we look together —
the proportions seem just right.

So, good luck,
dick, prick, dong,
lul, bite, schwantz,
wang, willie, weenie,
and all your other names,
if you've a mind to, now,
and I'd say you've earned it,
stand up, old friend, with me
and take a bow.

MARGARET MORGANROTH GULLETTE

ALL TOGETHER NOW

The New Sexual Politics of Midlife Bodies

Over the past decade or so, the experience of aging into the middle years has been changing, for men and for women, in separate, dramatic, unprecedented ways. For their part, men have begun to worry more obviously and anxiously about their physical aging. The signs of this are all around us, but I began to hear this news in most detail and with most poignancy from women friends.[1] As a student of the history of the middle years of life, I feel that men are in danger of falling into the same cultural traps laid in the twentieth century for "aging women."

At all ages, the male "body" (like the female "body") experiences itself mainly through the mesh of culture. Can anyone know "the body as such," even one's own corporeal body? With many other observers, I no longer think so. What I see in the mirror has already been affected by images from movies, magazines, old photos of myself, chance comments I've heard — associations so manifold and dank and dangerous it can make me tired to think of scrolling through them. What we do and say even in the privacy of love-making has been influenced by advice (maybe even manuals), yet more images, borrowed fantasies — by culturally-shared ways of living in a body of a particular age and gender.[2] These ways of living in a body are not eternally fixed; they change; history startles us. At the end of the twentieth century we find ourselves entering a new cultural situation. Where gender intersects the middle years, traditional norms are being crossed, traditional stereotypes are sliding around with alarming looseness. As the changes in men's relations to their midlife bodies become more visible, midlife women have a new perception of men to assimilate and a choice to make, of how to respond. At the same time, men have to respond to women's new attitudes and behavior, and so on, interactively, without forseeable end.

In the transition period, there is bound to be confusion — possibly wrenching but potentially liberating confusion. I discern one distinct trend: coming from very different directions of the cultural compass, women and men in their middle years are converging. Different groups and individuals are moving at different rates; as with all social developments, this one is uneven. But at the moment aging is becoming a unisex problem. For good or ill, for however long it lasts . . . we're all together now in a new era of sex, age, and gender politics.

*   *   *

"My brother went to the hospital to have his love-handles removed. Well, he wanted to have it done quick and get it over with, so he didn't tell them he had a cold, and he wound up spending a week in there with pneumonia. And what did he do it for anyway? He's been married for years; he's only just turned fifty."

"He's thirty-eight years old, and he's suddenly started wearing his high-school class ring. He's starting to babble about his girlfriends from the Sixties."

"I don't know what's come over him. He's turned into a forty-something punk-rocker — spike hair, gel, funny footwear."

"When he had his forty-fifth birthday, he decided he couldn't coach the basketball team anymore and he was giving up basketball for good. 'Why don't you start pickup games with people your own age?' I said to him. But no, if he can't play like a teenager, he can't play."

"He comes in from tennis and he's beet-red, puffing, winded, bent over — looks like death. 'Don't you guys ever take a break? Whaddya trying to do, kill each other?' Is this for *health*?"

"He was interviewed by the newspaper — big spread about all his theatre work for the last ten years — and he lied about his age. He took off five years. Why, I don't know *women* who do that any more."

Women I know are worrying aloud about their aging husbands and lovers and brothers and friends. Aging — we're all noticing this — depends less on biological givens like birthdays than on a person's state of mind. As women interpret the signs, these men are in a bad state, worried, looking anxious, giving up, acting out, succumbing to the cult of youth. No doubt these women are not telling me all they know about the feelings of these men. (Despite what men may fear, women — the women I know — are reticent about revealing the secrets of the men in their lives.) Possibly the men concerned would word their own interpretations differently. But behind the women's readings lies sorrowful speech they have heard directly: hints of misery in half sentences, "humorous" confessions of anxieties, bedtime conversations in the dark. They come in murmured forms because, like women, men also conceal their fears of aging. And perhaps these women erupted to me because codes of silence make it harder to speak plainly to their loved ones across the old age-and-gender gap. As they and I break the code, men may react angrily.

In the funny pages, though, Garry Trudeau goes public with the subject. Rick Redfern turning forty uses products supposed to prevent wrinkles, retain hair, prolong life; other midlife male characters in the strip are given stereotypical fantasies of seducing younger women. Rick's wife is advised to "lie" — presumably, about his looks.[3] During the Eighties, cartoons in the *New Yorker* — Ed Koren produced many of them — and birthday greeting cards for men thirty and above spotted or supported the trend toward jocular self-deprecation and joky self-pity. Like flypaper they fixed the language and the ideology that are still circulating. Koren produced the man floored at the cookout, with the caption, "Well, there's mid-life" — with the other three people present spatially detached from him, as if the rest of them are all merely onlookers at whatever "mid-life" [*sic*] has done to him.[4] Whatever went wrong with him is due to

Garry Trudeau, "Doonesbury" strip, *The Boston Globe*, August 17, 1992.

"Well, there's mid-life."

Ed Koren cartoon, *The New Yorker*, August 19, 1985.

age—or in some unspecified way, his reaction to age. The cartoon, mildly satirizing the label "mid-life," nonetheless leaves it intact, reiterates and authorizes the label—at least, for the man. Like Rick's wife, the woman who speaks is presented as unaffected; in Koren she's not only unmoved but blithe, not to say gleeful. It's all done in light pencil, but these cartoonists fix a new binary: men as decked, women as immune. Like me, they want to point out some changes they've noticed—some changes they believe everyone has noticed. But they want to show them as a *total reversal* of cultural norms, men and women simply changing places. The actual, more complex situation doesn't fit into the cartoon Weltanschauung: that some men now *share* the condition that women have been forced to live, that they have this intimate problem in common, that the genders are not opposed but in some freaky new way overlapping.

It's man against man, however, in Koren's Sunday in the Park, a dutiful herd jogging "scene."[5]

The joggers can be seen as lemmings, mass man (literally: the crowd is almost entirely male). Their foreground representative

"As for me, I'm in various stages of deterioration."

Ed Koren cartoon, *The New Yorker*, January 28, 1985.

looks trim, "healthy." The main male-male binary pits the Jogger against an isolated figure: the thicker, padded, hirsute, bespectacled pipe-smoker with a book under his arm, the intellectual zhlub, complacently asserting his "deterioration." Both men are smiling. Whom does the man reading the magazine want to identify with? Perhaps neither? (Do men ask themselves: Are there really only and always two sides?)[6]

The women who have been offering me these fragments from their intimate lives suggest that it isn't a one-line joke or sitcom material. They find themselves talking in unexpected ways about the bodies and behavior of men their own age, but they're troubled mainly about their states of mind. On the other hand, they don't assume that the situation will be repeated ad infinitum, and they wouldn't want to call this "self-delusion," label it a "midlife crisis," say he's "high in denial" or (without other issues) urge the guy into therapy.[7]

Women who are feminists, after all, recognize ageism; they see it as a cultural problem that spares no woman—they know it as a common burden. And they have practiced fighting against the culture. Some respond with love and reassurance. The first way to fight it is to go on admiring your loved ones and letting them know you do. This doesn't mean lying, but it does require anyone who does it to reject unceasing pressure to continue using anachronistic youth-standards for judging bodies and faces. It involves working our way into an appreciation of male midlife bodies and midlife forms of beauty — or, falling short of that, disregarding features that we cannot succeed in finding attractive. The woman whose husband gelled his hair went on to convince him that she loved him even though he couldn't hide his bald spot. "After all," (I imagine some women conveying), "I didn't marry you for your hair (waist, profile)." Or they convey instead, "Great legs! Great back! Great buns!" "Let me count the ways." But there are different ways to count. Some women really do want him to fit into the size 34 bikini underpants.

I hear in the voices of my friends, aside from concern and support, some anger and puzzlement and pity. Privately, they're irritated that men they know and influence can't deal with it better. They're mystified that the men are hit so hard. And they're astonished to be powerful enough to pity men. (Pity has a component of tenderness, but it also has a component of the condescension of power.) "Men! *They do age*." Of course women know that women are scarcely exempt from worrying about the passage of time, but they probably once thought that men would be. Men benefited sensationally from the "double standard of aging," as Susan Sontag described it in the early Seventies. She began her essay with a long explanation of the symbolic — and she believed widespread — phenomenon of *women* lying about their age.[8] Many women would swear that the situation remains unchanged: men, they say, can still take advantage of accrued male superiority, and women still learn to internalize female deficiency, as we all move through the life course. But many of the supports for the double standard have been weakening over the last twenty years. We need to understand that many men in middle life are having the same problems women have, caught in the head-trap of having to figure out how to "stay young." Stay young or, in the prevailing binary, feel they've "given up" and "lost out" in a race that has tremendously high stakes. Beyond Central Park, in the culture at large, both the Deteriorating Man and the Jogger are caught in the trap.

For the historically-minded, the new situation marks the decline of a piece of male privilege that once seemed eternal. Even those who know how much the appearance of "the natural" depends on culture may find these particular changes in age/gender relations baffling. "What's happening?" a historian asked me recently, knowing my scholarly interest in aging. "It used to be that men got 'distinguished' and women got 'dumpy.' It used to be that only women got called 'vain.' Now the opposite seems true. Is it just aerobics?"

*   *   *

It's a complex story. Two things have happened more or less simultaneously but independently. The way many women *see* men is changing. And the system that sells products based on fears of aging has turned its giant voracious maw toward that next great big juicy market, men. As scholar Lawrence Birkin told us in *Consuming Desire*, it's the era of the "genderless" consumer.[9] Age, not gender, identifies the system's next market. If they can get you to "feel your age" — to feel over-the-hill and wistful about youth — you are theirs. Since a male body can learn when young to take on the signs of male power through "mental body-images and fantasies . . . [,] muscle tensions, posture, the feel and texture of the body,"[10] it can also be taught later on that masculinity recedes. And if aging can be made anxious for men too, there's profit in it. The Baby Boomers are a cohort doomed by their numbers to have their needs manufactured their whole lives long. "During this decade, the number of people aged 45 or older will grow by 18 million, compared with no net increase for those under 45," noted one writer in "the magazine of consumer change." (The heading on his article was, "Looking and feeling good will be a priority for aging baby boomers.")[11] "Boomers will grow increasingly affluent as they reach their peak earning years around age 50."[12] But the target cohort is even more vast: it includes all men who identify themselves currently as in their middle years, and it potentially includes all the men born since the end of the Boom who although chronologically young are aging into the American cultural situation at this time.[13] Thus my son, now aged twenty-four, and his friends are at risk. The members of this vast group are all being battered with signs that they need or will need "help against aging." These needs are not rational: longevity rates are still going up, men of middle years are healthier than their fathers were at the same age. But the market reasons the need for all.

Men show they are becoming increasingly vulnerable to the commercial packaging of youth. All across the country they're buying hair dye. They're self-conscious about balding and willing to buy hair remedies to grow thicker hair.[14] Sy Sperling, the hair-insertion promoter, does over 10,000 male heads a year in a competitive and rapidly growing field. Designers are marketing perfumes and cosmetics for men; salons are doing facials. Men are buying exercycles, rowing machines, expensive athletic shoes, home gyms. Fine, maybe; fun, maybe. But there's a change . . . cultural critics who have been worrying about female consumption of youth products and practices would do well not to glide over this trend. Men are spending more than women on what are called "beauty aids" when women buy them. According to one study, men of fifty are as self-conscious about being overweight and far from their ideal body as are midlife women and young women; the three groups together thus distinguish themselves from young men, who alone feel relatively closer to their ideal body form. Dieting turns out to be correlated with cultural standing in the body-competition stakes.[15] Midlife men's sweatclothes are the same as those of the toned-up young: paintbox spandex. (As with women, sharing youth's exhibitionistic clothing ups the ante, teaches everyone to look for minute, age-related differences.)

Men are the fastest growing market for plastic surgeries — dermabrasions to create smoother and younger skin, "coronal lifts" on the forehead to erase lines ("that make a man look angry or tired," said one publicist to me); alterations on noses, ears, chins, bellies, eyelids; total face-lifts.[16] Men make up somewhere between 16% and 25% of the market. "Love handles" — extra flesh at the waist — was a new category to me; excising it is part of the "body-sculpting" movement. The newest craze on the West Coast is silicone body implants for calves and chests. Surgeons don't care whether that body part is male or female. Men are being taught to shop and chop their way to oblivion. "Men are proving a lucrative market for surgeons," according to a *Boston Globe* article on "The Male Makeover." One surgeon said, "Women must have reinforcement to give themselves permission to spend the money. But men always feel they deserve it."[17]

The next steps? Based on what we know of the ways women have been manipulated, we can fairly safely anticipate the moves to be made on men. The system needs to raise men's anxiety level about aging to unheard-of new levels. On the way to the higher levels of stress, the concept of aging at midlife — shorn of its accompaniments of poise, sexual pleasure, accomplishment, wisdom, and the like — is reduced to a state of subtractions, compounded of many and varied losses, with an emphasis on the visible, physical ones. The marketers of commercial rejuvenation and their media shills will smooth over the difference between fashion-consumption that is considered "normal" and the products they're in the process of normalizing. One way they teach women not to refuse facelifts is to say it's no different from lipstick. The system will teach men to be proud of their transformed body because it matches the way they feel "inside." "I want to look as young as I feel" — a standard line — creates an interior self that doesn't mature, at odds with a body defined as aging and disagreeable. (Maturity doesn't exist anywhere, in this scheme.) They'll tell men that a jowl-nip is just the next thing to buy after your exercycle, your new briefcase, your $1000 suit; that knowing more about your field is no substitute for looking young; that "everyone" is doing it. The media do not often protect men: recent magazine articles about implant surgery for men voice an antique gung-ho spirit. (There are more articles for women, but by contrast they almost all contain warnings.)[18]

These approaches work. One man said that "his wife's appearance motivated him to have a facelift, as he did not want his wife 'to look much younger.'" Because double-standard language lingers, reminding men that they can't afford to sound as if they care how they look, "some men may deliberately misrepresent [their concern for appearance] . . . complaining that they 'can't breathe' to cover up their wishes for a better-looking nose."[19] The ads also target the older man afraid of being down-graded or unemployed, who badly wants to look as if he's able to make it; they hold out the promise of maintaining middle-class status, and yet, of course (in this recession), have to hedge on the promise.

If men behave the way women have done, the most vulnerable in terms of practices will be in the higher income brackets, where the codes of perfection are stricter, the competition keener, the fear of failing greater, the marginal advantages of "youth" credibly higher, and the money available for expensive procedures, from workouts with massage several times a week to spas and surgery. But lower-income men, like lower-income women, will wind up psychologi-cally worse off, with their new desires for cultural "goods" denied to them, with age-anxieties they can't allay in any of the fashionable ways.

The system will teach men that their "midlife crisis," which has been viewable as an interesting self-reorientation available to some specially perceptive and future-looking individuals, is somehow both pathological and universal, linked to self-loathing and sexual "dysfunction." (Here therapists, writers of self-help guides, and pub-lishers add themselves to the commercial/media mix.) Victims of the crisis are meant to age "badly, increasingly obsessed with penile tumescence, increasingly estranged from any other life, from any other flesh."[20] They're meant to feel emotionally helpless without the practices and products being promoted. Films still offer the solution of seeking (and sometimes marrying) young female flesh, the solution-by-sympathetic-magic. This narrative often involves dis-prizing, if not abandoning, same-age female flesh. In solemn psy-chological tones, it constructs a hero tormented by his behavior — guilty, but somehow helpless to do otherwise, or think at all. In a story of midlife helplessness, the climacteric will loom much larger. They'll teach men that *their* aging too results from a hormone-deficiency disease and that it can be cured by buying chemicals or implants. Prostate cancer — mainly a slow-growing disease of old age — is now presented as if it were the next thing that happens after your fiftieth birthday. Already men with hot flashes and anxieties about their sexuality are being given testosterone. According to researcher John McKinlay, over sixty clinical trials are underway for a wide array of products — drugs, prostheses — targeted for the next market."[21] Already there have been scandals because scientists have been promoting for rejuvenation purposes unapproved products like Retin A and collagen after having received grants from the pharma-ceutical companies that produce them.[22]

The long decline in real wages over the course of the Eighties (affecting between seventy and ninety percent of Americans), and the recession, with its attendant unemployment or job insecurity, have softened up the market. This recession has hit men in the middle class as well as the working class. Those who might have relied on their economic security or professional achievements or seniority to maintain their sense of self have been weakened in their work lives — this core area in which (at least in comparison to their fathers and the women in their lives, if not to other men in their cohort) they had been relatively strong. Forced to expect less satisfaction from the job sphere, they back into private life looking for affective satisfactions — again, just as women did for so long. In that evermore crucial encounter, women are both the prize of achievement and the judges of failure. And it is precisely there in the world of love and sexuality that the system exacerbates their "problem," offers men an explanation and a solution: it confronts men with their own "aging" and offers its alleged antidotes. Little in mainstream discourse now warns men and women that national economic weakness raises their stress levels, makes them feel old, and kills them.[23] Instead, all of us are encouraged to believe that our problem, aging, is natural, inevitable, awful, but controllable. We're all supposed to concentrate on the private sector of body-control, solipsisticly competing with our own gender and (if heterosexual) keeping the other gender in the dark about it.

It will be fascinating as well as horrifying to watch how the system uses men's available vulnerabilities to get them to accept all

"In the last few months, Matthew has gone on twenty-four-hour alert for signs of aging."

Ed Koren cartoon, *The New Yorker*, June 18, 1990.

this. When looking in the mirror, they have to be brought to see themselves as older-than-young and thereby deficient.

In another cartoon a man does just that, fingering his under-eye area.[24] Again, this cartoon places women as spectators of male distress and commentators on it, exempt. "In the last few months, Matthew has gone on twenty-four-hour alert for signs of aging." One continuous form of preparation for the mirror scene is effected by ads—all those gorgeous unsmiling young men in the national glossies, selling their young kissers as the only true allure. We can expect to see Kinsey-style statistics proliferate, about how much young men are getting it, in an attempt to get older men to decide that they have sex less often than they used to and that it's not as good. No doubt we'll see a blockbuster book for men called *Masculine Forever* that makes men's sexual problems more public and humiliating than they are now, and that trumpets a medical magic bullet for male aging.[25] Eventually we may look back on today, and ask, "How come they didn't move sooner? The market was just sitting there, aging quietly, privately, and (relatively speaking) happily."

*   *   *

I, of course—speaking for a second as that supposedly essential figure, "a woman"—had nothing to do with all this. I try to dissuade women from liposuction and HRT and getting anxious about aging, so I'm not about to encourage men to follow suit. I've never sold a man an "anti-aging" product either directly or indirectly, either by innuendo, deprecation, or by admiring other men. I have been married for almost thirty years to a man my age, and he reciprocates: he doesn't produce my "aging" for me either. In many ways we share my project, which he thinks of as emancipatory. The worst I could be charged with as the years have passed is urging him into sexier and handsomer clothes; I've been instrumental in getting him to wear velvety sweaters and nontraditional patterns and colors. In general, men's dress clothes are becoming more visually interesting and varied; more textured, patterned and colorful. Men can wear velour, chenille, silk; soft sweaters, more lavish scarves, larger coats with more swing to them. Inside these clothes they can disport a more expressive body. Feminism can take some credit for this, in so far as it has supported crossing gendered boundaries in dress as in other social arenas.[26] And my own kind of feminism advocates that older men as well as women think themselves worthy of adornment. Not desperate for it. Men too need to try to distinguish between forces permitting them new pleasures and forces coercing them into new anguish and new expenditures.

For a long time I didn't even know there was a commerce in male aging. And if I had been told, I might have denied it or said it was trivial, because for a long time I believed that men manage capitalism entirely to their own advantage.

Quite independently, then, I discovered that I didn't see other men's bodies the way I was supposed to. When I went to my twenty-fifth college reunion (that instititution for cohort-gazing and cohort-comparisons), I noticed that the women looked better than the men — and I was surprised to notice it. It wasn't mainly that so many men were sagging, waistless, balding, jowly, or inappropriately "youthful." It was also the way some talked. "They bore themselves," one woman said sagely; "they're tired of being them. We're not." I tried to move beyond my first impression, a combination of shock and — I dare say — some relief. I was not displeased, at first, to notice that I noticed that men aged. But I soon came to other more firmly held and politically useful feelings, to which I'll return later. Of course there are also men in my cohort who can transfix the eye. Two or three of the beautiful boys I had assiduously cultivated at eighteen were still lovely to look at. Some men look their very best in their middle years: they've filled out the hollow chests and thin arms they had at twenty. I like the silky skin under their eyes, their laughlines, and the way some look at me now when I'm talking, no longer mesmerized by something in my face I never could see. Now they're seeing *me*, the once invisible me behind the young-female flesh. Others are well-kept shrines to boyhood. The joggers looked drawn, spent. Some heavy ex-jocks looked worst of all. The unmarried, hunting, didn't look as if they felt self-confident and lucky; they looked dispirited.

There was more pleasure to be got from looking at the women. There too were surprises, to one reared expecting to see female midlife decline. The women were larger and more lined than twenty-five years ago, but they looked womanly to me. Most of the beauties were still wonderful. Like the others, what mattered was their visual expressiveness. They broadcast vitality; there was so much individuality to be deciphered. "We've grown into our faces," said Connie, a friend of three decades, "we've earned them." My college favored a low-maintenance "natural" style, which became a habit for most of us sooner or later, and which serves most women at any age very well. Many women swim, jog, or dance—they've discovered their bodies as sources of pleasure and pride in midlife, and they are trying to stay on the far side of that line I mentioned, away from cultural/commercial coercion. (There were a few women in a bad state too, worried, looking anxious, giving up, acting out, succumbing to the cult of youth—but that I had expected; that's not news.) In Margaret Drabble's novel *The Radiant Way*, the heroine dressing for a party opens her make-up kit to "put on her face" (as women used to say) and then closes it. Knowing you look fine *as is* seems to be the new spirit. And the relatively unretouched body tells a new story about being female in the middle years, signals an attitude (that even a woman with the habit of make-up can share) of expectancy about future self-fashioning. A lot of the old formulas about women's aging demand revision. "A woman of about forty-five strikes us as a youthful, even unformed individual, whom we expect to make powerful use of the possibilities for development opened up for her. . . . A man of the same age, sadly, often frightens us by his psychical rigidity and unchangeability. . . . There seem to be no paths open to future development." This is the way Freud would—or could—rewrite "Femininity" if he were writing it today.[27]

What's the difference between then and now? Why are men in general more vulnerable than they used to be to age-conscious discourses and practices? Until recently, midlife men have not thought of themselves as a gender and age category. Although that is sometimes spoken of as a piece of their privilege, in this context it marks their lack: it makes each man an isolated individual, fragmented and competitive, vulnerable to commercial manipulation. Even now the men's movement, although targeted to midlife men and fueled at least in part by unhappiness about aging, doesn't seem to know that contemporary constructions of aging may be part of the problem; it's not investigating aging as a separate, historical construct.[28] Although men of mature years dominate critical theory, age is not being theorized. Meanwhile, women who wanted resistance to the youth-cult and to the denigration of the midlife have had feminism. Its anti-ageism may be inconsistent and occasionally perfunctory, but (as the articles warning women against plastic surgery suggest) most of the theoretical resistance and effective rhetorical opposition that makes its way into the mainstream comes from that source.

Among a million other things feminism made possible for me was that I aged past twenty-five or thirty under its friendly gaze. My professional interest in age as a category of cultural construction thickened the padding I needed to resist the culture's constant age-assaults. I take hits (like the recent movie *Death Becomes Her*, which tried to reinstate the double standard by glorifying Bruce Willis as an aging cosmetic surgeon who'd literally rather die than join women in their female aging frenzy). But after painful experience I've taught myself how to recover. Although not free from physical preoccupations, I quite like being my age. Frankly, I was never happy as a youthful sexual object. Around twenty — aside from loathing leers and ribald jokes, and preferring to think of myself as an intellectual — I was irritably self-critical about my appearance. I took my cultural burden seriously and I felt painfully inferior to beautiful women. In those days applying make-up required excruciating care, and nothing I could do to them softened me toward my stomach, my upper arms, my chin, my nose. One of the reasons I was mad at my gender was because I thought (oh how mistakenly) that boys didn't worry about their body parts. Now at fifty I like all the parts. A few years ago, I caught myself admiring my feet, my "broad, peasant feet," for the first time. Some of the parts I once disliked — or prided myself on — could now conceivably be viewed as problems. But they simply don't disturb me in the young way. If my appearance now saddens my husband, my friends, my mother, or my aunts, they haven't been letting me know. I earned my workers' hands and those keen lines around the eyes. I *waited* to get that silver streak that says, "This is a woman whose experience you can trust; listen to her. Pay her well."

Women who see the way I do turn to each other in wonder. "*That men didn't age, while women did* — we made men magical by repeating this preposterous idea over and over."

One sign that we have moved into a new era of gender/age relations is that it has become much harder to decide for sure now whether men were "really" at one time more "distinguished" in their middle years than women, or whether women "aged" sooner. Was it an age/gender ideology that made everyone see differently then?

It has to have been ideology. Discourse about male/female bodies is always (although not only) the surface of the lopsided power struggle. Women were taught to feel older but not to notice men feeling older, and rather than critiquing the difference they were pushed into explaining it. Why did they accept the explanation, "Men don't age as fast"? Compared to women, men have always had more access to money, security, comfort, power, and fame, and they often controlled even more of these good things as they aged. No wonder they continued to look desirable. And from desirable it's a short step to handsome. Understanding the mechanism, Proust once said wryly, "All duchesses are beautiful." I confess that once upon a time I had a sexual dream about Henry Kissinger. Can anyone think it was because I thought his body alluring? But I recovered pretty easily from my brief participation in American myth-making about "glamorous" middle-aged men. In my family, all the women but one worked and liked their work, and some — atypically for America — probably earned more than their husbands. Maybe it was just a coincidence that when I was growing up I never heard anyone glorifying my uncles' midlife attractions and denigrating my aunts'?

Understandably, some wives were complicit in the interactive process that produced their husbands as "younger" than they were. A friend who is a psychoanalyst writes, "I think Barbara Bush had definitely done this for George. Her accepting the burden of overweight and white hair has allowed George to seem/feel by contrast young and possessed of more horizons. Maybe 'good wives' always agree (tacitly/preconsciously) to speak up on behalf of both by making *a contrast between* wherein the man could feel superior." Some women thus used to let themselves lapse into the forms of "aging" that were culturally prescribed. But in contrast to the Deteriorating Man of the cartoon, who has Bruce Willis on his side, they probably did so in silence, without receiving gratitude. And they certainly experienced more public shame, because to perform their valuable emotional service they had to eschew the other cultural imperative for "older" women: looking young. Women were sold the-need-to-buy-youth — and when they dutifully did so were mocked for visibly trying to simulate youth. Now men may find themselves caught in this mocking view-finder: it's where Garry Trudeau places Rick. He's been found out in his simulations, and needing to simulate is ipso facto failure.

In the bad old days for women, when few had incomes and almost all were commodities, inevitably women felt intense pressure to package themselves for the male-dominated marriage market. Naturally, distinctions had to be invented to connote "marketability." And "Youth" was part of what older male buyers sought. The longing to be marketable still grips many young women, many poor women, and women of any age, race, class or income who still believe that male eyes and male preferences alone decide their value. But more and more, women in my cohort refuse to identify themselves as either that poor or that dependent. They've mostly finished raising their children, and if they did that — the hardest part — alone, they're not going to rush into marriage for money now. They're sliding or striding into the new age where "What I want" prevails over what the culture made us need, and "What I see" prevails over what the culture wanted us to see. Now *our* eyes judge. (If 62% of income equality can achieve this, what's next?) Feminism did help level that wage differential, and it is responsible for telling women over and over again that their eyes judge.

The gap remains. Midlife men have not become commodified in the same way women were; they haven't lost their economic edge or the personal power that can be borrowed from the larger context of inequality. But they may be on their way to losing the old easy access to young women. Educated women in their twenties now are less likely to marry older men out of fear of failing in the economic system; they can make it on their own. Demography is also against the midlife man who wants to marry a younger woman: the post-Baby Boom cohort is too small. In general, men's "prospects for marriage are declining. . . . Among men under 45, the remarriage rate has dropped by nearly half, to 58% of its 1970 level."[29] Divorced or widowed, independent older women I know are not hastening back into matrimony (even though the culture keeps shouting "Men are scarce" to frighten us into submission). Women who like men may want male companionship and amorousness and love, but more are refusing to pay for it the old high wages of female subservience to male deafness, bossiness, and psychological dependence. If some marry younger men, it's partly because younger men are likelier to be feminists: likelier to listen, to not think about everything in terms of sex, to see older women as irresistible, to appreciate *Thelma and Louise*. The ads imply that what women like in men is pecs and baby-skin. Let me tell you, it would be more useful for a man to say he believed Anita Hill than to have silicone implanted in his chest.

The culture handed men — all men — the double standard of aging. Older men traded on the double standard: many ignored same-age women, called us ugly, told jokes about our alleged frigidity, left the Peter Arno cartoons lying around, foisted on us those stereotypes we're still trying to lift off. Husbands out walking with their wives shopped younger women, pointed out their appetizing characteristics, implied unflattering contrasts. At parties, flirting with flattered girls, they flaunted their potential mobility. They flaunted their superiority through pornography, trophy brides, and sex practices that enhanced their dominance. Cultural power made them mean.

Female independence across the life course teaches men a whole lot faster than argumentation or fashion photos of gorgeous fifty-year-olds that women their own age or older can be desirable. Women aren't automatically knocking women any more, or knocking them over on the way to the nearest man. Unless they love the man and he's good to them, they don't have to overlook male paunchiness and rename gray hair "distinguished" when it appears on male heads. If now we decide that life's lines and silver streaks have beauty and "character," it may be because they look good on women we like. And *we* will decide, out of a better use of midlife power than men have made, whether it's only fair to like on the second sex what we like on our own.

*   *   *

Men may read this and say, Double whammy. And then, as the bad news brought to them by commerce gets worse, some may blame "feminists." Or all women. Let me summarize why they shouldn't.

Men have always known they aged, of course. There's an individual life, after all, modest and scared, that goes on beneath all the hype of the culture circus and the gender war. Looking in the mirror, how many midlife men see Jeremy Irons or Nick Nolte? Do they see an aging star — Robert Redford or Clint Eastwood (who are now touched up less in their movies and who announce this as a sign that they "accept" aging)? Ordinary men see themselves creased under the eyes, with deeper squints, a little dry fold under the chin, "hacked," as Saul Bellow has said, across the back of the neck, flabby-armed, lean-shanked, high-hipped. Human, like us. But what they see and what they feel about their bodies also depends on training. Men need to understand that from the opening decades of the twentieth century, various discourses have aged them in ways that biology alone never can. Every trick that is being used by commerce now was active earlier in the century. The male climacteric was moved back from old age into the midlife then. The generation gap, the cult of swinging youth, the desexualizing of midlife women, began then.[30] Having made men frantic about their aging, the culture offered them not just Retin A but remedies that involved objectifying and dominating and rejecting women, creating competition between young and midlife women, forcing same-age wives into facsimiles of age or youth — in short, carrying generic male socioeconomic power into private life in cruel and unjust ways. The manipulation of men was once less visible only because the subordination of *women* to age-grading was so vast, so prevalent, so discussable, so easily made public and ridiculous. The anger of women as they came to understand this story has frightened men, distracting them from understanding either their roles in the narrative or the cultural pressures that prodded them into those roles. In being offered tyrannies as modes of compensation for real and imagined aging, older men were victims too. They need to see this in order to free themselves and their victims.

*   *   *

So here we are together — more or less together, if we can dispassionately consider the idea — in the human condition. Both biologically aging, of course, and now both being aged by culture in more similar ways. But my sober final assessment is that this is not a cause for rejoicing for anyone. As it's going, it is not necessarily a trend toward age equality. Generally, it is a most dangerous moment for people of all ages, classes, races, and sexual orientations. What makes it perilous is that *both* genders are now wide open to psychological, medical and commercial exploitation. And *both* are now vulnerable to romantic and economic blackmail: "The younger-looking person will be the one who gets the lover/spouse/job." The pressure comes from the job-market, and from forces (like cosmetic surgeons, pharmaceutical companies) that use fear of youth-competition as their marketing tool, and from the media that naively pass along the cultural messages without querying their provenance. If the recession continues, it could get much worse much faster. In any case, it's likely to get worse, because markets need to grow. So my message to men is—as the kids say—"If you're dissin' the sisters, you ain't fightin' the power."

Whether the pressure on men to feel old and pay to get young will start coming from women too remains to be seen. In the unknown days to come, what's going to matter is what men do, say, and choose, how they act in the streets, at parties, on dates, at the breakfast table, in bed—all the places beside the workplace where behavior has political and ethical consequences. The women I quoted initially weren't mocking men for being in the fix they're in, nor were they demanding that men try harder to mimic youth; on the contrary. They want men to liberate themselves. But women are not all liberated; the evil done by the era of the double standard lives on. The kind of woman (or, for that matter, man) who has bought into the aging crisis is going to take it for granted that you'll buy in too; if you get a hair transplant, he or she can feel free to get a face-lift. Such people are not acting to harm, but to *help* you, out of simple blitheness: "It's a product you want, buy it."[31] Think twice. Anxiety about aging is not a simple purchase. You won't like added levels of stress.

As for women who think consciously as anti-ageists (feminists, in short)—who knows how each one will react? Women don't feel in control in their middle years; they're wary about becoming victims of male power; they'll wait to see whether this alleged trend toward male vulnerability will lead any given individual man to reciprocities—or to retaliations. "How sweet revenge could be. . . ." I envision some wanting to get even—thinking it would leave a good taste in the mouth. Here and there in this essay I've left traces of its preliminary savor. Yet maybe it is a new situation. There are other sweet emotions too. Fighting ageism in alliance with men might be one of them.

As far as I'm concerned, losing men to American ageism would be a disaster—for men of all ages, for the women who care for them, for women of all ages themselves, and (not least important) for the future of any anti-ageist movement. The way men were supposed to age—carelessly, unthinkingly, contented in their changed bodies—was to me one utopian idea, one proof that such an attitude could make a space for itself. Losing this possibility would undermine everything that people in age studies are trying to do to clarify the issues, to de-naturalize "aging" and fix it more explicitly as a product of cultural forces and thus a set of pressures that can be rejected.

Will men resist, though? And resist in alliance with women? I'm not always sanguine on either question.[32] When they need to evade age, people learn ingeniousness. Some men say there's nothing to resist; they're not buying the products, they say. . . . Well, they're not buying many. And what would be wrong with buying the products, or telling jokes about urination and impotence, or even having a midlife crisis — as long as they're not putting women down? If I say they're internalizing the discourses, they respond, in effect, "Let me be anxious and unhappy, let me try to buy my way out, let me stay me."

Men who come from ethnic or religious backgrounds in which aging is positively valued as an access to wisdom and its authority, sometimes say they feel less vulnerable. Some men in academe, who in their middle years usually have tenure, have told me they don't feel vulnerable at all. I take them all at their word, although I sometimes wonder whether self-reflection might bring out further, more complicated, more interesting truths.

Men who represent themselves as completely invulnerable spare themselves work whose results we need: the introspective task of picking out what in culture still needles them from what they have easily cast aside, the emotional task of admitting that they are in any way like women their age, the intellectual task of describing their sources of resistance to cultural pressures, for the sake of others. These are brave and altruistic projects. Men in this group certainly postpone taking a share in liberating other men from the forces they are free of (including warning the young). So when academics explain that it would be a travesty of oppression/liberation discourse for them to "play victim," I demur. Their attitude makes it less likely that age can soon be added to the historical and theoretical fields that need it, and (once age studies become established) postpones vital and inevitable debates: about the cultural construction of men, differences among men, and the ways in which age intersects with race, class, and sexual orientation.

And looking ahead I wonder whether by the start of the next century even the most privileged men in America are going to be able to feel truly, entirely, immune.

Other men may believe they have some personal interest in asserting immunity: by doing so they might maintain the double standard a little longer — and "get away with being less sensitive, less reliable, less analytic about human relations," in the words of a minister friend who would like men to take more responsibility for the ethics of private as well as public life. In any case, denial comes in many forms. Men may find themselves arguing that they're simply aging biologically, that deterioration is not a cultural label with a complicated origin but a set of physical facts. There's some deep fatalism around — an attitude meant to be stoical, and within its limiting context, admirable — but in fact helplessly naive. A gendered variant of this argues (as the cartoons do) that *women* don't age but men do. Resentment and self-pity fuel this mystified reading of the cultural situation. Men need to think more introspectively and deconstructively about all these issues, act in accordance with their findings, and move their discourses onto a plane beyond.

A complicated assignment. There are signs that some men have been taking it on. And when we strategize about change — as opposed to when we describe the culture — we should concentrate on the promising signs rather than the ferocious remnants of the double standard. We should all be on the lookout for spots where the system is breaking down, where midlife likeness between men and women is being stated, where conditions are right for moving on toward more age-equality. The past twenty years have been revolutionary for men too. In the Seventies a new concept of adulthood arose in social psychology that explicitly included men. It was sold as "gender crossover" (not an entirely felicitous marketing strategy), with men seen as developmentally tending toward "greater nurturance, passivity, dependence, or contemplativeness" in their middle years. Now we'd be likely to use such terms as care and interdependence. Bert Brim found such men as early as 1975, describing them as "more diffusively sensual, more sensitive to the incidental pleasures and pains, less aggressive, more affiliative, more interested in love than conquest or power, more present than future-oriented."[33] In the last twenty years, many men I know have lived with women who appreciated such traits and gave in return for them a less grudging, wary, and self-protective love than would have been possible earlier. In this context, what might have been perceived by men as coercion to behave differently, to be different, was absorbed by them as parts of their ego ideal. Or perhaps they set out on their own initiative to create a more just relationship: Not passively but actively, they made space for another, supported her goals as well as their own, shared in child-rearing. Or perhaps they set out to marry a feminist, even unconsciously, intuiting that adulthood would be easier with a partner. In such relationships, they might risk telling secrets, even scary secrets that might have humiliating consequences. And then, the conversation would be open for women to begin to talk about how they suffer from — and resist — menopause discourse or the "empty-nest syndome" or "Momism." Or perhaps some men admit they don't worry about aging, as a step toward assuring their wives that they needn't worry either. In all these versions, couples have lived their way into midlife age equality — not without tension, but with affection, relief, and growth.

In the arena of second marriage, where so much bitterness can be engendered by the double standard of aging, some men have learned to reinterpret their best interests. The increasing economic independence of women means that at remarriage, a man can feel better assured that the woman can't be said to have been bought. People have been inventive about relational changes in the longer post-parental period, a period that, in Janet Z. Giele's words, "traditional age-sex roles no longer easily 'handle.' "[34] Over the past twenty years, as the Baby Boomers have been moving through the life course, men have absorbed into their emerging concept of (midlife) masculinity new language and sexual behavior and attitudes. I know men who understand how the culture has condemned women to age unequally, yet don't feel exempt and don't need to exaggerate the gender difference. I want to hold out the possibility — the undocumented actuality — that men and women who bring more confidence and trust into their intimate lives, can admit their degrees of vulnerability, compare notes, and practice resistance together. Where are *these* midlife stories? What forces have kept them from being represented? These narratives need to be made public and accessible to everyone.

In the long run, for men, it simply makes good sense to join forces with like-minded people in this cause at this decisive moment. Good sense and personal happiness. I aged happily — and less — because feminism and age studies helped me walk past those shop windows. It's time for men to learn what women know about cultural resistance to age constructions, and teach what they know and haven't told. We'd all benefit from inventing the next strategies together.

NOTES

This essay is dedicated to Caroline Cross Chinlund and Stephen Chinlund.

[1]Therapists and midlife scholars also report these signs: see for example John A. B. McLeish, *The Ulyssean Adult* (Toronto: McGraw-Hill Ryerson, 1976), 2. On the whole there is remarkably little ethnography of male aging, and most important, a dearth of firsthand reports from men. I felt I could not use those that men friends and colleagues have shared with me without betraying their confidentiality. However, these private conversations have informed much of what I say about men in this essay. The approach I begin with — using the reports of women to gain some initial and oblique view of the subjective world of men — and many of my other methodological choices arise precisely from the dearth of written materials.

I would like to use this essay as a call for men to produce their own, multiple accounts. Women do not want to speak for the Other as men used to speak for them during the ages of resentment.

[2]Even sexuality, which seems so private, can be interpreted at most points only through concepts and values provided by the culture. This is shown in the lives of men by (for example) the work of G. J. Barker-Benfield, *The Horrors of the Half-Known Life* (Harper and Row, 1976) and Stephen Heath, *The Sexual Fix* (Macmillan, 1982).

[3]See Garry Trudeau, "Doonesbury," *The Boston Globe*, August 17, 1992, et. seq.

[4]*New Yorker*, August 19, 1985, 30.

[5]*New Yorker*, January 28, 1985, 27.

[6]The role of fiction in producing images of midlife men, and the relation of fiction to other popular and mass images would require a separate essay. In general, novels with midlife male protagonists assume readers who accept decline plots and decline tropes. John Updike, for example, who has been unfolding Harry Angstrom's life course for thirty years, could plausibly kill off the protagonist of his tetralogy — whom many men identify with — at age fifty-seven. Updike made Harry a Deteriorating Man beforehand: overweight, a compulsive nibbler. (He also made Harry's wife in her middle years newly fit and athletic.) For some sense of the ways in which midlife decline has been plotted, and the difficulties of writing an alternative genre, see my *Safe at Last in the Middle Years. The Invention of the Midlife Progress Novel* (University of California Press, 1988), Chapter Seven, and "The Deaths of Children and the Fear of Aging in Contemporary American Fiction," *Michigan Quarterly Review* (Winter 1992).

[7]As reported by Winifred Gallagher, several researchers associated with the MacArthur Foundation Research Network on Successful Midlife Development see "people prone to midlife crisis" as scoring "low on tests of introspection . . . and high in denial." "Myths of Middle Age," *The Atlantic Monthly*, May 1993, 34.

[8]Susan Sontag, "The Double Standard of Aging," *Psychology of Women. Selected Readings*, ed. Juanita H. Williams (New York: Norton, 1979), 462–478. This now reads as a chilling account of the way things were before there was any resistance, before any breaks in male superiority could be imagined. Many relationships continue to reproduce that model, of course.

[9]Lawrence Birken, *Consuming Desire. Sexual Science and the Emergence of a Culture of Abundance, 1871–1914* (Ithaca: Cornell University Press, 1988). Many historians of the turn-of-the-century are linking together changes in gender relations, the transition from a "productivist" to a "consumer" society, issues of social control,

and new sexological discourses. My contribution is to add age: specifically, to focus on the middle years as a zone where these forces and others intersect with special intensity contemporaneously.

[10]R. W. Connell, *Gender and Power: Society, The Person and Sexual Politics* (Stanford: Stanford University Press, 1987), 85. "My male body does not confer masculinity on me; it receives masculinity (or some fragment thereof) as its social definition" (83). Note Connell's astute use of the passive. What is received can be taken away. I would argue that age is relevant: masculine power is conferred at a certain age/stage and withdrawn at another.

[11]Jeff Ostroff, "Targeting the Prime-Life Consumer," *American Demographics* 13, #1 (January 1991), 30.

[12]Roger Thompson, "Baby Boom's Mid-Life Crisis," *Editorial Research Reports* 1, #1 (January 8, 1988), 3.

[13]On the age at which the pressures start, the uncertainty about when the midlife "begins," and the effects of this uncertainty, see Margaret Morganroth Gullette, "Rethinking Sexuality, the Midlife, and Aging," in progress.

[14]The binary (hairy/not so hairy) is supposed to mark proper masculinity in later life. Pushing hair to holy prominence in *Iron John* (Reading, MA: Addison-Wesley, 1990), Robert Bly insists that "what the psyche is asking for now is a new figure . . . a religious figure but a hairy one" (as opposed to "bald, ascetic"). See pp. 249, 248. Bly himself as pictured on the back of his book has quite a lot of (white) hair. Is the psyche of a bald man also asking for a hairy leader?

[15]Paul Rozin and April Fallon, "Body Image, Attitudes to Weight, and Misperceptions of Figure Preferences of the Opposite Sex: A Comparison on Men and Women in Two Generations," *Journal of Abnormal Psychology* 97, #3 (August 1988), 342–7. This rare two-generational family study included 97 fathers (M = 50.3 years) and 97 mothers (M = 46.5 years). 59% of the fathers, 60% of the daughters, and 67% of the mothers thought themselves considerably overweight, vs. only 33% of the sons. On the scale of responses – Dieting (often or almost always) – 50% of the fathers, 62% of the daughters and 73% of the mothers responded that they do; in comparison sons said they did so 33% of the time.

[16]As of 1986, according to one source, men were getting 95% of the hair transplants, 44% of the ear "revisions", 27% of the dermabrasions, 25% of the nose reshapings, 10% of the facelifts. John Camp, *Plastic Surgery. The Kindest Cut* (New York: Henry Holt, 1989), 224–5. "Statistics on the actual incidence of cosmetic surgery are virtually impossible to obtain"; likewise the gender ratio of users. But it is estimated that in 1988 more than 500,000 people in the United States had cosmetic surgery; one conservative estimate is that 90,000 of them were men. Diana Dull and Candace West, "Accounting for Cosmetic Surgery: The Accomplishment of Gender," *Social Problems* 38, #1 (February 1991), 55 and 54 n2.

[17]Carol Stocker, "The Male Makeover," *Boston Globe*, October 30, 1991, 63.

[18]My survey (*Academic Index*, 1986–91) found that the articles about men carried titles like "Want a Lift?" "More Males Having Aesthetic Surgery," "Now men too pumped to pump iron can turn up the volume with a set of pectoral implants." The articles about women, influenced by feminism, have titles about the dangers of silicone, the "Colonization of Women's Bodies," "Liposuction under Federal Review," "Fat Transplant Warning."

[19]Dull and West, "Accounting for Cosmetic Surgery," 66, 65. Although the authors wish to maintain that the double standard is still in full operation, their quotations

from the few men they included in the study support my argument about convergence.

[20]John Stoltenberg, *Refusing to Be A Man. Essays on Sex and Justice* (New York: Penguin, 1989), 99. Stoltenberg argues that men should think more conscientiously about the private relations of men and women in terms of politics, ethics, and justice.

[21]Private communication.

[22]Judy Foreman, "Drawing the fine line on Retin A," *Boston Globe*, November 23, 1992, 13, 15. Dr. Michael Greenwald pointed out in another article that the study linking balding and heart attacks was "financed by Upjohn Co., which makes minodoxil." Bob Hohler, "Medical News Taxes Patience of Many Doctors," *Boston Globe*, Feb. 28, 1993, 10.

[23]New studies (October, 1992) by M. Harvey Brenner of Johns Hopkins, and Mary Merva and Richard Fowles of University of Utah, estimate that bad economic times raise mortality rates from major diseases from 3 to 6 percent.

[24]Ed Koren, *New Yorker*, June 18, 1990, 41.

[25]Although attempts to sell women hormone treatments as an antidote to aging began early in the twentieth century, one of the landmark documents in the effort was Robert A. Wilson's text about the magic of estrogen-replacement "therapy," *Feminine Forever* (1966). To its credit, at the time the medical profession reacted strongly against the hyperbolic promotion. It has since weakened. See Margaret Morganroth Gullette, "Menopause as Magic Marker," forthcoming.

[26]Shifts in dress, aligned with changes in gender relations, were a subject for advanced thinkers in the first wave of feminism. See Mathilde and Matthias Vaerting, *The Dominant Sex. A Study in the Sociology of Sex Differentiation*, tr. Eden and Cedar Paul (George H. Doran, 1923), 119.

[27]Readers of "Femininity" will remember that it was actually "a man of about thirty" whom Freud stationed in the lucky developmental slot. See *The Standard Edition of the Complete Psychological Works*, edited and translated by James Strachey (London: Hogarth Press; New York: Norton), Vol. XXII, 134–135.

[28]Robert Bly's extremely popular book, *Iron John*, for instance, tells a historical narrative whose outcome is that fathers — spoken of as "the father-table, the groundwater," and "the salt" of life, by Bly — "get no respect" from their sons. But the text doesn't recognize that current age and generational issues might create part of the author's need to write the family narrative as he did. Bly doesn't cite scholarly work in men's studies and theoretical work on the social construction of masculinity, and men who read his work rarely seem to know about this other contemporary material. But age is not a concern here either. Even a quite brilliant theorist of gender like R. W. Connell writes as if the "social definition" of a man were fixed (at some undefined point in life) and remained fixed without alteration over the life course.

[29]"The decline in the male remarriage rate has typically been overlooked, because the rate is so much higher than that for women." Frances Goldscheider, "The Aging of the Gender Revolution. What Do We Know and What Do we Need to Know?" *Research on Aging 12*, #4 (December 1990), 542, 538. Goldscheider compares remarriage rates in 1970 and 1980.

[30]A chapter of my work in progress, *Midlife Fictions*, treats "The Invention of Male Midlife Sexual Decline, 1900–1935." Another chapter is called "Sex-Starved and Doomed to Disappointment; or, The Post-sexual Woman."

[31]Thus, the title of a study of the nineteenth-century medical exploitation of women, *For Her Own Good* (1978), by Barbara Ehrenreich and Deirdre English.

32For a contrary view see Alex Comfort: "The astounding resilience of human common sense against the anxiety makers is one of the really cheering aspects of history." *The Anxiety Makers. Some Curious Preoccupations of the Medical Profession.* (London: Nelson, 1967), 113. Much has happened since 1967 to deflate optimism in the particular field of age.

33Cited in Janet Zollinger Giele, "Adulthood as Transcendence of Age and Sex," in *Themes of Work and Love in Adulthood,* ed. Neil J. Smelser and Erik H. Erikson (Harvard University Press, 1980), 166.

34Giele, *Ibid.,* 167.

MARIO WIRZ

INBETWEEN ZONE: LIFE IN NEUKÖLLN

I no longer find sheep in the pasture of my night. Not one little bitty lamb that I might count in my hunger for sleep. The virus wolf has devoured them all during the last five years. One sheep after the other. Meals for one thousand eight hundred twenty-five nights. Morpheus is a capricious shepherd. This night, too, he celebrates his shepherd's hours with others. And why indeed should he want to embrace the horny infected buck who now lies on his bed sleepless and like a bookkeeper counts his T-4 cells? From one to four hundred twenty. That's how many there were at last examination three weeks ago. As late as a year ago my immune system disposed over a proud army of six hundred eighty resistance fighters. My virus wolf is voracious. From one to four hundred twenty. And once again from the beginning. Foolish numbers circus. Outside of my window snow is falling black and white. The descending snowflakes are my decreasing T-4 cells. By now, perhaps, I no longer have more than four hundred or three hundred ninety. Hysteric numbers acrobatics. You must fight and gain time. I am sure that soon they will find a remedy, says Andreas, who was no longer able to take my nightmares. My night is not his night. Now he sleeps at the side of Frank, who is 23 years old and who can talk about the future without stuttering.

With blond sentences that do not suddenly darken and drop into a bottomless abyss. Andreas has deserted me.

A cloyingly sweet sobby melancholy sits in my head and colors every thought. I don't want it, this bitterness which oozes from all my pores. Better to throw vases against the wall in raging jealousy than this larmoyant passivity which again and again dictates the same sentences to my cage. I have been condemned to understand Andreas. His panic. His fleeing. I am a threat to him, and he flees to those whose mortality leaps to the eye less insistently. When Andreas embraces me he embraces his fear. Of AIDS. Of disease. Of death. I understand Andreas, but my understanding is hell. Fire and Ice. I burn to death when I inhale, and I freeze to death when I exhale. Icicles grow into my heart which rebels and flails. From one to four hundred twenty. The small multiplication table of hope that weighs heavier than the fear. I am sick and tired of hoping. I am sick and tired of again and again trying out an optimistic posture, of bearing the unbearable. I am sick and tired of the phony endurance slogans with which in the morning I sentence myself to live through the day. With the hollow jolliness of radio anchorpersons. Get up! Don't let yourself go! Pull yourself together! Carry on! Head high! I am sick and tired of the many vitamins that I mercilessly stuff into myself. A kiwi fruit, a glass of carrot juice; another multivitamin capsule just to make sure, and I feel strong enough to uproot a tree that I have never planted. To do everything so as to feel strong enough to fool myself and others. Daily comedy of confidence. When darkness falls, the only thing that helps is vitamin A as in alcohol. The virginal carrot juice of the morning joins the sinful fluid of the evening in fraternal union. Of course, I am not an alcoholic. I only drink a bit regularly in order to appease the specters spooking in my head. I am sick and tired of being tired. From one to four hundred twenty.

The phone does not ring. It is night, and I invent a young man who cuts the telephone cord. Snip, snip. A phone that cannot ring makes no noise. I lie in my bed, sleepless, and the bed becomes a ship that sinks in my storm.

My T-4 cell count drops, and I drop deeper and deeper until at the bottom of my nocturnal sea a man catches me who, together with me, side by side, swims against the current. For a moment we breathe together, even into the fifth wind direction, and then my companion vanishes, and the sea washes me back onto the shore. My pathos does not save me. My bed still is in the room, and I am still in bed. Nothing has changed. Mercilessly the things insist on staying in their places. The couch. The desk. The chair. The shelf. The red touch-tone telephone that eyes me silently and malevolently. Red-plated turtle. Nobody tears my heart out of my body. Nor does it break. Bravely it beats and makes it through the night. That is all. I lie in bed and drive the young man crazy. Quickly I fictionalize myself from the second to the fifth floor and make the young man jump out of the window. A nice corpse for Andreas, who loves death and passion only in operas. The high C of my fear of death does not fill the evening. Are you again having one of your nocturnal hysterias? Pull yourself together! Don't you see that everything is all right, he would say if I now were to phone him. Andreas is crazy about Wagner's nightmares. I shall dedicate an operatic drama from Neukölln to him. From the second floor of my little back alley flat in the apartment complex. Da capo for a beautiful corpse! My rage is a metaphor in which I myself don't believe.

Perhaps I really am positive. I don't want to know, says Andreas, and strews confetti on the bomb. Did the virus teach me anything new? What have I learned in the school of my terrible fears? I too want to have nothing to do with DEATH. Get away from me and from this night and from this room. To leave the lonely prisoner behind me who lies in bed and dreams of Andreas.

To get up and prevent the light in my head from going out. My body obeys me and, well behaved, slips into the long gray underpants that with gray sullenness watch over my health. I cannot afford either vanities or colds. Relieved, the underwear disappears in the corduroy pants. The black Nicki sweater is a present given me by Andreas, but I forbid myself detailed memories. Turn up the central heating and be grateful that my one-room apartment was done over three years ago. The other tenants had their old coal stoves ripped out to get more space, but my stove stayed in its place, like everything else. For the last five years I have dreaded change. I cling to everything familiar as if thereby I could intimidate the enemy, time. My cold stove by the bed tells me a story, too, that concerns Andreas and me and the many nights during which we fell asleep together, but I am not listening. I could go to my gay bar around the corner and get tanked up. Let my wings sag with the other nocturnal birds and twitter with them while tieing one on. I could raid my condom supply and run to the nearest t-room in order to reel off the usual film. Guys who dream of sailors fool around with guys who are looking for a cowboy. Or at least a truck driver. Night after night the "unheard prayers" of rickety poem writers and romantic clerks end up in the toilet bowl of reality. I could defy the cold and roam through the park to hunt me some horny stag. In the moon's benevolent light to transform a willing frog into a fairy tale prince and to hope that he will manage the same metamorphosis also with me. But in this night I probably would find no more than a fat snowman to melt away in my arms.

What has changed in the five years since I have known that I, perhaps, perhaps not, but nonetheless probably . . . ? I have not been able to make my peace with what I consider my life. No philosophy that tames my disaster. No religion to defuse the bomb. My sex now is safe, but what is not safe are the days and nights. Every hour a mine field. To sit and to stare and to smoke. My room. My cage. My cell. My grave. Despotic insomnias that almost always reel off the same film in the movie theater of my head, or else bouts of wild compulsion to sleep that set in even as I am shaving. The razor blade a weapon in front of the stranger in the mirror who declares war on this day also. I lather the truths in my face and feel myself get tired standing in front of the clown's mask that lets the curtain go down. Insomnia or hypnomania, rarely anything in between. I am reeling from one extreme to the other not knowing which I fear more. The lack of energy that forbids even the most timid activity and drags me to bed, or else that panicky wakefulness that chains me to the images of my night. My room. My cage. The repetition of the retrieval of the repetition.

When worried friends ask about my day, I often invent a biography for the hours just so that I won't say the same things over and over again: I got up. Took a shower. Ate breakfast, and then, then I felt so weak and went back to bed. My room. My prison.

Days crazy with sleep, in which I sleep everything away so as to find everything again in my dreams. Monday or Wednesday or Friday. I breakfast with myself and try not only to be positive but also to think positive. An alert glance at the flowers I bought myself in order to appease my capricious soul.

Trash cans clang. Mrs. Schmidt above me screams something out of the window. Somebody runs down the stairs whistling. I lift the coffee cup as if it were a heavy weight and fall into the first great tiredness. Come on, take a walk! says the 34-year old man in his cage in a cheerful voice. Do something! Pull yourself together! Don't let yourself go that much! Work on your theater play! Give the day some order, an aim! My tyrannical fatigue ignores my commands and throws me on the bed. Is it my damaged immune system that tires me to my states of exhaustion, is it the confusion of my feelings? I deny myself to the day and flee under the covers. Bed the never-changing drumbeat in my head on the mussed-up pillows. Mrs. Schmidt and the gulf war and the deadly headlines of the living are outside in front of my window. You must gain time. You must fight, says Andreas, but once again tiredness has defeated me. Monday or Wednesday or

. . . I go into sleep as if into a trap. Hospital dreams. Oxygen tent dreams. White smock dreams. Karpos dreams. Dreams connected to plastic tubes. Rubber glove dreams. Cemetery dreams. "To die, to sleep / No more, and by a sleep to say we end / The heart-ache and the thousand natural shocks / That flesh is heir to" says Hamlet, but I don't die, and nothing is at an end. My tirednesses rehearse death with a slowness that is due to my dulled intellect. For the last five years I have been surviving myself. No living and no dying. I accommodate myself in the in-between zone and learn the uncertainties by heart. Day after day I shave a shadow. Spook around as a ghost even while still alive. Am a well-trained ghost. With a genteel smile and well-mannered habits. No revolt against the flowered wallpaper in my hell.

No outcry that might frighten the neighbor. Day after day I clothe the catastrophe in a fresh shirt and take it out on a walk. No stench that might betray me. No messiness to unmask me. I am pulling myself together. I don't let myself go. I carry on. Sapped of strength but well-behaved. Weak but with a freshly washed neck. My polite silence resides behind brushed teeth. People like me. I am a well-adjusted young man who soon will croak. Nothing further. Sometimes I design a new image of myself and of the possibility that in an extreme situation I might conduct myself differently. Design of a rebellious hour. Curtain up for a young man who accepts his fate heroically. Applause for a courageous one who breaks out of his chains and with his truth grows beyond himself. End of the dream. And I awake into my printed realities. Now it is night. I relieve myself where for once I would like to piss all around me. My little old mother can be proud even of her son's corpse.

I have instigated no revolt. Not even found a new question. I have left the lies in their proper order and have not turned anything upside down. Nothing has been changed by the voracious death that is now smacking his lips while nibbling at me. A piece of raspberry candy for someone who spoils nobody's good mood. Let us have fun. A big brownie point for one who has learned his lesson. In my next life I will die of leukemia. Lung cancer would be a decent alternative too. But perhaps by then AIDS will have established itself. Rock Hudson took the first step toward lending the shame a bit of glamour and dignity. Perhaps even AIDS will one day be numbered among the causes of death that can be mentioned in decent company. Like the heart attack, which is the privilege of the successful.

*

Did you tell anyone else that you are infected? The embarrassed fear in the eyes of my 75-year-old mother who is thinking of the people in Frankenberg. Of the mighty lawn dwarves in the idyllic gardens who have reared me too. Bad enough that the illegitimate son is gay. A drag queen. A transvestite. A cocksucker. An assfucker. A faggot who offers his ass. And now AIDS-infected to boot. A juicy sensation to spice up a small-town uneventfulness. A bit of pepper and paprika for the bored people in the beautifully decorated Tudor houses. AIDS is even more exciting than a divorce in the neighborhood or an abortion. In my head too the lawn dwarves are spooking. Failure, they cry. Unemployment insurance recipient! Gay, infected swine!

I sit on the couch and give myself poor grades. An E for lack of success. An E for my crummy one-room apartment in Neukölln. An E for my weakness. An E for my fear. An E for my bankrupt existence.

To hell with my mother and with Frankenberg. To hell with my hatred, which I am still forcing into handsome costumes. The ashtray is spilling over. I ought to smoke less and get myself a cat instead. Or a canary.

Now I am sitting on the couch smoking my lungs away. Does not matter any more. Maybe that is the freedom the Marlboro man talks about. The first and last adventure. Maybe death is an American cowboy who will shoot me in a gun duel at dawn. With a cigarette stub in his mouth and a Robert Redford smile. The phone does not ring. Andreas is sleeping with Frank. I must learn to take that. I have lousy cards in this game. Frank is the new Knave of Hearts. He shakes out his laughter like an ace from the sleeve. His blond harmlessness that makes me the envious loser.

Frank does not have any night sweat compelling him to change his T-shirt several times. No discharges separating him from Andreas. When Frank sweats, that is a sweat he shares with Andreas. No swollen lymph nodes to transform a love story into a history of illness. I am sitting on the couch and stare and smoke. The young man has jumped out of the window, and I am so sapped of strength that I could re-invent him into my room this night. I think of Andreas as of a deserter. He has fled and is abandoning me in my war against fear. You must fight and gain time. Goddamned crybaby. I sit beside myself and watch myself indulge in self-pity. I have had it with the heroic postures that I have trained myself to assume. I have had it with the false show of bravery that I act out for myself and the others. I have had it with my phony serenity. I have had it with my armored jolliness that forces every pain into a witticism. I am not the cheerful postcard that I write to my mother in Frankenberg so that she won't worry so much. Still the guilt-ridden son who refuses to speak his anger. I write to my mother as to a stranger, but I do write to her. My mother, too, profits from the chronic understanding for all things that I construct for myself. If the virus does not kill me, I will be killed by my understanding. I am not the sovereign ex-lover who is trying with clever remarks to receive loving attention from Andreas who expects intelligent sentences from me. I find it awesome how you deal with the situation, says Andreas, and asks me for the bill. Reassured, he pays for the meal to which he has invited me and goes back to Frank. Andreas harbors a protective liking for me, and I am not proud enough to refuse such alms. We meet regularly, and I try hard to play my role without forgetting the script. I don't allow myself tears or other disturbing eruptions of feelings.

It is night, and in front of my window thick flakes are falling. The central heating is chugging along gently, and that is not an unfriendly noise in the quiet of my room. I am sitting on the couch and I am alive. So far, the illness has not yet set in. To be sure, the virus wolf howls through my blood aggressively, but he has not yet poised himself for the deadly leap.

Early next week the AZT treatment begins. I had wished to get along without AZT through 1990, and I succeeded. No excessive wishes. Maybe I will tolerate the medicine well. In small dosages the risk of side-effects is negligible. Stefan has been taking AZT for a year, and his immune status has improved. The danger that I will develop resistance against AZT too early is something I have to take in the bargain. I have learned to live with that danger for the last five years. Why do I now think of Norbert, who also has been positive for five years and still has nine hundred twenty T-4 cells? His immune status is only minimally below the normal limit. Competitive thinking even in disaster. Arthur still has seven hundred and sixty T-4 cells, and Tom eight hundred twenty. In all cases that I know, the values vary, sometimes up, sometimes down. In my case they fall with stubborn continuity. What is really insulting is the calculability with which my counts go down not only continuously but in increasingly voracious downward increments. All this with a linearity that does not at all fit in with my chaotic history. Jörg swears by ozone therapy, and Marcus preaches the healing capacities of Vitamin C. Klaus believes in the power of the soul. Everyone creates his own magic rituals in order to escape the paralyzing feeling of powerlessness. I no longer give my credulous attention to every charlatan and miracle healer. I have stopped going through every newspaper and every brochure to look for promising new rumors that nourish my hopes for two weeks and then be even more ample food for the ensuing disappointment.

Perhaps I ought to examine alternative therapy more carefully, but I have decided to rely on the helplessness of my physician. The timid glances in the waiting room that is different from all other waiting rooms. They speak their silence into the newspaper or stare down on their shoes while their eyes like cameras catch the other guy's every movement. Sometimes a flu virus sits between the AIDS patients, insouciantly silent. Or it happens that someone whose illness has erupted visibly tells a funny story to his companion and spreads terrible merriment. Most of them have the certainty of death written into their faces. We are sitting in the same boat, but through our silence we place ourselves back into our own homes.

The dying takes place behind drawn curtains. Secretly, softly, but in well-bred manner. Only few put up a fight. Most of them croak in the anonymity of some clinic or return to their village where honorable mothers and fathers falsify the death of their gay son. And I? For five years I have been cheating myself around my sentence. I write boulevard comedies as if I was sitting in a box of chocolates. I too am a deserter. Run away from my topic. I am gay. I am positive. I call myself an author. Not without that disquiet in the stomach region every fourflusher is familiar with. I write boulevard comedies. I am a clown who jumps through flaming hoops smack into the grateful applause given by the lawn dwarves. Once again I stylize myself into sugarcoated poses. I am no clown but an uptight gay bluenose who has not reflected sufficiently.

Another cigarette. The spots on my right arm demonstrate the sensitivity of my skin. Nothing else.

No karposi. My neighbor with the expensive music boxes is asleep tonight. No noise to entertain my insomnia. No loudness to divert me from the buzzing in my head. I am scared of the quiet. The radiator no longer chugs. Not even Mrs. Deter's cat is crying today in the backyard. She has found her tom. No alcohol in the house. Now I regret my sudden bout of rationality. I know the resolution I made. No more getting stinko in my apartment. No more celebrations with my irresponsible bottle pals. Three, four mugs of beer in the dive, but no more alcohol at home. No more sherry. Tender-loving comforter of my afternoons. A few glasses, and everything weighed lighter. Pretty soon I needed half a bottle in order to tolerate a brief afternoon. Quit it now! No more gin. Three glasses, and for a few hours I lost my tyrannic memory. No more wine. I want to learn to take my sentence. Don't want to be too easy a prey for death. Dear God, I don't believe in you, but do give me a little more time. My two teddy bears are sitting on top of the old tiled stove. They were a present to the two of us from Andreas' mother, but the ex-companion of my life did not wish to acknowledge his infantile side so obviously. Both bears found refuge on top of my tiled stove. Andreas, do you remember our bear talk? Fiep, when we were so sad, and rghhh when we were longing for each other. I the Big-bear. Also Dumbbear and Wildbear. Goldpaw and Honeybear. Biggrowl and Littlegrowl. What is left of the two of us? Two orphaned bears on top of the tiled stove.

One a little lighter, the other a little darker. Sweet intimacy à deux. Opposites embracing. Together they keep vigil over the nursery of the 34-year old man who, with luck, will turn thirty-five in December. Infantility wrinkled with age. The small lion on the bookshelf helps to administer the lost kingdom. He is too young to put the grownups' spooks to flight, but he too guards the dreams dreamed by the erstwhile child who forgot his actual childhood in order to make room for a poetic fiction. How many childhoods I have invented! Often they last no longer than a short story, but my memory has always been designed so as to remember a fiction better than a fact. How many biographies I adopted, how many memories of non-existing marvelous fathers! Did I not have the right to correct a false reality? Forgive me, Mama. Not every hour needs to be corrected. You walked through the streets of the small-town boobs erect, at your side the illegitimate child. The bastard. You did not allow anyone to declare your last happiness a disgrace. All the many Protestant and Catholic monsters who expected the daughter of a decent family to lower her eyes and be ashamed for having loved once more at the age of forty. Forgive me for sometimes feeling contempt for you because of your fear of the hypocrites and church-goers. After all, I feared them too, that pious mob. You did not teach me to sabotage the fraudulent rules of their game.

"One has to blend in!" was the sentence you inscribed in my rebellious heart. I wish that now I could dedicate my resistance against this lesson to you. But I preferred to repress these things and to live in a phantom world. How can I resent your not having tossed bombs into the hypocrites' idyllic gardens? Before the noses drop off the lawn dwarves, we ourselves prefer to fall off the tightrope. But only on condition that we will be dead when we hit the ground of reality. There is nothing for which I can be angry at you, Mama. You never got out of the small town. In contrast to me. And I have managed to get no further than this couch in this room in this night. Foolish heroics of a chainsmoker. At my side two bears and a lion.

So there I sit on top of my bomb, fearful, and watch that it doesn't explode. I do everything to make sure that my neighbors won't learn anything. I have just barely managed to more or less stand by my gayness. Would old Mrs. Schmidt above me write a letter to the apartment house management demanding that the infected guy on the second floor get kicked out of his flat? Mrs. Schmidt, an eighty-year-old German woman who spends her time calling the cops when someone turns the music on too loud. Especially when this someone comes from Turkey. Beware of the eighty-year old women and men of Germany. But I am also scared of the young ones. I am frightened by the "sound instincts of the people" to which I submit with fear and silence.

I am that friendly gay person from the side wing who three times a week goes shopping for ailing Mrs. Stiller, ground floor right. Besides, I am considered an artist who once in a while even gets into the newspaper. In such a case the "sound instincts of the people" may indeed close one eye once in a while. I have made it easy for all of them. More macho than John Wayne, I amble across the back yard, as if walking to the garbage cans were a ride across the prairie.

I don't wear dirndl dresses or pleated skirts but a leather jacket that emphasizes my "masculinity," which I believe I owe to myself and to the world.

Once a year I allow the drag queen inside me to indulge in unre-strained screeching in some dimly lit gay bar. During the remaining 364 days, my internal he-man stuffs the drag queen's mouth. Tears the garish laughter from her face and sets a lean, hard smile into the right-hand corner of the mouth. A bit of James Bond, a bit of Rambo. The guy does his job thoroughly. It is easy to intimidate the fearful queen. Quickly she stops gushing about Liz Taylor and reciting poetry. Dutifully she practices speaking in monosyllables and looks cool like the other men. Once in a while her gestures get out of control, and her hands flutter away from her like excited birds, but the he-man quickly revokes the involuntary confession. Hands into the pants pockets or placed into a restful position. Stop that womanish gesticulating. What is most difficult to tame is that lecherous glance. These hungry eyes betray everything, this longing leer. So she lowers her eyes. Quits staring at other men. Quits sending distress signals. Practices, in the sweat of brave self-abnegation, the look of detachment, of boredom. Looks satiated rather than hungry. Denies herself ladylike liqueurs, which she prefers drinking, and orders hard stuff. Lifts the beer mug like a man and drains half of it. Another vodka, another beer. Laughs at the stupidest joke and is a good pal. Discusses the gulf war and has a masculine opinion. Everybody wants peace, but too much pacifism is counterindicated. Whoever is attacked must defend himself. Strike back. The drag queen would much rather be watching a Doris Day movie, but the he-man prevails.

How exciting the war on television. Thrilling like a soccer transmission, says the drag queen even though she can't stand soccer. But that is something she should not let every Tom, Dick and Harry know. In the case of Boris Becker she need not pretend. She really liked him. Honest! Didn't she just now let out too feminine a giggle? Quickly another hard-boiled statement about the gulf war. Air raid and ground offensive are muscular words in her mouth, macho words, every letter a clenched fist. Even a warm brother* can think like a cold warrior once the training is successful. The secret rapists of women are good animal tamers.

What is bothering our little Miss Sensitive now? laughs the athletic coach and gives the other boys a wink. I am standing in the gymnasium crying. I cry often. I am a mimosa. I am prissy. I am a crybaby. I am a mama's boy. I have not yet learned my lesson. We must not tease Miss Volker so much, shouts Uwe, the class spokes-

---

*Warm brother" is a German slang term for a male homosexual. (Translator's note)

man, whom they all admire. I too. A wave of laughter crushes me. I am thirteen years old and do not yet know what it is that prevents me from being like the other boys. Soft as pudding is the judgment of my schoolmates. I have no grit in my bones.

He lacks the firm hand of a father, say the neighbors. I am thinking of Charly's beer-guzzler father who beats him regularly. Petra's slimy savings bank-inspector father who licks the boots of every title and every high income. Soft-as-a-pudding runs out of the gymnasium. Runs to Mama who comforts him. Something happens in me that I don't understand. During the night I meet my enemy Uwe in my dreams, and he allows me to touch him.

"Let me ride piggy back, Daddy!" cries a blond TV movie boy, and a blond TV movie daddy laughs fondly and goes into a crouch so that the little boy can sit on his shoulders. "Higher! Higher, Daddy!" cries the same boy in another scene on the swing, and Daddy laughs fondly and gives the swing a push. "Higher! Higher!" Daddy goes with his son to the zoo and buys him an ice cream cone. Daddy tells his son a good-night story and tenderly strokes his hair. The loving smile never disappears from his face. Such fathers exist only in the movies, says my mother and gives me a guilty side glance.

It is Sunday, and we sit on the couch and watch television. Mother and son. An old married couple. My mother puts her arm around me, but I withdraw from her touch. Got to pee, I say coolly and run to the john where I can bawl. I am fourteen years old and am bawling because of a kitschy TV movie. Sissy! is what I am called by the other boys, who at this moment are playing soccer on the athletic field. I am trying to hide my fear of them and to strut about in the very same manly and hard-boiled manner, but they see through me. I imitate their loud gestures, but then I look like a lousy actor. I don't belong among them. I am soft as pudding and sit on the couch with Mama. I stuff candy and chocolates into my mouth, and one look at my rotten teeth unmasks the softie. Uwe has teeth almost as beautiful and white as those of the TV movie daddy. He laughs like one who is scared of nothing.

"Let me ride piggy-back, Daddy!" I am thinking of all the many ugly and self-satisfied small-town papas with their petty-bourgeois family bliss. Papa, Mama, child and dog. What's for dinner tomorrow? The same as every Wednesday. What's playing on the boob tube? A rerun of a crime story. But that doesn't matter. I have already forgotten who the murderer was.

Papa, Mama, child and dog. They no longer have anything to say to each other, but they stay together. For the sake of the children. For the sake of the dog. For the sake of the little house. For the sake of the lawn dwarves. The woman next door to us hates her husband, and her husband hates her. But they won't get a divorce. They need their hatred like air to breathe. If you get an A on your paper, you may wish yourself something, says the papa to his son, knowing that his promise will not entail any expenditure of money. If you bring home one more E you will be grounded for two weeks, shouts Mama, with red spots on her neck, knowing that her intimidated boy will divert her from her hatred of her husband for two weeks. Child rearing means revenge. Why should her son be happier than the unhappy Mama?

"Higher! Higher!" When I was a child, I used to marry my mother to all the handsome and young men of the town without regard to the age gap. Now I am fourteen and almost grown up. You are my little man, my mother often says with a loving smile. I want the loving TV movie daddy smile. Everything okay? calls my mother and gently raps on the door. Everything okay! I call back and open the water faucet so that my mother won't hear that her little man is sitting on the john bawling. From the couch in Frankenberg to the couch in my back alley flat in Neukölln. My room. My cell. My cage. TV movie daddies are still able to make me cry. Perhaps I will agree to get a cable connection after all. Tonight I would prefer a late movie in the television to the program in my head.

My night is not the night of Uwe, who at this moment probably is asleep by the side of his wife. In sync with himself and with the laws of normalcy. The superior force of the Uwe men. Uwe deeds and Uwe jokes. Uwe heroes and Uwe victors. Not torn to pieces and not stirred up. Harmless and invulnerable. Volker! Come and do an imitation of Miss Wagner! That is an order, and Volker obeys. Volker jumps through the hoop and apes the anile math teacher so they all laugh so hard their bellies ache. Regrettably no one dies laughing. No respite for the comic. And now do Theiss! Class spokesman Uwe gives the class clown a terse order. Oh yes, and now Theiss! cries the public and laughs on credit. Volker with a lisp puts the uptight German teacher on the stage and resolves to include a new number in his repertoire. Perhaps the asthmatic art teacher who always snorts like a locomotive. Or the heavily made-up English teacher who struts across the schoolyard like a fashion model.

Uwe laughs. That is a good sign and means that later in the gymnasium Volker perhaps will have nothing to fear. No terribly nasty remarks at his expense. Nerd and goof already sound like familiar caresses to his ear. The others know who calls the tune and adapt their mean epithets to Uwe's caprices. If he is in a friendly mood, the others are gentle also. Even more than the physical education period Volker fears the end of the hour when they all take a shower while he awkwardly steals out of the dressing room. Is Miss Volker bashful again? This is a nickname that Uwe who in good mood now slaps his thighs has hanged on him. Your Theiss is groovy, he calls, and the clown takes a bow.

What do I care about Uwe, who may now be tossing in his bed unable to sleep because the neighbor has sired a gifted child. Owns a faster car and a bigger house. What do I care about Uwe men and their ambitions? My night. My room. My couch. My overflowing ashtray. My T-4 cells. My insomnia. Again and again the old clichés terrorize me. Those self-assured TV movie men. The jolly picture magazine heroes. The daring commercial movie Tarzans. With broad-shouldered opinions and well-trained averageness.

What is the matter with our little Miss Sensitive? Even today I am threatened by that rumor which calls itself "masculinity." To act like a man. Not so hesitant and irresolute. To hit the table with the fist like a man. Not so sensitive and soft. Not so prissy and excessively vulnerable. To walk like a man. Not so wiggly and loose-limbed. To sit like a man. Not with one leg over the other. Not so queen-like, not so gay. To talk like a man. A man—a word. Not so flowery and arty. Be brief. To the point. The bare facts, and no unnecessary details. To feel joy like a man. A clear gesture, and that's it. Not so exaggerated and euphoric. Not so emotional. To feel pain like a man. Without losing one's composure. Stunned but in control. Not to become hysterical, not to weep, not to scream.

The animal training has been successful. Deep is my voice and firm my handshake. I never cry in public. I appear forceful and dynamic. I borrow the gestures of so-called normalcy and execute them like a rented tuxedo. Why, you don't look gay at all, friends say sometimes, and for a long time I was perverse enough to take this as a compliment.

How should I interpret my secret masochistic longing for those who deny me? Dreams woven out of self-hatred and inferiority complexes. As long as I am not like the other men, at least I pay them tribute by wanting and admiring them. Aping them and even trying to outdo them. Gays have to be especially good in whatever they do so that "mankind" will forgive them for being different. I have not begotten a child, but at least I am an interesting artist. Entertaining and witty enough to make you have a fit. I have built no house, but at least I am an empathetic and understanding friend who is liked by all women. I can confide in you about things that otherwise I would never tell a man, says my friend Sigrun. I have never planted a tree, but at least I practice the art of being a "nice guy." So friendly and so helpful, say the neighbors. My gay friend Norbert cleans the stairs with devoted thoroughness and basks in the approving glances of the super's wife, who refers to homosexuals as vermin. Norbert has scrubbed himself a place in her heart and can sleep peacefully. A pedestal for the image of my enemy that shall remind me every day that I must make an effort . Ever-present and all-powerful are the norms of the Uwe man. Even in my most arcane dreams the animal trainers crack their whips. I jump through the flaming hoop and vie for the applause of the crowd. You have got to adapt yourself, said my mother, and her sentence multiplied and formed metastases in every corner of my soul, which on occasions I allow myself. Even in my sexual fantasies I renounce individuality and try to achieve exchangeability. Sometimes I dream of a gay anti-world that is searching for its own values and does not so eagerly and subserviently ape the masculinity rituals of the heterosexual majority. It is night, and my head is on fire. My nocturnal fever is something on which by now I can rely.

At times it surprises me already in the early afternoon. My fever so eager for recognition. Climbs up and down and demands my attention. The magic of numbers. Just above 38 centigrade or far above 38. Again and again the same ritual. The gutsy coolness of the thermometer under my armpit, hypochondriac pleasures of one who is ailing. To sit and to stare and to allow my capricious fever to make a fool of me. Climbs up and down and jealously guards my hours. With all sorts of tricks. Roars through my blood. Steams in my ears. Makes it snow in my head. Burns behind the eyes. Makes me sleepy-lazy. Forces me to my knees. By now I know your repertory, my narcissistic fever. Don't try too hard, tonight the thermometer stays in the drawer. Ever-present and all-powerful, my fever, even on feverless days, ever-present in such cases in my astonishment over the fact that my thermometer indicates a normal temperature, all-powerful in the expectation of the following day. Compulsive counting game. My virus is a full-time job. Profession: HIV-positive. Is there anything else? My room. My cage. I watch the news show and current events and simulate an interest, but the virus is stronger and keeps reducing me to my AIDS reality. AIDS words and AIDS thoughts. AIDS dreams and AIDS feelings. The AIDS merry-go-round is turning.

A as in angst
I as in inevitable
D as in dark
S as in succumb.

And if once in a while I succeed in leaving my topic in my room, it will triumphantly greet me at the counter of some gay bar. Have you heard, Christian died last week. Which Christian? Well, the fat one who would always strip when he was drunk. Ah, yes, that Christian. They say that toward the end he was reduced to mere skin and bones, terrible.

Ever-present and all-powerful, the fever and the nocturnal sweating. The swollen lymph nodes and the T-4 cells. Mario, age 34, is sitting on the couch remembering Volker. What did it get me that I chucked my name and constructed myself a Mario identity? Nothing was to serve as a reminder of Volker, the class clown and bastard. Volker the crybaby. The mimosa. Volker soft and prissy. Little Miss Sensitive Volker. Mario was strong and self-assured. Generated admiration and was loved by all. Mario, my fictitious alter ego, my pubertarian hero, was to be Volker's avenger and was to show it to that goddamned little town. To the hypocrites and the guardians of normalcy. . . . Curtain up for Mario!!!

Mario, actor and poet, a shining star on the horizon of new names. Stupid Frankenberg was to grow pale in the face of my glory, to ask forgiveness for every humiliation. Have you heard? That Volker has become a famous author. Calls himself Mario. Who would have thought that faggot bastard would ever be so successful?

Even my ambition was an open wound. AIDS, an acquired immune deficiency. I have a notion that as early as in Frankenberg the lawn dwarves infected me. Soft as pudding, said Uwe, and the statement was poisoned and tasted of death. Bastard, murmured the neighbors, and their whisper transmitted the deadly virus. You are my little husband, said my mother, and her sentence strangled me. My death sprouted in the idyllic gardens, blossomed behind quarrelsome fences, peered out from behind the neighbors' clean curtains, grinned in the saleswomen's cunning friendliness. Brayed rudely in the other boys' voices that I tried to imitate. Murmured through the streets of Frankenberg and giggled. I bet that Volker is a queer. He walks so funny and talks so funny. And altogether he is so funny. Wrote on the blackboard with white chalk: One must adapt! One must not appear different!

One must be like all the others!

Translated from the German by
Alfred G. Meyer.

SUSAN BORDO

READING THE MALE BODY

> Through concentration to projection into the
> beyond. The male projection of erection and ejacula-
> tion is the paradigm for all cultural projection and con-
> ceptualization — from art and philosophy to fantasy,
> hallucination and obsession. . . . Male urination really
> *is* a kind of accomplishment, an arc of transcendence.
> A woman merely waters the ground she stands on.
> Male urination is a form of commentary. . . A male dog
> marking every bush on the block is a graffiti artist,
> leaving his rude signature with each lift of the leg.
> Women, like female dogs, are earthbound squatters.
> Camille Paglia, *Sexual Personae*
> (Vintage, 1991, 20–21)

> "It's just a piece of meat!"
> Kidnapped and handcuffed black soldier Jody,
> trying to convince Fergus to help him urinate, in
> Neil Jordan's *The Crying Game*

Luce Irigaray, in describing woman as "the sex which is not one,"
implicitly counterposes the radical plurality of female sexuality to the
sex which *is* "one," the sex which is man. Because Irigaray's dichot-
omy is not based on a notion of biological difference (or even on
differences in the lived experiences of men and women) but rather on
sexual difference as it has been constructed by a Western, phallocentric imagination, the identification of "man" with phallic unity is
justified. But actual *men*, even men who are unambivalent in their
acceptance of male domination as the natural order of things, are *not*
"one." For actual men are not timeless symbolic constructs, they are
biologically, historically, and experientially embodied beings; the singular, constant, transcendent rule of the phallus is continually challenged by this embodiment. Crystallizing this tension into its most

succinct form: The phallus is haunted by the penis. And the penis is most definitely *not* "one." It has no unified social identity (but is fragmented by ideologies of race and ethnicity). Rather than exhibiting constancy of form, it is perhaps the most visibly mutable of bodily parts; it evokes the temporal not the eternal. And far from maintaining a steady will and purpose, it is mercurial, temperamental, unpredictable. Of course, it is always possible to bestow phallic majesty onto even the most banal of the penis's possibilities, as in the Paglia quote. This is an old, stale story. Far fresher insights can be gained by reading the male body through the window of its vulnerabilities rather than the dense armor of its power — from the "point of view" of the mutable, plural penis rather than the majestic, unitary phallus. This is not to deny the formidable social, historical, and cultural actualities of male dominance, but to reveal the ways in which that dominance maintains not only the female body but the *male* body as a place of shame, self-hatred and concealment.

"What do women want?" was Freud's famous question; men have rarely similarly interrogated themselves as men, rarely found the question of what *they* want equally as fascinating to explore as the vicissitudes of the mysterious Other — for they generally have not appeared to themselves as men, but rather as the generic "Man," norm and form of humanity. When men problematize themselves as men, a fundamental and divisive sexual ontology is thus disturbed. New possibilities for communication are born as well; so long as men are transparent to, uninterrogating of, themselves, how can women have a real conversation with them about gender? This conversation has finally begun, and my paper would not have been possible without it — not without the discussions I have had with men, but particularly not without the men's writings which have emerged over the last decade, focusing on male sexuality as a subject to be explored rather than a subjectivity to be presumed. This essay describes itself as a reading of the male body; but it is as much a reading of those writings as well.

*   *   *

[W]ithin Western cultural practice generally . . . a male's body is not anatomized nor is it ever made an object of study in the same way as female bodies. The net result is that the penis is never made public, never put on the measuring line in the same way that female sexual body parts are put on the measuring line. On the contrary, a penis remains shrouded in mystery. It is protected, hidden from sight. What is normally no more than a swag of flesh in this way gains unassailable stature and power. . . . As an object perpetually protected from public view and popular scientific investigation, it is conceived not as the swag of flesh it normally is in all the humdrum acts and routines of everyday life but as a Phallus, an organ of unconditioned power.

(Maxine Sheets-Johnstone, "Corporeal Archetypes and Power," *Hypatia*, Vol 7, #3, Summer 1992, 69.)

Maxine Sheets-Johnstone is surely right that within dominant constructions of masculinity, the penis remains private and protected territory. The woman's body has become increasingly common cultural property; in 1993, any young boy who wants to learn what the female body looks like, how it functions, and what diseases it is prone to can get a liberal education from cable tv, Blockbuster video and Sally Jesse Raphael. A trip to the porno-store, the medical library, or even through the pages of *Playboy* is hardly necessary. Two years ago, *Newsweek* thought nothing of illustrating a cover-story on breast cancer with a photo exposing the cellular make-up of a naked breast, in profile and with the nipple fully visible. It is not impossible to imagine a similar "medicalized" cover-exposure of the female genital area; certainly, sexualized representations of the female body in magazines and films no longer shy from full frontal nudity.[1]

By contrast, outside of homoerotic representations (which I will discuss later), the penis has grown more, not less, culturally cloaked over time. Is it possible to imagine a *Newsweek* cover on testicular cancer, illustrated comparably to the cover on breast cancer? The phallus, of course, is always *symbolically* in evidence, from metaphors of war and weaponry (Fig. 1) to contemporary worship of the pumped-up muscle to the lascivious and swollen cartoon-camel of the cigarette billboards, proclaiming that he is "wider" and "smoother" than all the rest. (See Fig. 2 for an unusually transparent example of a automobile-phallus from the fifties, laughably literal by today's standards.) But only in pornography and homoerotic representations do we see the phallus embodied in the erect human penis, much less the human penis in non-phallic repose.[2] Indeed, the penis — insofar as it is capable of being soft as well as hard, injured as

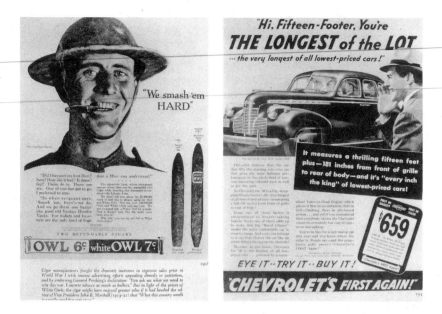

Fig. 1   Fig. 2

well as injuring, helpless as well as proud, emotionally needy as well as cold with will, insofar as it is vulnerable, perishable *body* — haunts the phallus, threatens its undoing. Patriarchal culture generally wants it out of sight.

A little girl can thus grow up in this culture with an acute sense of what phallic power and danger is all about without having any idea of what a penis looks like. My own father continually entertained his three young daughters with stories of his sexual exploits and daring, sometimes mildly criminal escapades as a young man growing up on the streets of Brooklyn; but he would rather have eaten glass than allow us to catch a glimpse of him naked from the waist down. I entered puberty, along with most of my girlfriends, more frightened of having to *look* at a penis for the first time than of engaging in various other forms of contact with it in the dark. Admittedly, those with brothers at home may have had a different experience. And certainly, times have changed. Fathers of the post-Woodstock generation may be less obsessive than my father was about making sure that bathroom and bedroom doors are shut while they are showering or dressing. In my day, classical sculpture was virtually the only realistic representational route to any anatomical knowledge of the penis. Today, AIDS has made facility with condoms a matter of life and death; teachers bring life-like models to fit in class demonstrations. Yet it is still highly unusual for male genitals to be shown in movies, even for a fleeting flash, and although male strip-shows for women are touted on *Donahue* as a "what's good for the goose is good for the gander" development, the Chippendales and their like do *not* ever exhibit themselves fully naked to women, the way female strippers do to men. What is eroticized in the male stripper routines is not the strip, not the exposure of nakedness, but the teasing display of phallic power, concentrated in the hard, pumped-up armor of muscle and the covered frontal bulge, straining against its confinements. Their penises they keep to themselves.

Not all men, however, are permitted to keep their penises to themselves. Instead, they are required to play the cultural shadow to the phallus; that shadow is always some possibility felt to be harbored by the male body and threatening to its masculine stature and status, whether it be the softness and vulnerability shared with the feminine body or the instinctual urges shared with the animal body. In *Male Fantasies*, Klaus Theweleit argues that for the German fascists, there existed two types of bodies: the up-standing, steel-hard, organized, "machine" body of the German master (see Fig. 3, in which the penis, while exposed, is visually overwhelmed by the muscular, upward-aspiring, phallic bodies of two stalwart "comrades") and the flaccid, soft, fluid body of the Other.[3] Although the woman's body provides the archetypal model for the soft body, and fascist fear of dissolution into feminine liquidity the original threat, the same horrors and revulsions get projected onto the body of the Jewish man. In anti-Semitic tracts

Fig. 3

and cartoons, the Jewish man is represented as dwarfish, soft, womanish, simpering, impotent, a castrate. Such stereotypes, albeit often in more polite form (e.g., the "nice Jewish boy," the ineffectual scholar, the meek husband or dutiful son dominated by the castrating Jewish Mother) continue to haunt Jewish men today[4], as Harry Brod's edited collection of essays on Jewish masculinity, *A Mensch Among Men*, documents.[5] A continuing theme in these essays is the second-generation Jewish man's struggle to dis-identify with these debasing images and achieve masculinity on the terms of a racist culture.

Sometimes women may become instruments of that struggle — as depicted, for example, in many of Philip Roth's novels, in which various male personae identify the achievement of "American" masculinity with winning the prize female icon of the culture: the blond-haired, blue-eyed *shiksa*. This is a masculine "strategy" of empowerment that has resonances with issues in the sexual politics of African-American culture, as well. It is important to recognize, however, that possession of the white or gentile woman is not simply a matter of vengeance, defiance of the white or WASP man's privilege by stealing his "property" (although this may figure in, as in Eldridge Cleaver's descriptions of why he raped white women) but of erotic attraction to she who is most emphatically "not-self."[6] For, to the degree that racist constructions of masculinity have been internalized, so too will be racist constructions of femininity.[7] Jewish women and Black women both often pay a heavy "double" price to racism here. One toll is paid to the dominant culture that de-feminizes and stereotypes them as dominating "Jewesses" and "Negresses" (a de-feminization that may include hyper-sexualization, as in the image of the Jezebel) and that constructs their racial bodies as ugly. The other toll is paid to those men of their own races whose quest for masculinity may feel threatened by or, at the very least, unrealizable with a woman of their own race, and whose erotic imaginations have been powerfully shaped by other images.

The predicaments of the Jewish man and the Black man are not equivalent, however. While the Jewish man is forced to carry the shadow of softness, the castrated, "feminine" penis in the cultural psyche of Western masculinity,[8] so the black man has been forced to carry the shadow of instinct, of unconscious urge, of the body itself — and hence of the penis-as-animal, powerful and exciting by virtue of brute strength and size, but devoid of phallic will and conscious control, therefore undeserving of worship or even respect. Frantz Fanon, discussing the racial fantasies of his white psychiatric patients, writes: "One is no longer aware of the Negro, but only of a penis: the Negro is eclipsed. He is turned into a penis. He *is* the penis."[9]

The black man as penis. This, of course, was the "intriguing concept," as Orrin Hatch put it, that the senator seemingly had so much difficulty comprehending during the Clarence Thomas confirmation hearings. In a cunning, risky, and ultimately triumphant move, Thomas had brought the mythology of the black man as over-sexed, over-endowed animal out of the shadows and onto the floor of the Senate, where it became a newfound ally rather than age-old nemesis. Believe Anita Hill, Thomas challenged, and publicly reveal your complicity with racist sterotypes; *deny* her, and you take public arms against them. (That Hill as a black woman might also be subject to racial stereotypes — as well as sexist projections — was not mentioned by Thomas and seemed not to occur to any of the senators).

Could it be that Orrin Hatch was truly the cultural innocent he appeared as he pushed Thomas to explain in just what way Hill's testimony played into racist stereotypes? Hatch: "And she said 'He described pornography with people engaging in oral sex.' Is *that* a black stereotype?" "No," replied Thomas. Hatch: "People engaging in acts of sex with animals?" Thomas: "No." Hatch: " 'Long Dong Silver' — Is *that* a black stereotype? Something like 'Long Dong Silver'?" "Yes," replied Thomas, "the size of sexual organs would be something. . . ." At first, I thought it was all simulation and strategy, designed to fuel public outrage with the drama of Hatch's slowly dawning recognition. "Well! I'm concerned!" "This bothers me!" he kept repeating, as he gradually "got it." Reflecting further, I've come to consider it possible that Hatch's ignorance *was* genuine, yet another educational deficit of the privileged dream-world in which most of these senators appear to live.[10] But in either case, Thomas's strategy was cynical and brilliant; so intent were the white senators on proving to the world that they (unlike Fanon's patients) did *not* see the black man as penis, that they apologized profusely every time they were forced to merely utter the *word* while questioning him. They only refered to "penises" when directly quoting from Anita Hill's testimony; their own preferred term was "private parts."

＊   ＊   ＊

What light through yonder TV breaks? It is Little Kimmi Johnson, with her blue dress threatening to ascend and her schoolgirl pumps aflutter with anticipation as she coos, 'I'm ready. I'm ready now.' An English teacher is 'tutoring' Little Kimmi. Mother is eager to engage her in incest. Mother's boyfriend (despite a stern warning delivered in the bland tones of video erotica) teaches her to fellate him — and more. Little Kimmi goes through it all with blithe assurance, taking sex in as if it were a calliope. . . . In reality, Little Kimmi would be a budding schizophrenic. In life, we would pity her and loathe her mentors. As testimony before a congressional subcommittee, her story would be stunning in its depravity. But in the video, Little Kimmi Johnson — played, I should point out, by a woman pushing 30 — is hot.

Little Kimmi Johnson is an icon of heterosexual pornography; by which, I mean, she turns me on. But how can I admit it? How can I acknowledge that, though this film arouses socially destructive passions, it also arouses me?

> (from Richard Goldstein, "Pornography and Its Discontents,", in Michael S. Kimmel, *Men Confront Pornography* [New York: Meridian, 1991], 81)

Clearly there was one site where the senators and Clarence Thomas met, neither in political collusion nor class/race collision, but as men. "This dirt, this sleaze," Thomas told the committee at the very beginning of his testimony, "is destroying what it has taken me 43 years to build. . . . How would *you* like to have this done to *you?*" Over and over again, he posed variants of this question to the senators, and I believe they felt his anguish. To be reduced to one's penis just as one is realizing the fruits of one's effort, the portals of phallic power — unthinkable, unbearable, unsayable. Yes, of course one could be cool with *Hill*; one could look *her* in the eye and not see oneself there (in fact, she was just about as "Other" as another could get). But Thomas, who had effaced his race in every way open to him and declared his primary allegiance to the white "brotherhood," was another matter; a border-being who was both other and self to the senators, he could shame them with his difference ("high-tech lynching") but also haunt them with his sameness: if the dirty secrets of his maleness could be so exposed, if that exposure could so threaten to undo all that he had accomplished — all the years of ambition, will, effort — so too could the senators' dirty secrets betray them. (For at least one of them, they already had.) Over and over, they attempted to distance themselves from the sorts of behavior that Thomas had been accused of, calling it "gross", "awful," "perverted", "sick"; the person who would perform such acts, Hatch declared "would not be a normal person . . . would be a psychopathic sex fiend."

The senators, of course, protested way too much. One of the virtues of Michael S. Kimmel's collection *Men Confront Pornography* is that it refutes the notion that pornography and the power-relations depicted in it are the preserve of the pervert. It is not just that the collection reveals — the senate hearings notwithstanding — that many intelligent, sane men buy or view pornography. More importantly, through a spectrum of intellectually diverse, personally honest, often insightful, sometimes brilliant, occasionally infuriating analyses and arguments, pornography becomes a window on key elements of the normative construction of male sexuality in our culture.

I learned a great deal from this collection, and not only on the level of detached intellectual insight or analysis. All my life I have felt, in my sexual relations with men, to be walking a perilously unsteady tightrope. An incautious overstep to one side of the rope, and I was seen as detached, remote, uncaringly separate; an awkward stumble to the other side, and I was experienced as sexually and emotionally "too much," overly needy, overly demanding. Men were supposed to want sex, and to be in a state of perpetual frustration because women didn't want it as much as they did; as I was growing up, that idea was conveyed in every movie I saw and everywhere I heard boys and men talking: in the playground, around my father's pinochle table, at basement parties. The thesis certainly seemed borne out when the first boy I fell in love with in high school rejected me in favor of a girl who was "faster" than I was, who was willing to "go farther." But then why did men not always seem to like it when, later in my life, my sexuality caught up with theirs? What *did* men want? My conclusion was that while I wasn't quite sure what it was, it seemed clear that there was something about *me* that it *wasn't*. Throughout my life, I remained haunted by a vague, ill-defined but powerful image of a woman who was not me, who *was* what men wanted, who was somehow both hot and cool at the same time, separate but responsive in just the right amounts, who was neither too remote *or* "too much."

Kimmel's collection helped me to fill in that image. Despite the diversity of the collection, certain ideas emerge over and over, ideas which require that we put to one side our revulsion or despair or anger over the degrading and disempowering representations of women depicted in heterosexual porn in order to explore a felt powerlessness at the heart of the psychology of male porn-consumption.[11] This felt powerlessness is the deep belief that women are in control of male sexuality and thus "manhood" itself, through our power to intrude on male subjectivity and arouse desire and then to reject that desire, leaving the man humiliated, shamed, frustrated—and, often, enraged. According to Timothy Beneke in *Men on Rape*, (New York: St. Martin's, 1983), this is a frequent theme in rapists' personal accounts. For example:

> Let's say I see a woman and she looks really pretty and really clean and sexy, and she's giving off very feminine, sexy vibes. I think, 'Wow, I would love to make love to her,' but I know she's not really interested. It's a tease. A lot of times a woman knows that she's looking really good and she'll use that and flaunt it, and it makes me feel like she's laughing at me and I feel *degraded*. (43)

Most men do not turn to rape when they feel degraded or humiliated. But many may find solace (and excitement) in pornographic images which degrade the *woman* and thus restore men's sense of pride, superiority, and power over the bodies which arouse them and then (as they experience it) leave them stranded, exposed, with "nothing but their dicks in their hands." Showing or describing such pornography to women, as Thomas did with Hill, can further right the power-imbalance. This is not to say that all women are disgusted or feel violated by pornographic images which depict male dominance and female subordination. Women may find them as stimulating as men. After all, phallic power *is* eroticized throughout our culture, and in many genres other than porn (some—for example, the romance novel—are designed just for women). Women "learn" *their* sexuality, too, at least in part through that eroticization. But whether a woman is turned-off or turned-on, being subjected to pornographic "discourse" at the office can only have an invasive, disequilibrating effect. It is no wonder, then, that Clarence Thomas, spurned by the attractive, highly professional and independent Anita Hill, sought to shake her self-containment and composure with talk of sex with animals and "Long Dong Silver." "You've invaded my space," such gestures proclaim, "Now *I'll* invade yours, with a vengeance!"

Many men in this book, however, protest the notion that the vengeful brutalization or humiliation of women is at the core of the pornographic experience for them. Rather, they suggest, pornography creates a fantasy-land in which male desire is always welcomed and the male body never rejected, no matter what it looks like or what it does. Pornographic motifs that may seem to women (and to other male writers in the book) to be quintessential expressions of a male need to degrade and dominate — for example, scenes which depict men ejaculating on women's faces — are, from this point of view, fantasies of unconditional acceptance, from which all possibility of rejection has been purged:

> From a male point of view, the desire is not to see women harmed, but to momentarily identify with men who — despite their personal unattractiveness by conventional cultural definition, despite the unwieldy size of their erections, and despite their aggressiveness with their semen — are adored by the women they encounter sexually. (from Scott MacDonald, "Confessions of a Feminist Porn Watcher," 41)

Pornography thus becomes a context in which the repressed penis, haunted by old guilt and embarrassment about secret masturbation, wet dreams, unwanted erections and ejaculations, taught that what spurts out of the body is disgusting, can come out of hiding and exhibit itself without shame or fear of rejection. And on this reading, it *is* the penis which has the stake here, *not* the phallus; for despite "the pervasive presence of erections" in pornography, these are erections that are exposed precisely in order to be validated. Their validation — the transformation of embarrassed penis into proud phallus — is the point of the pornography.

I think that all of us, male and female alike, can identify with the desire to be unconditionally adored, our most shame-haunted body-parts and body-fluids worshipped, our fears about personal excess and unattractiveness soothed and calmed. Only men, however, enjoy a culture of representations that enact such fantasies; and unfortunately, that culture often works precisely to reinforce *women's* shame, fear, and feelings of inadequacy. But one important insight that I gained from reading men's explorations of these fantasies is that what is going on in most of them is *not* "the objectification of women." Rather, the attempt is to depict a circumscribed female *subjectivity* that will validate the male body and male desire in ways that "real" women do not. The category of "objectification" came naturally to feminism because of the continual cultural fetishization of women's bodies and body parts. But here it is perhaps the case that our analysis suffered from mind/body dualism. For the fact that women's bodies are fetishized does not entail that what is going on in their minds is therefore unimplicated or unimportant. Rather, an essential ingredient in porn (at least, in one species of porn; clearly, different dynamics are at work in violent porn) is the depiction of a subjectivity (or personality) that willingly contracts its possibilities and pleasures to one — the acceptance and gratification of the male. "Here I am," that subjectivity declares, "uttterly available to you, happy to be yours no matter *what* you do or do not do."

The body in porn "speaks" this willing contraction of the self in gestures of total receptivity to the male — spread legs, for example. If this fetish really reduced the woman to the status of vaginal receptacle, she would be no more capable of expressing *receptivity* than the piece of liver that Portnoy masturbated with in his parents' bathroom. The woman in porn abdicates her will, her sexual discrimination, her independence, but not to become mute body for the man. For insofar as she is simply "meat," she has no power to reject, and thus her total acceptance of the man is unrepresentable. And, above all else, that unconditional acceptance *must* be represented, her body speaking with every gesture and through all its parts: "I exist wholly for you. I will never reject you. You *cannot* disappoint me."

This insight helps to reconcile two seemingly contradictory motifs that run throughout male representations of female sexuality. On the one hand, there is the male experience of woman's sexuality as voracious, "too much," threatening to engulf and obliterate the male — a motif that is at the center of Theweleit's analysis of fascist masculinity and that informs the "consuming woman" and "man-eating" imagery that upwells at certain historical junctures.[12] On the other hand, much pornography depicts women precisely as sexually aggressive, voracious, insatiable, presumably as an antidote to the constraints on male sexuality placed by "real" women, who are not sexual *enough*. The reconciliation is this: What is desired, and what much heterosexual pornography provides, is a world in which women are indeed in a state of continual readiness and desire for sex, but one in which female desire is incapable of "emasculating" the male by judging or rejecting him, by overwhelming him, or by expecting something from him that he cannot (or fears he cannot) provide. What is desired is a sexual encounter that does not put manhood at risk in any way — neither through female indifference to the male (leaving *him* feeling sexually "too much," exposed, ashamed) nor through "too much" independent, unpredictable desire, will, or need on the woman's part (eliciting anxieties that he will be unable to satisfy *her*). In pornography, women are indeed voracious, yet at the same time completely satisfied by anything the male has to give and non-needful of that which he cannot give. (Fantasy is not the domain of the reality principle, let alone correct politics.) Women in porn are hot, but in a crucial way their subjectivity is *cool*, undemanding, accepting, placid. This is surely part of the erotic appeal of "Little Kimmi", who blithely "takes sex in as if it were a calliope."

The notion that women have an awesome sexual power over men, in the face of which men struggle to maintain their equilibrium and control, is not new. Rapists have been acquitted on the basis of defenses constructed around this notion; poets, artists, philosophers and theologians have mythologized it throughout history; feminists such as Dorothy Dinnerstein have deconstructed those mythologies, and explored their roots in infant experience. Recently, both Camille Paglia and the mytho-poetic "men's movement" have revived those mythologies. Here, for example, is Sam Keen, writing in *Fire in the Belly* (New York: Bantam, 1991):

> We have invested so much of our identity, committed so much of our energy, and squandered so much of our power in trying to control, avoid, conquer or demean women because we are so vulnerable to their mysterious power over us. Like sandy atolls in a monsoon-swept ocean, the male psyche is in continual danger of being inundated by the feminine sea.(15)

The differences between notions such as Keen's and the analyses presented in Kimmel's collection are great, however. While Keen (and Paglia) present such notions as a kind of proof that women really *are* in control of the universe (social inequalities and injustices seen as trivial beside our awesome, "natural" power), most of the men writing in *Men Confront Pornography* recognize that men have been historically dominant vis-à-vis women in most ways. Indeed, as Michael Kimmel insightfully points out in the concluding essay to the volume, it is in response to the perceived eroding of that dominance that pornographic recreations of a lost world of "infantile omnipotence, when the entire universe revolved around the satisfaction of our desires" (315) have become all the more inviting to men.

Many of these authors, too, express intense ambivalence over their attraction to porn, recognizing that although the representations satisfy what they may consider to be benign male fantasies, women may feel differently, and often are affected by porn in less than benign ways. Although this is a collection of undeniably *male* responses to pornography, which rightfully insists that men's experiences and interpretations are meaningful and relevant and which never simply defers to women in the debate, the authors rarely forget that male psycho-dynamics are not the final word here. Despite that knowledge, these writers are brave enough to honestly reveal their sexual imaginations, "however barbaric" (as one writer puts it) or infantile. The most insightful understand, too, that the male experience of women as in control of the sexual arena (which most women — particularly those that have been raped, battered or harassed — certainly do not feel themselves to be) is the product of a variety of cultural sources, both representational and "material" — by the age-old, misogynist ideology of woman-as-temptress, by a mating system which has until very recently assigned men the role of pursuit and women the role of acceptance or rejection, and by a massive, contemporary industry in "intrusive images" (as Timothy Beneke calls them) which surround and bombard men with highly eroticized and arousing representations of female bodies, continually invading their sexual space every time they turn on the tv, go to a movie, or open almost any magazine.[13]

Collections such as Kimmel's and Brod's are important new intellectual sites for the continued elaboration of the feminist insight that the personal is the political — that social power and hierarchy are embodied not only in "external" institutions and forms of organization, but make their way into the very heart of desire, need, emotion, sexuality. Unfortunately, these collections (although the pieces are for the most part vividly and accessibly written) have been publicly eclipsed by sensationalistic, best-selling "reclamations" of masculinity such as Robert Bly's and Sam Keen's, reclamations which mythologize female sexual control over men and so are unable to move, despite their own avowed intentions, beyond reassertions of male potency and privilege.

Keen, for example, claims to be attempting to create a new, ecological, non-warlike, non-performance-oriented male archetype — "a new vision of manliness" which "perceives life and reality as a unified network of mutually interdependent entities whose well-being is enhanced by cooperation and compassion"(112–13). His prose, however, is so bursting with phallic adrenalin and metaphors that the medium destroys the message (which is mixed to begin with). "The phallic principle that gives man dignity and is worthy of worship is his ability to rise to the occasion, to answer the call of history," he proclaims (89). Today, the call is to create a "new race of giants," "fierce gentlemen," with "thunder and lightning in them," "men with "potent doubt," "manly grief," "virile fears." I know that Keen wants to *legitimate* male doubt, grief and fear here. But what can be the point of doing so through the invocation of "virility" and "potency," if not to "pump up" the image of the new man with a promise of phallic mastery? And if the new man is a giant and master, then in what sense is he "new"? (True ecological consciousness, I would think, requires that one see oneself as somewhat less exalted than a giant among creatures.)

A few key passages reveal how shallow and ultimately self-deceived Keen's "reconstruction" of masculinity is. In one, he criticizes gay men: "It strikes me that the lack of substantial manliness one finds in some gay communities is a result not of a homoerotic expression of sexuality, but of the lack of a relationship of nurturance to the young" (227). Here, under the guise of re-defining "manliness" to include traditionally "feminine" virtues, he continues to use the concept as a scythe to separate the girls from the men, the effeminates from those of "manly substance."[14] In another passage, he brags about how a female member of the audience paid homage to one of his seminars on "Understanding Men." "This weekend I feel like I have been in a room with giants," Keen proudly reports her saying, "I thank you for letting me listen"(9). In another passage, he describes looking in the mirror at the end of a night of sex: "The mirror reflected the image of a man I had never seen before — his cock, resting but proud, pulsated with life, his chest swelled with the joy of being, his sinuous muscles were full of power" (70).

This description — whose prose reminds one of the worst of D.H. Lawrence, or perhaps a Harlequin romance — is presented utterly without irony or humor. More remarkably, it comes at the end of an anecdote which is meant to demonstrate Keen's triumph over the sexual performance principle, on a night when he was "not ready" (his choice of words) for sex despite his partner's arousal. She reassures him, but he feels he has "failed the test of manhood" and drifts off "into a restless sleep." Then, in the middle of the night he awakes, fully erect, and enters her ("and [his] manhood," as he tells us) with barely a word; and they "moved together until the whirlpool sucked us down into the primal deep, and we slept as one body in the sweet darkness." The next morning he "roars like a lion" at the memory of his "passage beyond innocence."

From the textual context — a quite perceptive critique of "Getting Laid and Keeping Score" (Keen does make some good points in the book) — it is clear that he views this passage as having brought him to a recognition that sex can never be deeply satisfying to men so long as it is viewed as a test of potency and performance. I agree. The anecdote, however, seems not to demonstrate this so much as Keen's need to be the active, controlling, "deciding" partner in sex. It would be one thing if Keen were to explore this need (which is, after all, an important element in the construction of masculinity in this culture), but he is clearly more interested in creating a new masculine icon out of his own "transformation." He never questions *why* it was that his potency magically returned when his partner was passive, asleep. Although earlier in the book, he had analyzed rape as a response to the unconscious image of the woman as active initiator, an attempt to control what men imagine as the overwhelming erotic/spiritual power of women, he remains utterly oblivious to these dynamics in his own behavior. He might profit from reading the Kimmel volume.

*   *   *

"We've got to consider not only the rights of homosexuals but also the rights of those who are not homosexual and who give up a great deal of their privacy when they go into the military.
(Sam Nunn, on CBS *Face the Nation*)

Although heterosexual men generally do not get to shower and change with naked women as homosexual men have the privilege of showering and changing with other naked men, there are heterosexual arrangements that are similar. Consider life on the beach and around swimming pools where men and women wear as little as possible. Generally speaking, these arrangements for the stimulation of heteroerotic desire are not considered disgusting. . . . When a gay man looks at another man in the showers or locker room, it is never from the position of power that straight men have when they look at women at the beach or on the street. In fact, the erotic world that is invoked in homosexual voyeurism is one of equality in the gender myth and the paradoxical *violation* of masculine power rather than the orthodox, heterosexual *confirmation* of power difference that is fundamental to heterosexual desire. . . . Those who want to cling to their orthodox masculine power usually prefer to dis-emphasize the homoeroticism of their athletic environments.

> (Brian Pronger, *The Arena of Masculinity* [New York: St. Martin's Press, 1990], 205–6)

Recently, culturally repressed aspects of the male body have "returned" in several contexts to stir up the social psyche. Not surprisingly, in each context, it has been marginalized men, bearers of the shadow of the phallus, who have been the alchemical agents disturbing the (deceptively) stable elements. For me, the most powerful and moving scenes in Neil Jordan's *The Crying Game* occurred long before Jaye Davidson took off his robe, that cinematic moment with which the entire movie has become identified in the popular imagination. In fact, I had some trouble concentrating on the film after Jody was killed; my imagination and emotions remained haunted by the images of tenderness and brutality from the first part of the film, fixated on what was for me the most textured and dramatically realized relationship of the film — that between Fergus and Jody. Clearly, it was the relationship which most powerfully haunted Fergus as well. And arguably, the most culturally transgressive interraction was that moment when white, "straight" Fergus takes Jody's black, "bisexual" penis in his hand in order to help him urinate. But it was the film's more explicitly erotic relationship that had everyone talking, or rather — *not* talking. "Don't give away the secret!" "Don't tell the surprise!" The degree of collective collusion maintained, in a society where leakage of information is a national disease, was truly remarkable. Not even the shower scene in *Psycho* — shocking at the time not only because of its violence, but because it killed off the star so early in the film — was so carefully guarded. At times, the obsession to conceal "the secret" of *The Crying Game* bordered on crazy absurdity, as when Roger Ebert furiously scolded Gene Siskel for revealing "the secret" on their "If We Picked the Oscars" show, even though film clips had just been shown in which Jaye Davidson, nominated for best supporting *actor*, appears as a woman.

In the face of all this, it is tempting to conclude that the scene is deeply subversive of conventional notions of "femininity" and "masculinity." And in theory, it could be—for what the exposure of Dil's penis might be taken to reveal here is that its presence or absence is not the ultimate arbiter of gender. Does Dil become less a woman simply because he is revealed to be biologically a man? At least one (heterosexual) male friend of mine said that Dil never ceased being a sexually attractive woman for him, even after the Big Moment, and even after Fergus cuts his hair and dresses him as a boy. To the viewer who responds this way the film may indeed be subversive of deep cultural assumptions about gender. Psychologists Suzanne Kessler and Wendy McKenna showed subjects two sketches: one with all the expected female sexual attributes—breasts, hips, long hair—but *with* a penis, and one without breasts, hips, or body hair but *with* a vagina. They found that the presence of penis was the single most powerful, *the* definitive cue for gender-attribution, 96% of their subjects judging the figure with the penis as male despite the breasts and other female cues, while 33% of their subjects "were able to ignore the reality of the vagina as a female cue" in the other figure.[15] To the degree that the presence of Dil's penis does not obliterate a continued reading of the character as female, this conventional, phallocentric schema of gender attribution is disturbed.[16] But, more deeply than this, so too is the notion that gender flows simply and naturally from genital difference. Instead, it has to be acknowledged as a complex formation which is successful only to the degree that all of us—not just cross-dressers or transvestites—learn to perform the culturally required gestures and to wear the appropriate "drag" of the gender to which we have been assigned.

It seems to me, however, that the film's surprise subverts the notion that gender has a natural basis only to the degree that audiences experience (or allow themselves to experience) Dil's femininity as my friend did, as something which endures beyond the surprise. To the degree that Dil "becomes" a man for audiences once his penis is revealed—that is, if the revelation is experienced as a revelation of the *truth* of Dil's gender—then it functions as a disequilibrating jolt of a purely perceptual and more superficial nature. It profoundly disturbs the universe for a moment (hence its strong entertainment value for novelty-craving, sensation-seeking postmodern audiences) but then, everything re-configures into its more familiar shape. "Boy, I was sure fooled! Amazing how he managed to really *seem* like a woman, isn't it?" The deception, to be sure, is more titillating to heterosexual audiences than other cinematic magic tricks they've experienced; the possiblity that one can be thoroughly fooled about who has a penis and who doesn't is unsettling stuff. But for such audiences, it doesn't unsettle notions about the naturalness of gender, it reveals how artfully the "reality" of gender can be disguised. It thus may also raise the disturbing possibility of masquerade all around. Just how can one be sure who is who anymore?

Interestingly, in the context of the furor over gays and the military, it would seem that the most homophobic among us don't *want* to know who is who when it comes to sexual orientation. To me, this is one of the most revealing elements of the current debate—the fact that those who have argued against the disclosure of sexual orientation but who recognize that there have always been plenty of homosexuals in the military, seem perfectly happy to have had gays in the shower *so long as they didn't know who they were.* So long, that is, as they could efface their own knowledge of the fact that homosexuals were indeed in there with them. (If they *know* who is who, such effacement would be impossible short of complete cognitive dissociation.) What is starkly demonstrated here is that the arguments against "integrated" locker rooms and showers are not about regulating gay behavior but about protecting *heterosexual* men from certain unacceptable thoughts and feelings of their own. No one suggested that gays be segregated *before*—even though everyone "knew" that they were there. For that knowledge was general, abstract; very few knew just *where* "they" were. In the concrete experience (e.g., of the shower) they could thus deceive themselves about the possibilities. Described bluntly, this is a situation in which it is being proposed that the civil rights of one group are less worthy of protection than the *illusions* of another.

Once we recognize that the issue at stake is the maintenance of protective heterosexual illusion, we must ask what the illusion is protection against. Two fascinating recent books, Brian Pronger's *The Arena of Masculinity: Sports, Homosexuality, and the Meaning of Sex* and Richard Mohr's *Gay Ideas: Outing and Other Controversies* help provide an answer.[17] In *The Arena of Masculinity*, homosexual and heterosexual men describe a diverse variety of personal experiences in locker rooms and showers. Sexual activity, it appears, rarely occurs. But "looking" is always at issue. Some homosexual men attribute heterosexual discomfort at being looked at by gay men to a psychological flight from attraction to and admiration for the male body:

> We all play voyeur, straights play voyeur all the time. I've seen just as much cruising from supposedly straight guys as I've seen from gay guys. Gay guys just make it more obvious. Straight guys do just as much comparison and cruising as anybody does. I've noticed that a lot of guys will not shower anymore in the gym, they refuse to. If you ask them why—'too many faggots around here.' . . . Anybody who's that homophobic, I automatically question their sexuality. What are they worried about, 'You've got twenty-inch biceps, fella!' It tells me they are really uptight about their sexuality and have problems dealing with it. Anyone who is sure about themselves isn't going to be concerned when someone is looking at them.(196–7)

In another quote, a heterosexual man suggests that the "dirty" feeling some heterosexual men get when they feel they are being looked at by another man comes from "equating it with what they do to women":

> . . . that is that it's dirty, the sneaky peeks at women, and therefore it's what they would be doing and what they would be thinking about women. I think we tend to relate things to what *we* do, and so what they're thinking about women they realize somebody's thinking about them. (197)

Pronger himself suggests a more subtle dynamic. The gaze of the homosexual male, he argues, is paradoxical in its relationship to masculinity. On the one hand, it shares with orthodox masculinity a celebration of masculine power. Indeed, it invests that power with intense erotic meaning (as the preponderance of phallic imagery and symbolism in homoerotic art testifies). But for the homosexual male—unlike the heterosexual female, who may be equally phallus-worshipping—the penis in which the phallus is incarnated is a site of sameness with the object of desire rather than difference from him.

Here is where the paradox lies. If masculinity itself is a construction premised on, parasitic on, gender *difference*, then the eroticization of gender *sameness* is a violation of masculinity. Homoeroticism is paradoxical because it "both embraces and violates masculinity"(71).

There is thus (in striking contrast to Sam Keen's odes to his phallic manhood, played utterly "straight") a certain playful "deconstruction" of the icons of male power, even as they are worshipped. Brian Pronger quotes a gay gymnast, drooling over male muscles: "I don't know what it is but there is something about men's tits that just does a number on my brain! A man's chest is just irresistible!"(272). In the ironic labeling of male pecs as "tits," the essence of the parodoxical relationship to masculinity is revealed; that is, gender difference and the male power on which it is premised is at once revered and undone. The same ironic sensibility, Richard Mohr argues in *Gay Ideas*, imbues the hypermasculinist imagery of much gay art, as in Tom of Finland's 1976 hitchhiker (Fig. 4) where the very overabundance of phallic power-icons — biker's tattoo, pirate's earring, gladiator's cuff, police cuffs, frontal bulge, muscles — negates the oppressive masculinist meanings of any one of them, and of the image as a whole. Says Mohr:

> Here, the masculine is eroticized, but not in a way that affirms the oppressive features of traditional masculine roles. The various roles' iconographies undermine each other. In pinning these uniformly gendered but clashing images on himself, the fellow cannot plausibly be taken to assume the privileges of any — not even one — of the roles to which his adopted postures allude. Indeed, the hitchhiker's total presentational package exposes the stud to the charge of 'faggot'. Far from endowing him with privilege, his public hypermasculine posture exposes him to violence. (197)

If Pronger and Mohr are right, then the knowledge that gay men may be looking at them could be threatening to "orthodox" heterosexuals not because (or not only because) it stirs up their own suppressed homoeroticism or because they imagine they are being looked at in the demeaning way that *they* look at women, but because they experience their masculinity as violated. But we need to analyze this violation further. I suggest that it is composed of three elements. First, and on the most general level, the undoing which is dreaded is the "deconstruction" of masculinity as active,

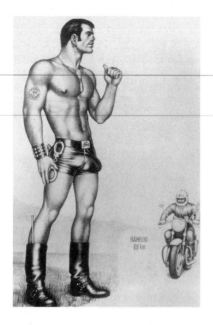

Fig. 5

Fig. 4

constitutive consciousness itself. Another man's look has far more power than most women's in this regard. For it is men who have been given the cultural role of the subjectivity which actively defines, shapes, and evaluates "reality" and which *never* allows itself to become that which is passively defined, shaped, and evaluated by another's consciousness. The latter is the proper role of the woman, the sex which is the appropriate object of another's defining gaze. Who can stare the other man down? Who will avert his eyes first? Whose gaze will be triumphant, turning the other into a "woman"? Such moments are a test of macho within street culture. Orthodox masculinity dreads being "stripped" of whatever armor it has constructed for itself, dreads being surveyed and determined from without.

Second, if the determination is of a sexual nature, the look of the other will be all the more threatening to orthodox masculinity, as we saw in my reading of Sam Keen's anecdote. Now, it is of course possible that Keen's initial lack of arousal had to do with tiredness or distraction. But in his own description, the date had been romantic, relaxed, emotionally non-coercive. Something interferes with the flow, an interference that is neutralized when his lover is asleep. Her judging eye is closed (or more correctly, what he experiences as her judging eye is closed); she is no longer watching him, evaluating him. Another illustration is suggested by Maxine Sheets-Johnstone, in her brilliant critique and re-casting of evolutionary theory, *The Roots of Thinking* (Temple University Press, 1990). Why, she ponders, has the significance of every aspect of bipedality in human evolution been explored except one: the fact that when primates stand up, the male genitals are visibly exposed while the female genitals become relatively hidden. The change would suggest that penile display rather than female sexual signaling might consequently become important to sexual behavior and selection, especially since penile erection seems "an evolutionary elaboration of the basic male [display] pattern [in birds, for example] of erection/ expansion," of "making some part stand up or inflating it" (98). But instead, although "virtually no description of nonhuman primate social life is without reference to display behavior," with hominids, "display behavior suddenly drops out of the primate evolutionary picture" (95) and is replaced by the concept of year-round female receptivity. Clearly, for male evolutionary theorists to imagine the bodies of their male ancestors as on display, their penile size scrutinized and evaluated, awaiting selection (or rejection) by our female ancestors, has been unthinkable.

And finally, there is the *specific* sexual meaning of the homosexual gaze. Both Pronger and Mohr theorize acts and images of male anal penetration as key "moments" when orthodox masculinity is violated. And certainly, this is the act that orthodox heterosexual men find most threatening. What exposure is most feared in the shower? Not the scrutiny of the penis (although this prospect may indeed make heterosexual men uncomfortable), but the moment when one bends down to pick up the soap which has slipped from one's hands. It is in the imagination of this moment that the orthodox male is most undone by the consciousness that there may be homosexuals in the shower, whose gaze will define him as a passive receptacle of *their* sexuality, and thus as "woman." There is a certain paradox here. For although it is the imagined effeminacy of homosexual men that makes them objects of heterosexual derision, here it is their imagined *masculinity* (that is, the consciousness of them as active, evaluating sexual subjects, with a defining and "penetrating" sexual gaze) that makes them the objects of heterosexual fear.

The conceptual/sexual system which sustains all this — the association of masculinity with the "doer" not the "done to," the penetrator not the penetrated, the desiring sexual subject rather than the "receiver" of the desires of another — runs extraordinarily deep in our culture. As an explicit ontology, one can trace it as far back as Aristotle, who describes the male principle (as well as the male contribution to reproduction) as the "effective and active" element, and assigns to woman the role of passive, penetrable "matter." These assignments are at the very heart of sexism — not simply because they conceptualize reality in terms of a gendered duality (active male / passive female) but, more importantly, because they so powerfully privilege the active over the passive, as in the following passage from Hegel:

> The difference between men and women is like that between animals and plants. Men correspond to animals, while women correspond to plants because their development is more placid and the principle that underlies it is the rather vague unity of feeling. . . . Women are educated — who knows how? — as it were by breathing in ideas, by living rather than by acquiring knowledge. The status of manhood, on the other hand, is attained only by the stress of thought and much technical exertion. (*Philosophy of Right*, 263–64)

In David Gilmore's cross-cultural study, *Manhood in the Making*, the "category of achievement" is described as a central component of masculinity in many cultures; he finds a "constantly recurring notion that real manhood . . . is not a natural condition that comes about spontaneously through biological maturation [as femininity is imagined] but rather is a precarious or artificial state that boys must win against powerful odds."[18] (See Fig. 5.) Gilmore tends to overuniversalize this as a phenomenon, ignoring or discounting evidence of other cultural styles of manhood and choosing illustrations that tend to confirm his thesis. But there is no doubt that he has isolated an important element in many social constructions of masculinity.

The deep associations of masculinity as active, constitutive (and self-constituting) subjectivity and femininity as a passive, "natural," bodily state underlie the equation of penetrability with femininity. (The equation only *seems* as though it is demanded by the anatomy of the female body. For the vagina could just as easily be imagined as actively holding, containing or enclosing the penis as being "penetrated" by it. In misogynist images — of the "devouring woman," the *vagina dentatis*, and so forth — the vagina *is* imagined as active, albeit terrifyingly and destructively.) Thus, Richard Mohr argues, there is something deeply subversive of sexism in homoerotic representations which "neutralize" the dominance of the penetrator and depict a kind of "democracy" of sexual position, in which active/passive roles appear as easily reversible and none is privileged.

Such sexual subversion, however, is not "built into" gay masculinity, as Mohr and Pronger both seem at times to be suggesting. When the role of penetrable male is identified with subordinate status, the act of being penetrated constructed as an act of submission to a master (as in prison cultures and racist pornography), or assigned only to the not-yet-developed youth (as in ancient Greek culture, which found it totally unacceptable for a learned, mature, socially powerful man to be sexually receptive), or associated with "wimpiness" (as Richard Fung argues is the case with the depiction of Asian men in gay male pornography), then pernicious gendered dualities are being re-inscribed, not challenged. This is strikingly the case in many Latin cultures, where homosexuality as North Americans understand it — as defined by the choice of a sexual partner of one's own sex — does not even exist; the system of sexual categorization is "based on a configuration of gender/sex/power that is articulated along the active/passive axis" rather than sexual object choice. Within the Mexican/Latin-American sexual system, for example, as Tomás Almaguer describes it:

> [The] homosexual world is divided into *activos* and *pasivos* (as in Mexico and Brazil) and *machistas* and *cochons* (in Nicaragua). . . . It is primarily the anal-passive individual (the *cochon* or *pasivo*) who is stigmatized for playing the subservient, feminine role. His partner (the *activo* or *machista*) typically is "not stigmatized at all and, moreover, no clear category exists in the popular language to classify him. For all intents and purposes, he is just a normal . . . male." In fact, Lancaster argues that the active party in a homosexual drama often gains status among his peers in precisely the way that one derives status from seducing many women.[19]

Clearly, in order to challenge the "penetrable woman / impenetrable man" duality that "maintains the system of gender sterotypes" (as Mohr quite accurately describes it) it is not enough to simply portray men as penetrable. Nor is it enough to portray women as capable of being as *impenetrable* as men (as in *Terminator II*, in which Linda Hamilton's expression barely changes throughout the movie) or to depict them as being as adept with symbolic phalluses as men are (as in the *Alien* movies, *La Femme Nikita*, *Lethal Weapon III*, and so forth). It is necessary to re-think and "re-vision" the qualities of penetrability and impenetrability themselves — and, I would argue, in terms of their broadest meanings: emotional, intellectual, and social as well as sexual. In our culture today, as I will suggest in the last section of this paper, we have been moving largely in the opposite direction.

*   *   *

There is something extremely depressing to me about the fact that when masculinity gets symbolically "undone" in this culture, the deconstruction nearly always lands us in the territory of the degraded, while when femininity gets symbolically undone, the result is an immense elevation in status. The description of male pecs as "tits" gets its irony from the *reduction* of an overbloated symbol of phallic power to a demeaning slang term for women's breasts. But when Linda Hamilton's or Sigourney Weaver's maternal devotion turns them into muscular, fierce warriors, their ascension into the masculine is nothing but admirable, even thrilling, to the popular imagination. (Thelma and Louise, of course, never become cold, hard warriors. If they had, the film would have been much less upsetting to the "orthodox" men who saw it as male-bashing. The macho-woman pays homage to the heroic myths of masculinity; the deeper transgression of *Thelma and Louise* is that it portrays men as frequently helpless human beings, even the best of whom cannot fulfill those heroic myths, cannot save the heroines.)

Gay and straight, male and female, blue-collar and white-collar, everyone in our culture today (who can afford to) is getting hard and ripped. The ideal of muscular fitness has changed dramatically. Buster Crabbe's body was considered in the thirties to be a paragon of masculinity; by today's standards, it seems "soft," without definition. Today, the ideal is to have a body that is hard as a rock, without looseness or flacidity anywhere; here, as I have argued in *Unbearable Weight*, we use the surface of our bodies to code superior will-power, control over desire, and the ability to manage and shape one's own life (see Fig. 6) and those of others (Fig. 7). Whereas

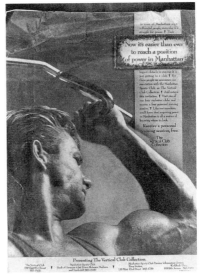

Fig. 6   Fig. 7

muscles once signified the brutely "natural," the primitive, and thus were usually reserved in cultural representations for the bodies of blacks, slaves, prize-fighters and manual laborers, muscles today have been re-located to the "civilized" side of the nature/culture duality. Unless developed to the point where body appears to overtake mind completely (as seems expressed, for example, in the massive bulk of competitive body-builders), muscles today are the mark of mind over matter.

As muscles have ceased to align with the "natural" — anyone can develop them, as the ads for gym membership and exercise equipment assure us — they have also become available to women, and taken up as an expression of equality with men. The word "muscle" itself comes from the Middle French *mus*, meaning mouse. The connection is that women of the *ancien régime* were supposed to faint away at the sight of both. Muscles have in the past been a quintessential symbol of masculinity as a "natural" (rather than achieved) difference from femininity. This symbolism still lingers today, as a recent *Time* cover illustrates (Fig. 8), and advertisements still frequently romanticize and idealize the visual motif of male muscularity/female frailty (Fig. 9). But we have also developed competing representations featuring the "new woman," unconstrained by biology or old social roles. Nike and Reebok have designed very artful and manipulative campaigns, capitalizing on the equation of physical fitness with resistance to old constructions of femininity as "softness." "I believe," declares the athletic young woman in Fig. 10, "that any man who wants something soft and cuddly to hold should buy a teddy bear."

It makes sense, of course, that as women have begun to enter the spheres of patriarchal power and privilege, a fashion for female muscles has emerged. But while the emergence of female muscles expresses a real breakdown that is occurring in the gendered division-of-labor in this culture, it also demonstrates the asymmetry of that breakdown. So far, the transformation has chiefly gone in the direction of permitting (and even eroticizing) *hardness* in women, but never softness in men. Reebok, in the "I believe" ad depicted in Fig. 10, tells women "Life is Short. Play Hard." The model's expression is hard, her body is hard, her attitude is hard. Yet although we have recently elected a "soft" male to the presidency — one who likes to hug cuddly beings of either sex, and whose body seems to resist getting hard, no matter how much he exercises — the virtues of his "softness" are continually being represented as feminized defects. The fact that he is a negotiator and consensus-seeker means that he is "trying to please everyone" rather than taking a "firm" stand. His genuine commitment to diversity gets translated as "caving in" to interest groups. "Can He Play Hardball?" reads the headline of an article in *Newsweek*. Even Clinton's eating habits are feminized. Traditionally, hearty appetite is a mark of the masculine. "Manwich," "Hungry Man Dinners," "Manhandlers" are products which boast of their ability to satisfy men. Even when men advertise diet products, they brag about their appetites, as in the Tommy Lasorda commercials for Slim-Fast, which feature three burly football players (their masculinity beyond reproach), declaring that if Slim-Fast can satisfy *their* appetites, it can satisfy anyone's. Clinton's love of food, on the other hand, continually gets represented as embarrassing, out-of-control, feminine "binge" behavior. He just can't resist those goodies, like the rest of us girls.

The asymmetry here reflects the social reality: to the extent that the rigidities of a gendered division of labor have been challenged in this culture, the challenge has consisted largely in permission for

women to do men's work and embody a masculinist ethos and aesthetics (at least, so long as they are at work; when they start their
"second shift" as wives and mothers, they are expected to become
"real women" again). It remains taboo for men to take on most jobs
that have traditionally been women's, and when they do, they often
"masculinize" them in an attempt not to be seen as soft or "sissy." So,
for example, Laurel Davis, in an extremely interesting article on the
world of male cheerleading, finds that when men become cheerleaders, feats of strength, stunts and "stiff" arm movements replace
the energetic, dancing-to-music routines which women perform.[20]
Jobs that resist such masculinization (such as child care) continue to
be seen as suspect fields for men.

I understand the attractions of the hard and impenetrable. Once,
one summer, after a long-standing and important relationship
ended, I found myself drawn into what began as a little bit of casual
weight-training but which within a few weeks became a daily compulsion, lasting for longer and longer periods each day. I remember
very distinctly the thrilling experience of flexing the thighs which

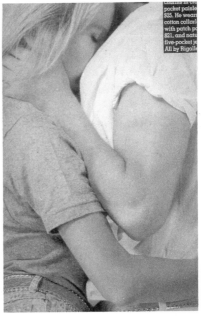

Fig. 8   Fig. 9

Fig. 10

had shamed me with their softness and seeing muscles tighten in them; I also remember the way having definition in my upper body made me feel when I walked by men — not just more attractive, but powerful. For the first time, I felt that their eyes did not penetrate me and reduce me, but glanced over me with admiration, as though I were an equal. The feeling, I am certain, had nothing (or little) to do with a real change in how men saw me. My pecs never got *that* developed; by today's standards they were very marginally defined. Rather, my feeling of invulnerability and power had everything to do with the sense that I had banished my then-hurting femininity out of the country of my body, replacing it — not with masculinity exactly, but with an armored femininity. I no longer felt that my body coded my soft and bruised feelings; instead, it coded independence, toughness, emotional imperviousness.

Whatever the meanings embedded in the aesthetics here, muscular bodies can be very beautiful. And there is nothing condemnable, it seems to me, about wanting some "phallic" armor when you need it, or indulging in a little phallus-worship as one of many possible erotic modes (particularly if you keep your sense of humor about it). The problem is that in our culture, to expect to engage in any of these in

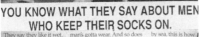
YOU KNOW WHAT THEY SAY ABOUT MEN
WHO KEEP THEIR SOCKS ON.
They say they like it wet.   man's gotta wear. And so does   by sea. this is how

Don't just serve. Rule.

Fig. 11   Fig. 12

moderation is a bit like wanting just a touch of anorexia nervosa. The
muscular male bodies that men and women idealize today really are
starting to look more and more like those depicted in Nazi posters and
sculpture, not only in their aesthetics of physical perfection, but in
their unsmiling postures of ascending power and superiority (Fig. 11),
with that power often explicitly thematized in the copy of advertisements and commercials (Fig. 12). Women are exchanging their eating
disorders for exercise compulsions, and their old addictions to controlling, masterful "phallic" men for addictions to self-control and mastery of their own bodies. And, judging from discussions in Pronger
and surveying the changing styles of representations in Allen
Ellenzweig's *The Homoerotic Photograph*, a non-ironic, fetishized
macho aesthetics is becoming more and more dominant within gay
cultures. The deep aim of the "masculinist fervor" in contemporary
gay art, Ellenzweig suggests, is usually not to deconstruct masculinity
through excess, but to "dispel effeminate homosexual stereotypes," as
in a gay picture magazine's definition of "macho":

> Today's gay is the opposite of all that. Today it's mustaches and
> beards. Levis and leather. Muscled torsos and *very* hirsute chests.

Not to mention other heavy-hanging equipment. And a consciousness raised to the nth degree. An infinity of variety. Sensitivity —
yes, we said sensitivity. All allied with a rough, tough, butch edge
to it. That's *macho*. (quoted in Ellenzweig, 142)

Really, it's not very different from Sam Keen's vision of the "fierce
gentleman."

Does my critique above mean that we need to replace the reign of
the hard with a new reign of the soft? I think rather that we need to
refuse that old opposition as a guide. Here the repressed penis — the
motif with which I opened this paper — can stimulate the imagination. Let's not look to the figure of the "soft" penis. This would seem
the most obvious route to re-visioning masculinity; but we're trying
to refuse "hard/soft" now. So, let's rather allow the imagination to
play with the figure of the *aroused* penis — aroused (as in a state of
feeling), rather than "erect" (as in a state of accomplishment and
readiness to perform). This liberation of the sexually excited penis
from its phallic signification allows us to radically re-imagine the
erotic charge of what we usually call the "erect" penis. Its charge
becomes connected not to an imagination of where it can go, what it
can do, etc. (the imagination that privileges its "hardness," its ability
to penetrate, its performance) but to an imagination of what it is
feeling — that is, arousal. The penis has a rather unique capacity to
make erotic arousal visible and apparent to the other person; it
wears its "heart" on its sleeve, so to speak. That transparency of
response can be profoundly sexually moving; it can also be experienced as a moment which empowers the one who has stirred the
response, allows her or him to vitally experience her or his capacity
to move another person. Looked at in this way, the "erect" penis is
anything *but* "armored." Such a reading, however, has been culturally occluded by the construction of male sexuality in terms of the
opposition hard/soft, within which the aroused penis is valued
because it is "hard" and armored, ready to storm the castle, and
disdained when it loses its armor and becomes "soft."

When the aroused penis is revisioned in terms of its capacity for
feeling rather than power and performance, the coldness of most
contemporary homoerotic photography (e.g., Mapplethorpe,
Giard, Ritts, and, earlier, George Platt Lynes) becomes underscored. These photographs are often stunning, arresting. But they
are austere, stark, distant. As in contemporary sports-equipment

Fig. 13

Fig. 14

and exercise-club ads, men with carved-marble bodies gaze vacantly into space or stare grimly at the camera. Couples may be depicted standing or sitting next to each other, but they are merely contiguous statues; they do not look at each other, they rarely touch each other, and no one ever smiles. The only contemporary photographs in Ellenzweig's volume that depict warmth and feeling are, strikingly, the "non-erotic" ones such as Chantal Regnault's (Figs. 13, 14, and 15), photos in which men's faces and bodies openly reveal their love, affection and loyalty to each other.

Although Regnault's "West Street, NYC" and "Gay Pride Day" date back only ten years, they already appear as relics of another time. (As I waited in the store for my reproductions, I met a gay photographer who, leafing through *The Homoerotic Photograph* with me, commented that he found Regnault's work "hackneyed" and "old.") Yet, of course, we know that the *reality* of life today among gay males requires (and has produced) a level of loving care for each other that is equaled only by that of mothers for their children. How is it, then, that emotional attachment, tenderness,

Fig. 15

and loving attention find no place in erotic representation? Certainly, the desire to dissociate from a "feminine" eros plays a role here, as it does for orthodox heterosexual men. But other cultural factors enter in as well: the contemporary artistic preference for the "cool" over the "sentimental," the social escalation of mistrust and fear over the physical and emotional dangers of deep erotic feeling (much "safer" to keep one's distance), and the economic incentive to retain the competitive edge by keeping our cards close to our vests ("Don't ever let them see you sweat!" urges a recent deodorant commercial). Within this cultural context, which strongly idealizes and eroticizes cool facade and self-containment (increasingly in women as well as men), Chantal Regnault's photographs seem far more counter-normative than Mapplethorpe's commercially successful "transgressions." (Mapplethorpe's work shocks and outrages the puritan, to be sure. But it really doesn't take much to do that; Madonna does it all the time.)[21]

I find Regnault's photographs very moving. To be sure, they are not homoerotic in the sense of depicting or stimulating sexual arousal; rather, they depict *eros* in the more general (and classical

Freudian) sense, as the urge for attachment, for connectedness, for building larger human unities out of the atoms of separate selves. Perhaps because the most *verboten* cultural context for such attachment is between men and men, I find that it is precisely images of men (both homosexual and heterosexual) openly loving each other, in couples and in community, that are most stimulating to my imagination of a "revisioned" masculinity. Another such image is presented in Mitchell Duneier's *Slim's Table*, which introduces us to a neighborhood circle of older urban black men who congregate daily at a South Side Chicago cafeteria, Valois. (I personally remember the place, having worked for many years in a bookstore not too far from it, but I never realized the world it contained.) The men of Valois, far from the popular stereotype of the violent, warring, alienated Black street youth, have created what Duneier describes as a "community of caring" among themselves which is utterly unconcerned with proofs of masculinity, and which is harshly critical of those who pursue what bell hooks has called "an unattainable life-threatening patriarchal masculine ideal." This is a community in which affectionate teasing, non-competitive conversation and continual subtle rituals reinforcing affiliation and connection are the stuff of everyday life. These are men, too, who confide in each other about their romantic vulnerabilities and longings rather than brag about their conquests; "Rather than presenting themselves as lovers and exploiters," Duneier tells us, "they are straightforward about their weaknesses . . . [M]any are anguished by their inability to meet women who share their ideas and values."[22]

The men who congregate at Valois are far from macho, but they never perceive themselves as "soft" or feminized. They never long, as Sam Keen and Robert Bly do, for some lost "deep masculinity." Rather, the oppositions soft/hard, masculine/ feminine have no purchase on their sense of manhood, which is tied to other qualities: sincerity, loyalty, honesty. Their world is not divided between the men and the wimps, but between those who live according to certain personal standards of decency and caring and those who try to "perform" and impress others. They are scornful of and somewhat embarrassed by the "cool pose" which has been adopted by many younger black men. And *Slim's Table* does suggest, as I have been arguing in this section, that emotional "impenetrability," although not unique to contemporary styles of subjectivity, *is* a particularly strong element in the contemporary construction of the successful self. In such a culture, those who have been marginalized — women, blacks, gays — may be more likely to view personal armor rather than the strength of community (devoted not only to political consciousness and action but the nurturing of cultural "difference") as the route to self-esteem and resistance to oppression.

But it has not always been so. Just as a previous generation of gay men may have been less obsessed with proving their masculinity to a culture that has "continually berated . . . their version of manhood" (Ellenzweig, 142), so a previous generation of black men may model something very different for us than a "cool pose" masculinity. Bell hooks recalls the men of her childhood who "touched her heart," men who "were caring and giving . . . who chose alternative lifestyles, who questioned the *status quo*, who shunned a ready made patriarchal identity and invented themselves" (*Black Looks*, 88). It may be that men of many races and ethnicities — if they look in the right places — can find in the lives of their fathers something other than either a (now lost) "deep masculinity" (what the culturally dethroned "orthodox" WASP man seems today to be searching for) or an emasculated manhood from which to dissociate oneself (as it has appeared to some Jewish and Black men). The experience of social marginalization, to be sure, may confer an "advantage" here. But clearly, it is not a sufficient condition of the self-invention that hooks refers to. The men of Valois have been historically thrust into a world apart from the "mainstream"; they've had no choice in that matter. But, unlike many of the present generation, they refuse to model that world after the image of the culture that has shut them out.

Slim's Table also helps me to more precisely elaborate the sexual metaphors I am exploring here. I do not want the image of the unarmored, aroused penis to slip inexorably into gendered cliché: e.g., "Why can't men be more open, more expressive about their feelings?" Sam Keen's book, after all, is literally throbbing with feeling! And some of the most "orthodox" masculinities — Latin and Mediterranean norms of manhood, for example — are hardly repressive of male emotionality. There are many cultural contexts in which men are encouraged to "let it all out." Indeed, they may be encouraged to "let it out" to the point where the preservation of *eros*, of relationship, is utterly sacrificed to the unhampered expression of their own desire, need, passion. These thoroughly "active" male emotionalities thus often have the ultimate effect of *obliterating* the other (that is, the other's desires, needs, feelings) in a tidal wave of emotional solipsism.

The men of Valois, in contrast, express their attachment to each other not through extravagant gestures which might embarrass or overwhelm the other person, but through a finely attuned attentiveness to the specific needs of the personalities they interact with. Much of the time, in fact, their communion with each other is silent, marked by gestures of subtle recognition. The expression of their love for each other is continually disciplined by *knowledge* of the other person's needs, strengths and limitations. I want now to map this refinement of the concept of expressive feeling onto the erotic domain. Earlier, I explored the construction of orthodox masculinity (whether heterosexual or homosexual) as the subjectivity which actively defines and constitutes ("penetrates") reality and which never allows itself to be defined and constituted ("penetrated") by the subjectivity of another. Under such conditions, in order for sexual desire to be sustained it becomes imperative that the subjectivity of the other *not* be experienced too strongly or distinctly. Here, femininity and masculinity are truly the mirror-image of each other, for while orthodox men's desire may "wither" under too powerfully defining a gaze, the "feminine" woman may require constant external "definition" (that she is attractive, desirable) from the gaze that (she believes) constitutes her.

The "erotics" of friendship among the men of Valois might help instruct us in imagining a different sort of sexual paradigm — one in which the subjectivity of the other is experienced neither as threatening nor as essential to the validation of the self, but as offering opportunities for *knowledge* of the other, and thus the possibility of real intimacy with him or her. Here, the erotics of the gaze no longer revolve around the dynamics of "looking at" or "being looked at" (of penetrating or being penetrated by, of activity or passivity), but around the mutuality of truly *seeing* and being *seen*, a meeting of subjectivities in which what is experienced is the recognition of knowing and being known by another. "Their eyes met and held each other's": a romantic cliché, but how frequently do we really experience the erotic charge of such meetings and "holdings"? To do so requires a responsive attentiveness, an ability to *notice*, the cultivation of consciousness, of awareness, and, frequently, patience — none of which are encouraged in our instrumentalist culture.

Finally, let me draw a concluding image from Neil Jordan's *The Crying Game*, not to the scene in which the biological "reality" of Dil's penis is exposed but to the dis-arming of the cultural phallus that is represented throughout the movie by the figure of Fergus. In the "big moment" of the movie, we learn that Dil is "not really a woman" — that is, anatomically. But we had already learned, from Fergus's relationship with Jody, that Fergus is "not really a man" in a different sense. He has a penis, sure. Moreover, when we first meet him, he's working with a macho terrorist group. But he's probably the least phallic hero the screen has seen. Has there ever been a male character in a movie that exhibited the pure emotional responsiveness that Fergus does in those early scenes? It's not a volatile or "active" emotionality; Fergus almost always appears tired, worndown. But he's utterly unarmored; Jody (and later, Dil) is easily able to enter his emotional life, and to touch him. We continually see it on his face. (I remember thinking how beautiful that face appeared to me, and realizing that I had never before seen a male actor simply registering that kind of "penetrability" to another.)

Fergus's attachment to Jody is not describable through any labels formed out of a gendered system — "homoerotic," "just friends," etc. Rather, the movie insists that at its most fundamental level the world is not divided into men and women (or blacks and whites), but into (as the twice-repeated fable has it) the scorpions and the frogs: those whose "nature" insists that they kill and those who are open to others, even if it kills them. Fergus's terrorist ex-girlfriend can put on the costume of femininity, but (unlike Dil) it's just a masquerade that disguises her classically phallic personality (near the end of the film, *she* appears dressed as the one truly in drag, not Dil). She's a scorpion, and thus could never be "right" for Fergus, whatever her biological sex. As for Fergus, he's totally without masquerade; we know he's a frog from virtually the first scene. In a culture in which we wear our various costumes and "cool poses" — including our muscled, surgically perfected and preserved bodies — as protective armor against others, as symbols of invulnerability to them, the character of Fergus presents itself not only as a revisioning of masculinity but an indictment of modern subjectivity, with a caution to women as well as a message to men.

ACKNOWLEDGMENTS

The final version of this piece owes much to the support and suggestions of friends and colleagues Janet Bogdan, Barron Boyd, Stanley Clarke, Laurence Goldstein, Patrick Keane, Michael Kimmel, Richard Mohr, Jonathan Schonsheck, Clarence Taylor, and Deborah Tooker. I would also like to thank all those who participated in the informal seminar on "The Male Body" that I led at the University of Notre Dame; that conversation left me with a great many ideas to stimulate my continued work on the essay. Special thanks to Le Moyne College and the Joseph C. Georg Professorship so generously awarded me by the college; without the extra research time afforded me by the professorship, I would never have been able to undertake the writing of an article this length during the teaching semester. And finally — as always — my deepest appreciation goes to Edward Lee.

NOTES

[1] The female orgasm has become public property, too; explicit facial and vocal transport is a requisite convention of contemporary sex-scenes. If we can assume that actresses draw on their own experiences here, then it is safe to conclude that film-going and video-renting audiences of 1993 have intimate (albeit impersonal) knowledge of how countless female stars look and sound while having orgasm (or, at the least, how they imagine they should look and sound). Rarely in these scenes do we see male faces or voices manifest the same sense of open capitulation to the other, and to the body, that actresses today are routinely required to exhibit. Al Pacino's orgasmic scream in *Frankie and Johnny* doesn't count; it was more a comic than an erotic moment. In fact, I can recall only one U.S. film which closes in on the man's orgasmic abandon, reflected as transparently in his face as it conventionally is in the woman's. That shot, significant not only because of the turn-the-tables theme of the movie, but for other reasons that I will shortly discuss, was of Eddie Murphy in *Boomerang*. (A friend who read an earlier version of this paper tells me that *Damage*, which barely escaped with an "R" rating, focuses on Jeremy Irons' face during orgasm.)

[2] Academics, particularly of a Lacanian bent, are not exempt from privileging the symbolic, disembodied phallus over the penis. Some very interesting recent articles, however, have begun to explore the meaning, consequences, and stability of positing a "transcendental signifier" phallus disconnected from the penis. See, in particular, Charles Bernheimer's excellent piece, "Penile Reference in Phallic Theory," in *Differences*'s "The Phallus Issue," 4; 1 (Spring 1992), 116–32.

[3] Klaus Theweleit, *Male Fantasies*, volumes 1 and 2, translated by Stephen Conway (Minneapolis: University of Minnesota Press, 1987).

[4] These stereotypes can crop up in unexpected places, such as David Gilmore's anthropological study *Manhood in the Making* (New Haven: Yale University Press, 1990), where Gilmore notes that "Even secular, assimilated Jewish-American culture, *one of the few in which women virtually dominate men*, has a notion of manhood" (p. 127, emphasis mine). One wonders where Gilmore got his anthropological data — from jokes about "Jewish Princesses"? From Hollywood's continual caricatures of the suffocating Jewish mother? From stand-up comedians' misogynist routines?

[5]Harry Brod, ed., *A Mensch Among Men* (Freedom, CA.: The Crossing Press, 1988).

[6]This dynamic, of course, is not limited to heterosexual attraction, as is thematized in *Tongues Untied*, Marlon Riggs' powerful documentary about gay, black males, where the discovery of beauty in men of one's own race is shown to be an arduous and "revolutionary" accomplishment.

[7]These dynamics are so powerful that they are reproduced unconsciously even within cultures that fully recognize that femininity is a construction. Bell hooks, in *Black Looks* (Boston: South End Press, 1992), criticizes *Paris is Burning*, Jennie Livingston's documentary about black drag balls, for unproblematizing the fact that within the world she depicts, "the idea of womanness and femininity is totally personified by whiteness" as the impersonators reveal an "obsession with an idealized fetishized vision of femininity that is white" (147–8).

[8]Not only Jewish men are represented as castrated in the Western psyche. Richard Fung, in "Looking for My Penis: The Eroticized Asian in Gay Video Porn" (in *How Do I Look? Queer Film and Video*, edited by Bad Object Choices, Bay Press, Seattle, 1991), argues that Asian men have been dominantly "consigned to one of two categories: the egghead/wimp, or . . . the kung fu master/ninja/samurai. He is sometimes dangerous, sometimes friendly, but almost always characterized by a desexualized Zen asceticism . . . defined by a striking absence down there."(7) In gay male porn, Fung argues, this absence is perpetuated by the continual portrayal of Asian men as submissive in anal intercourse ("the role of bottom") rather than active subject (the one who penetrates, and whose ejaculatory pleasure, according to Fung, is privileged in the narrative).

[9]Frantz Fanon, *Black Skin, White Masks* (London: Paladin, 1970), 120. Thus, while Jewish men may seek to prove their masculinity, as did my father and many of the young men I went to high school with, through wild, "uncivilized" behavior (Roth's and Mailer's characters provide many prototypes of this rebellion against the "nice Jewish boy" image), the strategy of young Black men may be to cultivate an impervious facade, a "cool pose" of detachment, ironic distance, and emotional composure, with subtle and complicated cultural styles of performance and communication. Richard Majors and Janet Mancini Billson, whose *Cool Pose: The Dilemmas of Black Manhood in America* (New York: Macmillan, 1992) provides a detailed sociological exploration, view "cool pose" as a defensive response to social disempowerment, a means of warding off anxieties over the dangers of being a black man in this culture, and a demonstration to white culture that he has not been destroyed by it, that he is not a *man manqué*:
"By acting calm, emotionless, fearless, aloof, and tough, the African-American male strives to offset an externally imposed 'zero' image. Being cool shows the dominant culture and the black male himself that he is strong and proud. He is somebody. He is a survivor, in spite of the systematic harm done by the legacy of slavery and the realities of racial oppression, in spite of the centuries of hardship and mistrust."(5)
All of this makes sense. But I think that Majors and Billson overlook the way in which "coolness" and the elaborate cultural apparatus which defines it also stands in opposition and challenge, not to a "*zero* image," (that is, not only to a lack) but to the all-too-substantial racist imagery of the black man as pure body, pure instinct— without control, culture, or "mind." "Cool" is not only toughness and fearlessness, it is style, language, art, precision, subtlety. The pose it attempts to project, for all the violence and self-destruction that it may actually engender, is that of mind over matter, culture over instinct, phallic self-containment over the penis-as-animal.

[10]Despite the pervasiveness of racist representations of the black man's body, there

has been relatively little detailed analysis of those representations by academics, black or white. Here, as elsewhere, one needs to turn to gay scholarship and culture in order to find the penis. A very interesting context for debate about the hyper-sexualization of the black male body, for example, is the interpretation of Robert Mapplethorpe's photographs. Critics such as Essex Hemphill argue that Map-plethorpe's work hyper-eroticizes and objectifies the black man's body, feeding into racial stereotypes. (The notorious "Man in Polyester Suit," which depicts a huge penis emerging from the open fly of a black man in a conservative business suit, has been a special target of such criticism, despite what is arguably a satirical point.) But Allen Ellenzweig, in the lavishly illustrated and perceptively documented *The Homoerotic Photograph* (New York: Columbia University Press, 1992), points out, while acknowledging the racial problematics, that a cold, objectifying formalism and fet-ishizing of body-parts is characteristic of most of Mapplethorpe's work, not only his photos of black men. Perhaps the most textured, complex commentary on the Map-plethorpe debate is contained in a set of two articles by Kobena Mercer. In the first, "Imaging the Black Man's Sex" (*Photography/Politics: Two*, ed. Pat Holland, Jo Spence, and Simon Watney [London: Methuen, 61–69]), Mercer argues (reading the photos "as a black man") that Mapplethorpe's photographs fetishize black bodies as sexual objects, much as women have been represented. In the second, "Skin Head Sex Thing: Racial Difference and the Homoerotic Imagery" (*How Do I Look?*, 169–210), Mercer re-evaluates the univocality of his earlier reading, suggesting that when one "reads" the photos as a *gay* man, that is with their homoerotic specificity at the foreground, one's understanding of the author's "gaze" is altered; it can no longer be seen as unequivocally objectifying, "since sexual sameness liquidates the associa-tive opposition between active subject and passive object"(182). This shift in perspec-tive allows Mercer to view Mapplethorpe as subverting rather than re-inscribing racial stereotypes.

[11]This is not to say that all the explorations of male sexuality in this book empha-size male powerlessness. There are also classic, strong condemnations (such as John Stoltenberg's "Pornography and Freedom") which view pornography as reflecting and reproducing a sexuality grounded in domination and subordination, as well as anti-feminist tirades that seem utterly oblivious to the pain, or even existence of real women (such as Robert Christgau's cold "Pornography as Ideology and Other Ways to Get Off"). Still other pieces (such as Richard Goldstein's fascinating "Pornography and Its Discontents") manage to combine an appreciation of the human need for transgression, excess, and extremity with a keen sense of the sexist and racist power-relations that provide the content of those experiences in a sexist and racist culture. As I've said earlier, this is a very diverse collection. It's only major lacuna is the minimal attention given to racial issues. The one article which deals with black attitudes toward porn ("Blacks and Pornography: A Different View," by Robert Staples) is bland and insubstantial; in none of the articles is adequate attention paid to racial (or class) motifs in pornography.

[12]See Bram Dijkstra, *Idols of Perversity* (New York: Oxford University Press, 1986) for a fascinating discussion of the prominence of such imagery in the second half of the nineteenth century, coincidentally (but not accidentally, Dijkstra argues) with the rise of evolutionary theories of "race," race purity and race degeneration. This correspondence is discussed, as well, by Theweleit, who follows its flowering in fascist Germany. See my *Unbearable Weight: Feminism, Western Culture and The Body* (University of California Press, 1993) for analysis of the re-emergence of anxi-ety over women's "devouring" hungers and desires in the context of contemporary gender backlash.

[13]These images, of course, also materially affect the way "real" women evaluate,

"correct," and present their bodies to the world, as I detail in *Unbearable Weight*. And emulating these images may indeed give women a way of experiencing the "power" of their sexuality and beauty (an experience that may be hard to relinquish in a culture that has afforded women few other avenues to self-validation.) But the ideals which beckon women with a promise of power, invulnerability, and control, ultimately tyrannize them with their impossible standards of physical perfection, youth, slenderness. Humiliated and angry men. Obsessive and self-hating women. One would think that men and women have a common interest in critiquing the eroticization and sexualization of women's bodies. (I'm not talking about censorship here, but simply the raising of critical consciousness and discussion among men and women.) Instead, we remain in thrall, convinced that our lives will be fulfilled if and only if we can sexually possess or embody the tantalizing images.

[14]And where did he get the idea, anyway, that gay men have no nurturing relationship with the young? Many gay men *have* children. And in any case, does one have to have one's own in order to nurture them? One aspect of gay male relationships that Keen ignores (or simply has no knowlege of) is the unusual degree of emotional mentoring and protection that older gay men often provide for younger ones. This is a gay "tradition" that goes back as far as ancient Greece.

[15]Suzanne Kessler and Wendy McKenna, *Gender: An Ethnomethodological Approach* (Chicago: University of Chicago Press, 1978), 151.

[16]In this context, it is perhaps significant that Dil's penis is not erect in the scene; if it had been, could a reading of him as female be sustained?

[17]Richard Mohr, *Gay Ideas: Outing and Other Controversies* (New York: Beacon Press, 1992). As the title of Mohr's book suggests, it deals with a variety of controversial topics (and does so most originally and interestingly). In this essay, however, I will be discussing only one of his chapters, " 'Knights, Young Men, Boys': Masculine Worlds and Democratic Values."

[18]Gilmore, 11. Many of the tests that boys must pass in order to win their manhood, involve "facing up" to the look of other men in various symbolic ways.

[19]Tomás Almaguer, "Chicano Men: A Cartography of Homosexual identity and Behavior," in *Differences*, 3; 2, 1991, 78.

[20]"Male Cheerleaders and the Naturalization of Gender," in Michael Messner and Donald Sabo, *Sport, Men and the Gender Order* (Champaign: Human Kinetics Books, 1990), 153–161.

[21]Regnault, it might be worth pointing out, is the only living photographer represented in *The Homoerotic Photograph* who agreed to release her work for reproduction in reviews; all the others, one suspects, enjoy much too booming a business in postcards, posters and the like to allow their work to be reproduced for non-commercial uses.

[22]Mitchell Duneier, *Slim's Table* (Chicago: University of Chicago Press, 1992), 41.

CONTRIBUTORS

Rudolf Arnheim published his first book in 1928; since then he has authored classics in many fields, such as *Radio, Film as Art, Art and Visual Perception, The Dynamics of Architectural Form, The Power of the Center,* and *To the Rescue of Art.*

Margaret Atwood is the author of more than twenty books, including poetry, fiction, and nonfiction. Recent novels include *The Handmaid's Tale* (1986), *Cat's Eye* (1988), and *Robber Bride* (1993).

Christianne Balk has published two volumes of poems: *Bindweed,* the 1985 Walt Whitman Award winner, and *Desiring Flight* (1995).

Ruth Behar, Professor of Anthropology at the University of Michigan, is the author of *Translated Woman: Crossing the Border with Esperanza's Story* (1993). She received a MacArthur Fellowship in 1988.

Mitch Berman has published a novel, *Time Capsule* (1988), and coedited a book on China, *Children of the Dragon* (1989).

Robert Bly's best-selling book of 1990, *Iron John: A Book About Men,* initiated much of the current debate about manhood and masculinity. *Selected Poems* appeared in 1986.

Susan Bordo is Professor of Philosophy and the first recipient of the J. C. Georg Chair at Le Moyne College, New York. Her book *Unbearable Weight: Feminism, Western Culture, and the Body* appeared in 1993.

Leo Braudy is the Leo S. Bing Professor of English at the University of Southern California. He has written books on Edward Gibbon, Jean Renoir, film theory, and in 1986 *The Frenzy of Renown: Fame and Its History.*

Andrew Campbell has completed a Ph.D. in the History of Art, and an M.A. in American Culture, at the University of Michigan.

Edward Field's book *Counting Myself Lucky: Selected Poems 1963–1992* appeared in 1992.

Sam Fussell is the author of *Muscle: Confessions of an Unlikely Bodybuilder* (1991) and the novel *Missing Person* (1994).

Laurence Goldstein is Professor of English at the University of Michigan and editor of *Michigan Quarterly Review*. His book *The American Poet at the Movies: A Critical History* appeared in 1994.

Nathan Griffith received his Ph.D. in the History of Art from the University of Michigan in 1993.

Margaret Morganroth Gullette, author of *Safe at Last in the Middle Years* (1988), is at work on a companion volume to be called "Midlife Fictions: The Construction of the Middle Years of Life, 1880–1930."

Brenda Hillman is the author of five books of poetry, including *Bright Existence* (1993). She teaches at St. Mary's College in Moraga, California.

Charles Johnson is the author of a book of stories, *The Sorcerer's Apprentice* (1986), a novel, *Middle Passage* (1990, winner of the National Book Award in Fiction), and *Being & Race: Black Writing Since 1970* (1988). He is Pollock Professor of English at the University of Washington.

Michael S. Kimmel, Associate Professor of Sociology, SUNY at Stony Brook, has published *Men Confront Pornography* (1990), *Men's Lives* (1992), and *Against the Tide: Pro-Feminist Men in the*

United States, 1776–1990 (1992). He has completed a study entitled "Manhood: The American Quest."

Evelyn Lau was born in Vancouver, Canada, in 1971. She is the author of an autobiography, three books of poetry, and two books of short stories.

David Lehman's books include *Operation Memory* (1990), a volume of poems; *Signs of the Times: Deconstruction and the Fall of Paul de Man* (1991); and *The Line Forms Here* (1992), a gathering of his essays on poetry.

Phillip Lopate has published two books of poetry and two novels. His nonfiction includes *Being with Children* (1975), *Bachelorhood: Tales of the Metropolis* (1981), and *Against Joie de Vivre* (1989). He holds the Adams Chair in the Department of English at Hofstra University.

Joyce Carol Oates is the author of many books of fiction, including *Foxfire: Confessions of a Girl Gang* (1993) and the story collections, *Where is Here?* (1993) and *Haunted: Tales of the Grotesque* (1994). She lives and teaches in Princeton, New Jersey.

Fred Pfeil is the author of *Another Tale to Tell: Essays on Postmodern Culture* (1990) and a work in progress, "White Guys: Studies in Postmodern Domination and Difference." Active in social justice work in Hartford, Connecticut, he teaches at Trinity College.

Nicholas Samaras received the Yale Series of Younger Poets Award for his collection, *Hands of the Saddlemaker* (1992).

Brad Sewell worked eight years in the steel industry, six of them in northeastern Indiana. He is a graduate of the University of Iowa Writers' Workshop.

David R. Slavitt's translation of Ovid's *Metamorphoses*, as well as his translation of *The Fables of Avianus*, are recent examples of his renditions from the Greek and Latin. He has also published some fifty volumes of poetry and fiction.

Alan Soldofsky is Director of the Center for Literary Arts at San Jose State University. He has published work in *Antioch Review*, *Grand Street*, and *Indiana Review*.

Cathy Song is the author of three books of poetry, including *School Figures* (1994). She lives in Hawaii.

John Updike has published many books of fiction, poetry, and non-fiction, including *Collected Poems 1953–1993* (1993) and a novel, *Brazil* (1994).

Mario Wirz was born in 1956 in Marburg, Germany. The author of several volumes of poetry, he has also published fiction and non-fiction, and worked actively in the theater. The work in this issue is taken from *"Es ist spät, ich kann nicht atmen." Ein nächtlicher Bericht* ["It is late, I cannot breathe." A nocturnal report], published by Aufbau-Verlag in 1992. His translator, Alfred G. Meyer, is Professor Emeritus of Political Science at the University of Michigan.